A Risk-Information Perspective on the Marketing of M&A Advisory

European University Studies
Europäische Hochschulschriften
Publications Universitaires Européennes

Series V
Economics and Management

Reihe V Série V
Volks- und Betriebswirtschaft
Sciences économiques

Vol./Band 3087

PETER LANG
Bern · Berlin · Bruxelles · Frankfurt am Main · New York · Oxford · Wien

Ute Kristin Schuler

A Risk-Information Perspective on the Marketing of M&A Advisory

PETER LANG
Bern · Berlin · Bruxelles · Frankfurt am Main · New York · Oxford · Wien

Bibliographic information published by Die Deutsche Bibliothek
Die Deutsche Bibliothek lists this publication in the Deutsche Nationalbibliografie; detailed bibliographic data is available on the Internet at ‹http://dnb.ddb.de›.

British Library and Library of Congress Cataloguing-in-Publication Data:
A catalogue record for this book is available from *The British Library,* Great Britain, and from *The Library of Congress,* USA

Thanks to…

… Luca for inspiring me to pursue this subject.
… Martin for reviewing drafts and keeping my spirits up.
… my family for proofreading and their animated support.
… Mergermarket for their trusting cooperation.
… Prof. Dr. Andreas Herrmann for his helpful supervision.

ISSN 0531-7339
ISBN 3-03910-434-9
US-ISBN 0-8204-7150-X

Hochfeldstrasse 32, Postfach 746, CH-3000 Bern 9, Switzerland
info@peterlang.com, www.peterlang.com, www.peterlang.net

Abstract

Risk and risk relievers, in particular information search and evaluation, have been shown to play important roles in purchase behaviour. While empirical research in the field of consumer goods has been manyfold on this topic, only little research has been conducted in the field of industrial goods, let alone industrial services.

The research presented in this thesis proposes that risk plays an important role in a company's choice of its M&A advisor, for both its perceptions and actual behaviour. More specifically, perceived risk is found to be strongly driven by the risk associated with the underlying M&A transaction, the prominence of the role the investment bank is expected to play in the M&A project (consequences), and the company's investment banking experience (uncertainty). Perceived risk associated with choosing an M&A advisor being high on market level, the orientation at a bank's reputation, and the initiation of a competitive selection process, which allows further information search, represent the risk relievers most commonly employed by prospective buyers. But it is also suggested that, while sales presentation does decrease perceived uncertainty significantly, its power to do so is inferior to other devices, decreasing its role to a mere "hygiene factor". As to more powerful risk relievers, the re-engaging of banks with which a company has already made good experience during previous projects is found to be highly efficient, both from an uncertainty and subsequent satisfaction perspective. A major setback is provided by its availability, which does, in contrast to sales presentation, not lie in the buyer's ad hoc power. Further, it is proposed that the utility of relying on the quality of previous execution decreases if a company does not "cherry-pick" the banker, which, from the perspective of M&A advisory's high degree of non-automation, is highly sensible. An exception to this rule is provided by highly renowned banks, hinting at reputation's reassurance and certification benefit. Further, the importance of reputation, from both a justification, as well as self-selection mechanism perspective, is being elaborated. The power of commercial banking relationships as cross-selling platform for M&A advisory is found to be only modest.

Against the background of restricted availability of risk relievers in the market, which mostly stems from M&A advisory's nature, it is proposed that banks should provide their potential buyers with risk relievers not yet available in the market. In particular, banks not having an excellent reputation may want to consider the offering of alternative "hostages" to their potential buyers (satisfaction-dependent variable compensation), and make the highly useful "previous execution" type information available to a broader buyer base (referrals).

From a banker-bank perspective, it is proposed banks should create an environment that attracts, develops, and retains gifted individuals by virtue of a stronger "build" as opposed to "buy" focus, and a better balancing of incentives. These measures should be complemented by the creation and enhancement of "corporation-owned" customer benefits.

Contents

List of figures XIII

List of tables XV

Preface by Prof. Dr. A. Herrmann XVII

Preface by Dr. L. P. Marighetti XIX

Part I **Introduction**

1 Goal 3
1.1 Research objectives 3
1.1.1 Theoretical perspective 3
1.1.2 Practical perspective 5
1.2 Organisation of the document 7
1.2.1 Structure 7
1.2.2 Lists 8

2 Motivation 9
2.1 Market development 9
2.1.1 Market size and structure 10
2.1.2 Drivers 11
2.1.3 Protagonists 17
2.1.4 Current situation and outlook 18
2.2 Practical pitfalls 19
2.2.1 General issues 20
2.2.2 Business-service-specific issues 23
2.3 Theoretic interest 25
2.3.1 Service specifics 26
2.3.2 Industrial good specifics 28

3 Basic concepts 31
3.1 Marketing concepts 31
3.2 Investment-banking-specific concepts 33
3.2.1 Definitions 33

3.2.2 Investment banks' tasks 36
3.2.3 Solicitation for mandate 39

Part II **Theoretic foundations and preliminary conclusions**

4 Risk and its explanatory power 51
4.1 The concept of risk 52
4.1.1 Perceived risk 52
4.1.2 Risk components 53
4.1.3 Corporate and personal risk 57
4.1.4 Underlying risk and transfer lever 59
4.2 Risk reduction methods 62
4.2.1 Thresholds 62
4.2.2 Uncertainty and consequence relievers 63
4.2.3 Mode of action risk reliever typology 64
4.2.4 Inherent risk and handled risk 73

5 Information and its utility 77
5.1 The concept of information 77
5.1.1 Types of uncertainty 77
5.1.2 Uncertainty of compliance in M&A advisory . 83
5.1.3 Cost, benefit, and utility of information 85
5.2 Natural information typology 86
5.2.1 Cognitive vehicle 88
5.2.2 Reference 94
5.2.3 Affinity 96
5.2.4 Source 101
5.3 Reputation, relationship, information search 103
5.3.1 Reputation 103
5.3.2 Benefits of a good reputation 105
5.3.3 Relationship 110
5.3.4 Information search 112

6 Product classifications in the light of risk and information . 115
6.1 Review of characteristics 116
6.1.1 Select approaches 116
6.1.2 Further classification parameters 120
6.2 Parameters' impact on the consequence component of risk 122

6.2.1 Product characteristics affecting the consequence component of risk 122
6.2.2 Product characteristics not affecting the consequence component of risk 123
6.3 Parameters' impact on the uncertainty component of risk 124
6.3.1 Product characteristics affecting the utility of information for quality uncertainty decrease . . 125
6.3.2 Product characteristics not affecting the utility of information for quality uncertainty decrease 129

7 The M&A advisor choice from a risk perspective 131
7.1 Consequence associated with the M&A advisor choice 131
7.1.1 Influence of M&A risk on M&A advisor choice risk 131
7.1.2 Risk associated with an M&A transaction . . . 132
7.2 Uncertainty associated with the M&A advisor choice . 139
7.2.1 Drivers 139
7.2.2 Relievers 140

8 The M&A advisor choice from an information perspective . 145
8.1 Vehicles a company might base its choice on 145
8.1.1 Most important concepts 146
8.1.2 Characterisation by means of natural characteristics 148
8.1.3 Assessment of information type prerequisites . 150
8.2 Signal vehicles' role in the marketing of M&A advisory 156
8.2.1 General importance of signal vehicles 156
8.2.2 Importance of signal vehicles for repeat buyers 159
8.2.3 Signal vehicles' "natural owner" 160
8.2.4 Signal vehicles' utility for uncertainty decrease 162
8.2.5 Satisfaction with execution and re-engagement intention 163
8.2.6 Importance of signal vehicles by type of selection procedure 165

Part III **Research and discussion**

9 Data collection and analytic methods 169
9.1 Data 169

9.1.1 Instrument 169
9.1.2 Sample 170
9.2 Methods 177
9.2.1 Measurement 177
9.2.2 Operationalisation of specific concepts 178
9.2.3 Dissonance reduction 180
9.2.4 Philosophy of science background 181
9.2.5 Data analysis technique 181
9.2.6 Statistical package 185

10 Review and discussion of results 187
10.1 Risk associated with the advisor choice 187
10.1.1 Consequence component 190
10.1.2 Uncertainty component 193
10.2 Information used to determine the advisor choice . . . 197
10.2.1 Importance of signal vehicles in general 200
10.2.2 Importance of signal vehicles for repeat buyers 204
10.2.3 Signal vehicles' "natural owner" 206
10.2.4 Signal vehicles' utility for uncertainty decrease 211
10.2.5 Satisfaction with execution and re-engagement intention 213
10.2.6 Importance of signal vehicles by type of selection procedure 219

11 Complementary and deepening analyses 221
11.1 Convictions and perceptions 221
11.1.1 Investment banking experience 221
11.1.2 Importance of investment bank's role in M&A 222
11.1.3 Risk associated with the M&A project 223
11.1.4 Consequence component of risk associated with the bank selection 224
11.1.5 Uncertainty component of risk associated with the bank selection 225
11.1.6 Banker-bank importance 227
11.1.7 Summary 228
11.2 Actual behaviour and implementation 229
11.2.1 Incidence of selection types in market 229
11.2.2 Quantity structure of the purchase funnel . . . 230
11.2.3 Specific banks' conversion rates 232
11.2.4 Summary 234
11.3 Revealed importance of signal vehicles 235

11.3.1 Data and method 235
11.3.2 Vehicles' influence along the purchase funnel . 237
11.3.3 Vehicles' influence by selection and buyer type 241
11.3.4 Summary 245

12 Synthesis and outlook 249
12.1 Theoretical perspective 249
12.1.1 Power of applied frameworks and further explanation needs 249
12.1.2 Limitations and broadening research needs . . 251
12.2 Practical perspective 252
12.2.1 Risk and risk relief perspective 252
12.2.2 A broader perspective on remuneration schemes 258
12.2.3 Signal vehicle perspective 262
12.2.4 A broader perspective on goodwill creation . . 271
12.2.5 Individual-corporation antagonism perspective 274

Appendix 283

Bibliography 297

List of Figures

2.1 Development of the European M&A advisory market . 11
2.2 Directions of potential value creation through M&A . 13
3.1 Self-explained task focus of M&A advisors 37
3.2 Solicitation types by initiative and degree of competition 40
3.3 Types of M&A advisory mandates 43
3.4 M&A advisory customer decision funnel 44
4.1 Risk components 54
4.2 Measures for the consequence component of risk . . . 57
4.3 Underlying risk and transfer lever 60
4.4 Examples for uncertainty and consequence relievers . . 64
4.5 Mode of action-based reliever typology 66
4.6 Mode of action-based reliever characteristics 70
4.7 Examples for mode of action-based risk relievers . . . 72
4.8 Risk thresholds and implied buyer behaviour 74
5.1 Uncertainty types 84
5.2 Characteristics used to differentiate information types 87
5.3 Utility drivers for search and experience 93
5.4 Utility drivers for result and plan/potential/process . 97
5.5 Utility drivers for related information 100
5.6 Utility drivers for third party information 102
6.1 Characteristics' impact on the consequence component of risk 124
6.2 Characteristics' impact on information utility 129
7.1 Consequence component of risk associated with M&A 135
7.2 Uncertainty component of risk associated with M&A 137
7.3 M&A advisor choice from a risk perspective 142
8.1 Information types transmitted through vehicles 149
8.2 Cognitive vehicle perspective on M&A advisor choice . 151
8.3 Reference perspective on M&A advisor choice 152
8.4 Affinity perspective on M&A advisor choice 154
8.5 Source perspective on M&A advisor choice 156
9.1 Respondents' geography and company position 171
9.2 Companies' role in the M&A project assessed 173
9.3 Size and geographic reach of M&A project 174
9.4 Representation of lead advisors in survey sample . . . 175
10.1 Questionnaire excerpt I 188

10.2 Test results on M&A advisor choice risk 196
10.3 Questionnaire excerpt II 199
10.4 Signal vehicles' general importance 203
10.5 Signal vehicles' importance for repeat buyers 204
10.6 Role of individuals in relationships 209
10.7 Role of individuals and implied loyalty transfer 210
10.8 Customer satisfaction by choice and bank type 214
10.9 Customer satisfaction by choice and bank subtype . . 217
11.1 Self-perceived investment banking experience 222
11.2 Perceived importance of lead bank's role 223
11.3 Perceived risk associated with the M&A project . . . 224
11.4 Perceived importance of M&A advisor choice 225
11.5 Perceived difficulty of capability assessment 226
11.6 Perceived importance of banker vs. bank 228
11.7 Incidence of selection procedures 230
11.8 Quantity structure of purchase funnel 231
11.9 Conversion rates by bank group 233
11.10 Vehicles' explanatory power along funnel 238
11.11 Reputation assessment by relationship bucket 240
11.12 Heteroscedasticity assessment for fourth funnel step . 241
11.13 Vehicles' explanatory power by selection/buyer type . 242
11.14 Switchers' vs. repeat buyers' relationship situation . . 244
11.15 Market positioning by bank group 246
11.16 Market positioning by bank 247
12.1 Satisfaction with the lead bank's execution 256
12.2 Recommendations from a risk/risk relief perspective . 258
12.3 Share of completed transactions by satisfaction bucket 259
12.4 Alternative M&A advisory remuneration scheme . . . 261
12.5 Escalation of experience type utility increasers 267
12.6 Perceived quality of sales presentation/discussion . . 269
12.7 Recommendations from a signal vehicle perspective . 271
12.8 Moving up the reputation-relationship matrix 273
12.9 Recommendations from an individual-corporation perspective 281

List of Tables

10.1 Consequences associated with the M&A advisor choice 191
10.2 Uncertainty associated with the M&A advisor choice and most basic relievers 194
10.3 General importance of signal vehicles 201
10.4 Importance of signal vehicles for repeat buyers 205
10.5 Importance of signal vehicles by banker as opposed to bank choice 207
10.6 Signal vehicles' effectiveness for uncertainty decrease . 212
10.7 Satisfaction with the bank by signal vehicle importance 215
10.8 Signal vehicles' importance by selection type 218

The Implications of Risk for the Marketing of Professional Services – a Preface by Prof. Dr. A. Herrmann

The choice of a financial advisor represents one of the basic challenges to a company in the context of mergers and acquisitions. Real life examples illustrate the prominence of such an advisor's role, for instance with respect to the transaction price, and show that substantial risk is associated with their choice.

In light of these facts, it is surprising that an examination of the choice patterns used to select an M&A advisor, or, taking the investment bank perspective, an examination of the key factors to succeed in mandate acquisition and retention, have not been more prominent in the literature. Two facts may provide an explanation for this gap. The high degree of confidentiality in the industry makes data collection particularly difficult, and, from a theoretical perspective, the identification of a framework providing the starting point for a sound hypothesis-driven approach is not an easy task.

Aware of these challenges, Mrs. Schuler approaches the problem of M&A advisor selection by means of the concept of perceived risk, combined with selected paradigms from information economy and principal agent theory. On these grounds, the first sound theory-driven approach to this highly practical problem is achieved.

By means of a European-wide company survey, Mrs. Schuler uses the derived hypotheses to identify important dimensions along which M&A advisors are chosen. This results in highly valuable insights into the determinants of advisor choice and a valuable guideline along which they may re-consider and improve their positioning. Mrs. Schuler uses this analysis to make conclusions regarding successful investment bank marketing strategies, as well as conclusions regarding potential organizational and cultural implications – topics of high practical value that have not gained much attention in the literature to date.

I consider this thesis a valuable contribution to marketing research and recommend it strongly to both scholars and practitioners.

Prof. Dr. Andreas Herrmann is Director at the Centre of Business Metrics at the University of St. Gallen, Switzerland. Besides others, he is member of several scientific editorial boards, and evaluator for the European Journal of Marketing, the Zeitschrift für betriebswirtschaftliche Forschung, and the Schmalenbach Business Review.

Of Chocolate Bars and Investment Banking – a Preface by Dr. L. P. Marighetti

What is the difference between choosing a chocolate bar and selecting the lead banker for a major M&A transaction? To the financial professional the question itself might sound anathema. In fact, if you asked a banker the standard answer would probably be: "Sorry guys, totally different things – do not even try to compare". To the marketing professional, however, the question would sound trivial. His standard answer would probably be: "None – at least in principle". I would argue that neither one is right and settle for a salomonic: "more than you think, less than you believe".

With that we are right at the core of Mrs. Schuler's fine piece of research and why it is worth reading. Acknowledging the simple fact, that the picking of a lead banker for an M&A project necessarily follows a purchasing process, she embarks on a thorough analysis of what is involved, i. e., the risk associated with the choice and the information gathering necessary to reduce the uncertainty prior to making a hopefully right decision. A major merit undoubtedly consists in having worked it out specifically for the M&A "product" while providing empirical proof.

As surprising (or trivial) as it might sound, this process is structurally comparable to the process a consumer is going through when choosing a chocolate bar. This is based on the belief that if the purchasing decision follows a rational, albeit sometimes unconscious, process, and if the process has proven influenceable for other product categories, then there is a high likelihood that too in the category "M&A advisory" marketing activities can influence purchase behaviour.

Assuming the above is right, the next question is then: what exactly can influence the behaviour of let's say a CFO choosing the banker for the next acquisition as opposed to the same CFO choosing a chocolate bar during a coffee break? As pointed out by the research at hand, the answer can be found in the different nature of the need and of the offer. I take the freedom to briefly evolve on this, since the understanding of this difference provides the crucial anchor point for any further analyses of the purchase process and subsequent marketing recommendations.

I will start with the chocolate bar example. Like most physical goods, chocolate bars are purchased regularly, are serially manufactured to given specifications and quality standards, and have a good name (or brand) standing for it. When choosing one, our CFO has two basic choices. He will either go for a known make (e. g., his usual brand) or try something new.

In the first case he expects the same taste as experienced in former occasions. He will perceive no risk as far a taste specifications are concerned and negligible uncertainty with regard to the actual bar to deliver them. Without realising it, and based on former experience, he will simply assume a stable production process that ensures constant quality delivery. In the second case he will perceive a much higher risk quantifiable in e. g. the amount of money wasted if the bar proves distasteful and the length of time during which the potentially bad taste will last in his mouth. He might be willing to take them under the condition that the new make promises to deliver a significantly better taste experience.

Two parameters will guide him when making the decision: the price of the bar and his ability to reduce uncertainty by gathering proper information. This establishes a clear context for a chocolate bar manufacturer trying to win new customers. He has two options: i) Lower the price for a trial to nil (e.g. through distributing free samples) and ii) Reduce the burden of gathering information by clearly communicating (e. g., through advertising, packaging copy etc.) what the unknown bar is all about, i. e., why it is worth trying. Both strategies have proven to work, as each of us has probably already experienced several times.

Let us now look at the same CFO confronting the task of choosing a bank for a significant M&A transaction. For simplicity purposes I will assume we are talking about the CFO of a large company with a history of such transactions as this makes it more easily comparable to the chocolate bar case. I will return later to the significance of more complex cases.

Like for the chocolate bar, our CFO has a significant experience of the offer, i.e., he is a regular purchaser of the service and has again two choices. He can rely on a firm with which he made good experiences in the past, or go for a new one. In both cases we can easily identify three significant differences vs. the chocolate bar example: i) At the time of the purchase, the product is not yet available for consumption (probably the reason why investment banks are remunerated *after* the transaction); ii) The risk associated with the choice is incommensurably larger in absolute terms (a successful career or a fat bonus vs. some distaste and a few cents might be at stake), so large that it remains relevant even after calibrating for any mental accounting effects, and iii) The gathering of the information necessary for making the purchase decision can not be made readily available by the manufacturer, translating into high search costs following high uncertainty for the CFO.

This again sets clear parameters for our CFO. He will seek to minimise both, his risk exposure and his search cost. This in turn establishes a clear context for the seller of M&A services. The latter has four options: i) He might refer to positive past experiences and/or trusted relationships; ii) He can play on market reputation (usually referring to league tables or to third party references); iii) He might try to impress through a good presentation (especially relevant in a pitch situation); finally, iv) He might be the one coming up with the transaction idea to start with, hence demonstrating his unique competence. We can see in real life how these strategies are been pursued by the selling side.

We now need to recognise that the above case is the easiest, and it is worthwhile remaking here that the detailed analysis of all cases is undoubtedly one of most intriguing aspects of Mrs. Schuler's contribution. CFOs of smaller companies, CEOs, company owners, short anybody in charge of selecting the advisor for an M&A transaction with no or limited experience will face an even higher level of uncertainty, exploding search costs, and hence an even more difficult decision process.

But, were the same people facing the task of selecting a chocolate bar, so they would continue to be fully comparable to our best case CFO. This points to a further peculiarity of the M&A support offering: because the seller has limited scope for satisfying the information gathering needs of the buyer and no chance of minimising the price for a trial (as outlined in the research at hand, the "price" paid for a distaste goes far beyond the price paid for the service), risk perception and search cost relate to experience and tend to compound. As a result, the buyers' propensity to experiment in the M&A area will tend to be low.

In summary, our unlikely comparison between the high end of investment banking and chocolate bars leads to two conclusions. First, the sale of M&A support does indeed require a quite substantial marketing effort. Second, because of the tailor-made nature of the product, this effort can hardly be performed by a marketing function shaped in the fashion a chocolate bar manufacturers would do it.

From there specific marketing strategies can be developed. We could regard "relationship building" as key to retain the loyalty of experienced buyers, "reputation building" as key for new market entrants, i. e., a new entrant would need to start with experienced buyer, as opposed to e. g. small companies, because experienced buyers have a higher propensity for trial and because reputation follows positive experience by a buyer. Further, we might conclude that incumbents need to take small assignments for full if they are to keep their stronghold on the market, otherwise small companies might be forced to go to new entrants despite of their trial adversity, giving them a chance to build a reputation this way. I could continue this list, but I believe it would exceed the scope of these introductory notes.

I come now to a final remark. The above outlined examples for marketing activities can be broken up in three types: pure advertising and promotion, strategic planning, and customer relationship management. A chocolate bar manufacturer would regard all three as being part of the marketing function. This would not work in the M&A area, if only because the "product" is not manufactured upon previously defined specifications but rather individually tailored to a specific situation. Hence the confinement of marketing to the "advertising and promotion" area, a point Mrs. Schuler does not fail to evolve upon.

Seen from this angle it appears fair to conclude that the purchasing process of M&A banking can indeed be influenced and that therefore the shaping of marketing activities should be high on the agenda of firms engaging in this business. This will however require an approach that departs from the actual purchasing process and peculiarities of the offer as opposed to attempting adaptations of marketing strategies that proved successful in other industries. Mrs. Schuler's work should be regarded as a sound basis from which to depart.

Dr. Luca P. Marighetti retired last year from active business life. He now sporadically and selectively advises financial institutions on a number of strategic issues. Prior to that, he held senior positions at Procter & Gamble, SC Johnson Wax, McKinsey & Company, and lately Deutsche Bank.

Part I

Introduction

1 Goal

To start, this thesis' research objectives from both a theoretical and practical perspective shall be outlined. Therefor the theories to be applied shall be briefly introduced. Besides, the most important problems from a practical standpoint shall be addressed[1].

The remainder of the chapter is going to detail the structure of this thesis, in order to help the reader's easier orientation.

1.1 Research objectives

The objective of this thesis is to research the main levers through the influencing of which an investment bank can more consciously and successfully steer its marketing activities. Most important building blocks for such goal are a better comprehending of how specific levers work, by understanding their importance and impact from an M&A advisory user's perspective[2].

1.1.1 Theoretical perspective

The choice of the research topic was strongly driven by practical interest[3]. A blend of theories that could help to elaborate problems from a generalisable perspective, and that offered the tools for a hypothesis-driven approach, was then identified. Accordingly, the following provided the theoretic foundations for the research of the M&A advisor choice:

---

1 The basic concepts used in this thesis, as e. g. "M&A advisory" or "buyer", are clarified in chapter 3.

2 That is, from the perspective of a company that wants to engage an investment bank as its M&A advisor.

3 Cf. chapter 2.

- **Risk theory.** For the last 40 years, risk theory has provided a valuable instrument for the explanation of buyer attitude and actual behaviour[4]. Among others, risk theory has been used to explain the buyer's appetite to search for (additional) information, rely on provider's reputation, or to explain his unwillingness to engage at all into purchases that surmount his tolerable risk level. In this thesis, risk-theoretic foundations shall be used to make propositions on the risk level associated with M&A advisor choice, and in order to assess the availability and potential benefits of according relievers to companies

- **Information economy.** Information economy deals with the question how markets that are characterised by an asymmetrical information distribution between participants work, and which implications can be drawn from the latter's differing information costs on the market process[5]. In this thesis, information-economic considerations shall provide the foundation for the discussion of the respective importance of different signalling mechanisms in the case of M&A advisory

- **Principal agent theory.** Principal agent theory is concerned with designs to be implemented into principal-agent relationships[6], in order to preclude problems arising from informational asymmetry, mutual conflict of interest, and exogenous uncertainty[7]. Principal-agent-theoretic perspectives having played an important role in the assessment of contract goods' marketing specifics – since these products offer the agent a multiplicity of opportunities for hold-up or moral hazard –, it would be inappropriate to neglect this perspective in the case of M&A advisory. A review of the M&A advisor choice problem from a principal-agent perspective shall yield the identification of designs that preclude investment banks' deliberate quality deception

- **Product classification approaches.** In order to better capture the marketing specifics of respective product subclasses,

4 *Bauer* was the first to identify risk as important antecedent for buyer behaviour, see Bauer[20].

5 See Fischer[90], page 445.

6 As the one between company and investment bank in the case of M&A advisory.

7 Cf. Picot[185], page 370.

scholars have developed segmentation approaches for both services and industrial goods. M&A advisory belonging to both of these classes, this thesis shall review the most common product characteristics employed, in order to assess their implications on risk perception and information utility. These general findings shall then be applied to assess the M&A advisor choice from a product characteristics perspective.

While a hypothesis-driven approach shall be applied in general, some of the findings will be complemented by descriptive analyses. The latter are meant to deepen the insights gained by the former. In particular, descriptive analyses shall be used to provide a perspective on what is common practice in the market. By an examination of what relevance certain concepts actually do have for companies choosing their M&A advisors, the hypothesis-driven findings' practical relevance shall be ensured[8].

1.1.2 Practical perspective

The topics of practical interest, addressed by this thesis' research, may be organised around the following areas:

- **Risk and risk reduction in the M&A advisor choice.** Here, the drives of perceived risk associated with the selection of an investment bank shall be researched, as well as the measures that may be taken by the company in order to reduce risk. The research of this area should provide answers to questions like the following
    - How big is the perceived risk in the M&A advisor choice?
    - What drives the perceived risk?
    - How is the risk associated with the M&A project linked to the risk associated with the M&A advisor choice?
    - What are according measures taken by the companies that have to choose an M&A advisor?

8 For instance, if it known that risk influences buyer behaviour in a certain way, such analyses shall research what risk perception in the overall market is, and whether a very high risk perception is more of a common or more of a rare observation.

  - Which information types can be considered useful for risk relief?

- **Public reputation, investment banking relationship, execution of previous projects, sales presentation, and commercial banking relationship.** A company may know a buyer himself, or by virtue of information gained from third parties. The reader's attention may in particular be drawn to the commercial banking relationship, which universal banks have eagerly defended to be their important competitive advantage over investment banks, when it comes to mandate solicitation. Questions concerning the role of these vehicles include

  - How does the relative importance of these vehicles change, dependent on whether M&A advisor selection is competitive or not?
  - How does the relative importance of these vehicles change, dependent on whether a company chooses an M&A advisor for first or repeat time?
  - Which of these vehicles are most important prerequisites for a bank
    - To be considered for a certain M&A project?
    - To be invited?
    - To be awarded the lead mandate?
    - To be awarded repeat business?
  - What are selected bank types' strength/weakness profiles with respect to these vehicles?

- **Individual-corporation antagonism.** M&A advisory constituting a highly non-automated service, individual skills can be expected to influence delivered product quality significantly, thus valorising the importance of individuals[9] as opposed to corporations[10] in the buyer company's perception. Questions comprised by this topic area include

  - What is the perceived importance of individuals, as opposed to the corporations employing them, in the choice of an M&A advisor?

9 I. e., bankers.
10 I. e., banks.

- Does the relative importance that is attributed to individuals in the M&A advisor selection differ by bank type?
- How does the question whether the choice decision is based on the banker, rather than the bank, affect the company's satisfaction with the subsequent execution?
- If the M&A advisor choice decision is based on the bank, rather than the banker, how does this affect the relative importance that reputation, investment banking relationship, etc., play?

Empirical findings in these areas shall be used to provide guidance for the development and implementation of successful marketing strategies.

1.2 Organisation of the document

To conclude this introductory chapter, the structure of this thesis shall be outlined.

1.2.1 Structure

The thesis is composed of three major parts: introduction (part I), theoretic foundations and preliminary conclusions (part II), and research and discussion (part III).

Following the outline of research objectives in this chapter, the motivation for choosing this research subject shall be depicted in chapter 2. Basic marketing and investment banking concepts which are going to be used throughout the thesis shall be explained in chapter 3.

In part II, the theoretic background, by means of which hypotheses shall be derived, is being developed. More specifically, chapter 4 deals with risk and its explanatory power. The discussion of risk reduction strategies is taken further in chapter 5, where the marketing situation is being developed from an information-economic perspective. Chapter 6 discusses marketing-theoretic product classifications from a risk and information perspective. Chapters 4 to 6 are then being used to assess the M&A advisory marketing situation from a risk and information perspective in chapters 7 and 8. This assessment culminates in the derivation of the hypotheses, which are going to be tested in the final part of the thesis.

Part III depicts the background, results, and further perspectives of the empirical research. Thereby, chapter 9 explains the data collection approach and the methods of data evaluation chosen, while chapter 10 provides the actual test results, including a discussion of unexpected results. Chapter 11 comprises descriptive analyses that are meant to deepen the hypothesis-driven findings of the preceding chapter. In chapter 12, a synopsis of the results is being given, and implications from a theoretical, as well as practical point of view are being discussed.

1.2.2 Lists

Besides the text itself, the thesis contains three lists which may facilitate the reader's orientation. Pages VII to XI contain the table of contents, while a list of figures is provided on pages XIII to XIV. Figures are being used to compactly illustrate major thought lines. Finally, the list of tables is being provided on page XV. Tables have been employed to give an overview of statistical test results.

2 Motivation

The following thoughts gave motivation to the subject. The highly attractive economics of the M&A advisory market, its tremendous development in the recent past and highly encouraging forecasts for its mid-term development, combined with pessimistic diagnoses regarding its current and near-future development, make it look an attractive while difficult-to-win market – thus a business which banks should be eager to "re-think", in particular marketing-wise.

If marketing-averse attitudes are prevailing in business and professional service environments, they may provide a complication to such endeavours. It is one goal of this thesis to overcome such attitudes. More specifically, this thesis is meant to show that market insights may be valuable also for practitioners, by helping them to understand the key success factors of the M&A advisory business.

But the marketing of M&A advisory is also a topic of high marketing-theoretic interest, due to the product's unambiguous affiliation to the classes of services and industrial goods, which academic literature has started to deal with only recently. The high complexity of the product, its immaterial nature, the high degree of interaction during production, and the supposedly high pressure for choice justification, are some of its most prominent features which have implications on its marketing.

The drivers and consequences of these phenomena shall be reviewed in the following paragraphs, which thus aim at detailing the thoughts that gave motivation to the subject.

2.1 Market development

Let us briefly revisit the most recent market development. This review shall be restricted to the *European* M&A and M&A advisory market[1], which shall also constitute the field of research in the remainder of the thesis.

2.1.1 Market size and structure

Between 1995 and 2000, the M&A market volume and with it the M&A advisory market volume have been growing tremendously[2]. This holds for the number of deals as well as their size.

Transaction size of top deals has increased so strongly during the past years, that average transaction size has more than doubled between 1995 and 2000. The market is highly concentrated around the top deals[3] – less than one percent of advised deals account for more than half of the transaction volume, and top 10 deals account for more than 20 percent of the volume[4].

On the M&A advisory supply side, the market is highly concentrated around the three leading, so-called *bulge bracket*[5] investment banks that have been able to take advantage of the demand side concentration: Goldman Sachs, Morgan Stanley Dean Witter, and Merrill Lynch have a market share of well above 20 percent in the M&A advisory business, where the bulk of their income stems from high volume transactions.

1 I. e., transactions where at least one of the counterparts is European.

2 For longer-term development, cf. for example Müller-Stewens[178], pp. 2–4, Jansen[127], pp. 20–29, resp. Achleitner[5], pp. 97–136, 142–144, where the M&A market development is analysed in the context of historical and legal development.

3 In terms of transaction volume, cf. also figure 9.4 on page 175. In Europe, this tendency has strengthened in the recent past.

4 Similar, although slightly weaker, results hold for the transition from transaction volume to fees charged (margins are of diminishing scale with respect to transaction volume). Margin effects cannot be adjusted for, though, because fees are often kept confidential.

5 A clarification of the term "bulge bracket" is provided on page 36.

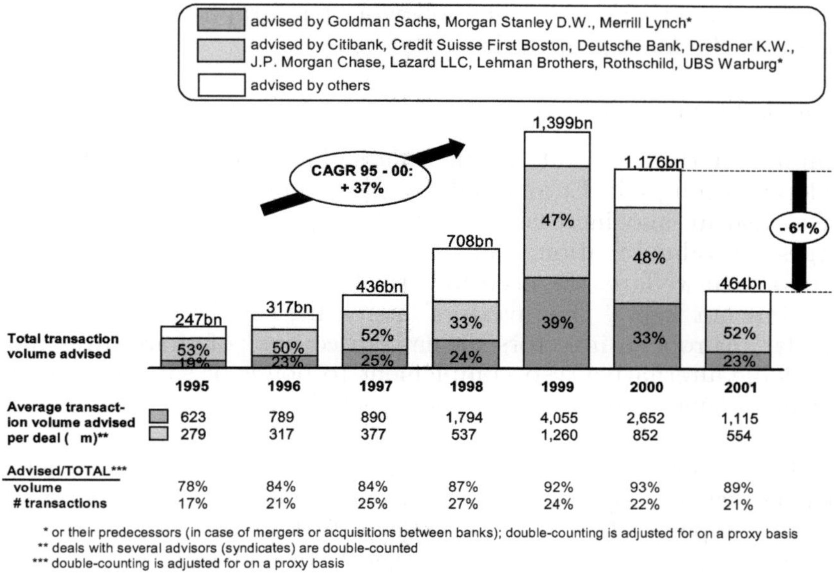

Figure 2.1: Development of the European M&A advisory market *(Volume advised; source: Thomson Financial Services)*

2.1.2 Drivers

The drivers for the M&A market's impressive growth are basically three-fold: shareholder value orientation, convergence resp. deregulation, and technological progress[6]. Besides these drivers, which have mainly increased the demand for M&A and M&A advisory, M&A advisory's comparatively increasingly attractive economics (as opposed to other banking businesses), can be considered a supply-side driver

6 Literature commonly suggests globalisation be one of the driving forces for M&A activity besides others such as deregulation. Contrarily to such reasoning, one can consider globalisation to be no more than just an intermediary force, which itself results from convergence/deregulation, as well as from technological progress. It is interesting to note that M&A literature hardly discusses the latter as a driver for industrial globalisation, but rather its consequences on the competitive investment banking landscape, as well as for best practices in investment banking, cf. also footnote 21 on page 15.

for the market's growth. The following paragraphs shall briefly expand on the main growth drivers.

Shareholder value orientation

Capital market orientation and shareholder value culture have developed strongly in Europe only in the recent past[7]. The formation of a wealthy and increasingly demanding investor generation, that urges for value creation, can largely be attributed to high general economical welfare, the need for private retirement provision, and – last but not least – the investors' increasing sophistication – in particular, European investors' recent "discovery" of share investment as viable alternative resp. complement to bonds or saving accounts[8] during a time of strong economical growth.

Having exploited the means of internal value creation – such as restructuring or operational effectiveness improvement programs –, many companies face the challenge to further increase shareholder return while acting in mature markets[9]. In many cases, this means that companies try to grow by acquiring, respectively merging with, direct competitors, aiming at the realisation of synergies, or to grow into new markets, such as new geographies or new industries, thus widening their geographic reach or product portfolio. Figure 2.2 illustrates these directions of potential value creation. Depending on the company's competitive position and on the targeted market's development stage, such growth may be achieved internally or externally[10].

7 Unlike in the US, where they already have tradition, cf. for example Müller-Stewens[178], page 13, Achleitner[5], pp. 43, 44, 144.

8 Cf. Jacob[124], page 19. This discovery may have been fuelled by the US stock markets' example, mediated by modern information technology.

9 Cf. for example Picot[186], page 10, Müller-Stewens[178], page 14, Achleitner[5], page 145.

10 Most of today's deals being strategically motivated, see for instance Achleitner[5], pp. 143–145, Jansen[127], page 55, this thesis concentrates on their rationale. *Bower* differentiates between five types of M&A according to their strategic goals, providing case examples as well as recommendations, see Bower[39].
Besides, mergers and acquisitions may be financially motivated, cf. for example Müller-Stewens[178], page 6, or Achleitner[5], pp. 138–142, Picot[186], page 10. A comprehensive discussion of envisioned M&A benefits can be found in Zenz-Spitzweg[244], pp. 7–13, or Dietzsch-Doertenbach[74], pp. 3–8.

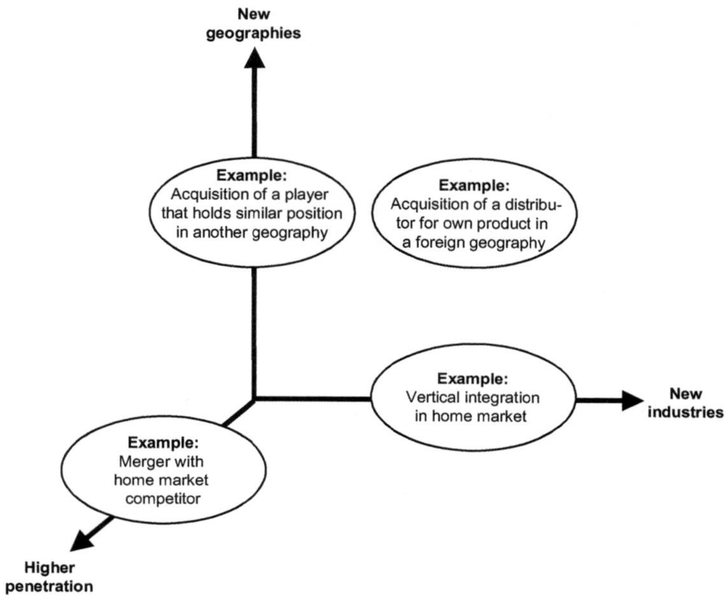

Figure 2.2: Directions of potential value creation through M&A

The establishment of a shareholder culture does not only urge for M&A activities, but it also fuels the liquidity of capital markets. Since such liquidity is a necessary precondition for investment banking activities[11], shareholder value orientation drives M&A activities also in an indirect way[12].

Jansen[127], pp. 54–89 researches potential benefits from the perspective of various economic theories, and discusses in how far they can be verified by empirical data.

11 A deeper discussion on the question in how far M&A activities depend on the capital market can be found in Dibelius[73], pp. 33–34. *Achleitner* discusses commercial banking as an alternative to investment banking combined with the capital market, cf. Achleitner[5], pp. 34–43.

12 Besides record equity market valuations, historically low interest rates and growing internal cash balances have provided the means for an inexpensive financing of M&A activities.

Unlike in North America, the majority[13] of mergers and acquisitions in the European market are not advised by third parties[14]. But an increase in the share of advised transactions can be expected, since the further development of capital markets is likely to go hand in hand with the tightening of legislative requirements for investor protection. An increase in the share of advised transactions in the mid-term growing M&A market can thus be expected to provide an additional boost for the M&A advisory market.

Convergence and deregulation

Both convergence[15] and deregulation[16] are catalysts for M&A activity. By the convergence of markets, the increasing assimilation of markets with respect to each other is being addressed, while deregulation denotes the abolition of legal restrictions within a market.

Widening the competitive arena, convergence and deregulation offer a wide field of strategic opportunities, as well as threats. On the one hand, companies may be able to access markets that offer attractive growth opportunities which they could not access before[17], and they may move, build, or buy operations in low wage countries or countries that have less restrictive legal environments, e. g. regarding R&D[18]. On the other hand, companies in converging and deregulated markets are forced to concentrate on and to leverage core capabil-

13 In terms of number, not transaction volume.

14 The share of advised deals in Europe is estimated to amount to only about 20 percent, see Achleitner[5], page 147, or figures provided in figure 2.1. An important reason for this is that the legal requirements in Europe are less restrictive, so that, unlike in Anglo-American geographies, companies are not forced to be advised externally on transactions, see for instance Deiß[70], pp. 489, 490.

15 See for example Müller-Stewens[178], pp. 9, 14, 20, 25, Achleitner[5], pp. 72, 145, Picot[186], pp. 28, 29.

16 See for example Jacob[124], pp. 18, 19, Jansen[127], pp. 6, 7, Müller-Stewens[178], page 9, Achleitner[5], pp. 71, 102, 124. Deregulation has often been driven by the competition of different geographies' capital markets for capital and opinion leadership.

17 See for instance Jansen[127], page 5, Müller-Stewens[178], page 20. This may be particularly important when home markets are already mature, so that growth opportunities there are restricted.

18 Cf. for example Jansen[127], pp. 57, 58, Müller-Stewens[178], page 14, Achleitner[5], page 145.

ities (to achieve economies of scale and of scope) in order to hold their ground under increased competition, while companies outside such huge single markets may feel pressured to secure their access to these markets[19]. Mergers and acquisitions constitute one mean to take advantage of new strategic opportunities offered by convergence and deregulation, as well as to fend off their threats[20].

Technological progress

Technological progress, which, by decreasing costs of information as well as of access, puts suppliers closer to the buyer, and thus competitors closer to each other, is another catalyst for globalisation. A world in which different competitors are only one mouseclick, phone call, or some hours' flight from each other, does not only offer tremendous business opportunities, but it also forces companies to compete with the best, which formerly were far away. Although this aspect of technological progress has not constituted a subject of M&A literature[21], it may be considered an important perspective on M&A market development in the "internet age".

Yet another aspect of technological progress are high R&D expenditures for technologically complex products, that only pay for themselves if return on them is high enough[22]. One strategy to increase return on such investments is to broaden the income (and thus amortisation) base, for example to other geographies, or to other areas by vertically integrating businesses that also profit from such

19 See for example Achleitner[5], page 145.

20 Prominent examples for the convergence of markets are the creation of the European Union, and the opening of the Eastern European markets towards Western-style market economy, as well as the creation of the North American Free Treaty Area (see for example Achleitner[5], page 145, Müller-Stewens[178], pp. 5, 9). As to deregulation, the recent revocation of taxation in the case of companies selling parts of their cross-shareholding (cf. for example Müller-Stewens[178], page 9. In fact, German regulators have not only weakened their restrictions, but are also looking for a European-wide convergence of M&A regulation, cf. for example Atkins[15]) by the German government, may serve as an illustration.

21 *Jacob* and *Klein*, as well as *Achleitner*, discuss in how far information and communication technology development affects the structure of the investment banks themselves, cf. Jacob[124], page 21, Achleitner[5], page 71.

22 Pharma may serve as an example for such industries.

research. Mergers or acquisitions may constitute a useful means to leverage R&D to a broader base[23].

Additional drivers for the German market

It is worth mentioning that, in Germany, M&A demand is resp. has in addition been driven by two German specifics. First, the privatisation of many of the Eastern German public enterprises conducted through the Treuhand following the reunion in the 90s[24] contributed significantly to the growth of the German M&A market. Second, unsolved successor problems in many of Germany's numerous and strong small- and medium-sized companies ("Mittelstand")[25], which constitute the backbone of Germany's economy, have led many of their founders or owners to consider their sale.

Economics

Not only has demand for M&A advisory increased due to the phenomena discussed in the previous paragraphs, but so has competition. M&A advisory's attractive economics have provided the most important basis for the latter – although one might argue that, to some extent, this has also resulted in an increase of the overall M&A advisory market volume, since banks may, by virtue of inventive project proposals, have helped a perking up of demand that formerly had not been achieved.

The financial intermediary acting *in the broader sense*[26], M&A advisory offers a bank the chance to achieve extremely high re-

23 See for example Jansen[127], page 6, Zenz-Spitzweg[244], page 15, Müller-Stewens[178], page 20.

24 Cf. for example Jacob[124], pp. 21, 22, Deiß[70], page 489. Müller-Stewens[178], pp. 9, 17, 27, Achleitner[5], pp. 143, 144.

25 Cf. for example Zenz-Spitzweg[244], pp. 27, 28, Müller-Stewens[178], pp. 21, 24, Achleitner[5], pp. 145, 146.

26 Which means, the intermediary does not act as counterpart of deals, and thus does not take on risk (for a more complete definition of "intermediary in the broader sense", cf. for example Bitz[33] or Achleitner[5], pp. 30–32). This means that no economic capital is needed to protect against unexpected losses, which again means that extremely high returns on economic capital can be achieved. Proprietary trading, or underwriting, compared with that, are examples for other investment banking businesses that do need economic capital. *Jacob* and *Klein* discuss in how far capital shortage may restrict investment banking activities, cf. Jacob[124], pp. 30, 40.

turns on economic capital. In times where the European universal banks' traditional corporate business is characterised by shrinking margins[27] and, even worse, severe credit losses, M&A advisory has thus been considered an attractive business alternative by European universal banks[28].

2.1.3 Protagonists

Investment banking has a long tradition in the US market, where it got earlier focused attention by providers than in Europe, presumably due to the differences in market regulation[29] and a further developed capital market orientation.

In contrast, one could say that European demand for M&A was born at a time European suppliers (i. e. banks) were not at all prepared to meet it with adequate offers – up to this time, investment banking activities had been one offer among others in the universal banks' portfolios, which did not get strong attention due to a generally weak capital market orientation accompanied by the "housebank" relationship phenomenon[30]. As European M&A activities were fuelled by the opening of the markets and an increasing shareholder value orientation at the beginning of the 90s, Anglo-American investment banks were committed to seize the opportunities, but still had to establish a broader local presence to do so. The tremendous business opportunities, as well as the threatening competitive

27 Cf. for example Deiß[70], page 490, Achleitner[5], page 6.

28 Cf. Currie[65], pp. 92, 93.

29 Regulatory differences can mainly be attributed to the 1929 US stock market crash and the consequences drawn from it: since many of the banks that had focused on security business were not able to pay back the liabilities they had to other banks, some of the latter went bankrupt, too, so that also many non-security investors lost their money. This induced the government to pass the so-called 1933 "Glass Steagall Act" and other regulatory measures (most prominently among them, the 1927 McFadden Act and the 1956/70 Bank Holding Acts), urging for a strict separation between commercial and investment banks, cf. for example Achleitner[5], pp. 5–7, pp. 113–117, or Jacob[124], page 9. Definitions for commercial as opposed to investment banking can be found in Achleitner[5] on page 9, Jacob[124], pp. 10–15.

30 I. e., customers took usually all services from one bank – unlike in the US, where regulation made this impossible by forcing banks to concentrate on either investment or commercial banking services.

power from overseas, induced many of the leading European universal banks to acquire rather than build investment banking capabilities in the nineties. Take-over targets were mostly situated in the United Kingdom (merchant banks[31]) or the US – such banks provided the specialised skills needed, while being too small to survive market deregulation autonomously in the longer run.

2.1.4 Current situation and outlook

While many of the European banks have been struggling with the integration of their foreign investment banking subsidiaries – which proved more difficult than expected due to huge cultural differences –, foreign investment banks have expanded geographically into Europe, mostly by building rather than buying local capabilities. This makes Europe look a mere battlefield, where some of the European players have already managed to gain a foothold in the "very upper" market, while most of them still struggle to do so. In fact, very big deals usually have not happened without the participation of one or more of the US-American M&A advisors, who up-to-date have scored first in European league tables[32].

In general, industry experts agree on the need for further mergers or acquisitions in Europe and consider the market's perspectives promising in the mid-term[33]. At the same time, its strong dependency on the economy is considered a threat to its shorter-term development – indeed, recent indications for economic slowdown have already affected the investment banks' profit reports and forecasts in an awful way, and the period to come is considered difficult[34].

31 Such merchant banks had for historical reasons business portfolios similar to the ones of US investment banks, cf. for example Achleitner[5], pp. 6–8.

32 To give an indication, the three market leaders have been involved in about 80 percent of the global M&A deals in 1999, cf. Currie[64], page 50.

33 *Müller-Stewens*, *Spickers*, and *Deiß* give further restructuring for shareholder value creation, clearing-up of historically grown cross-shareholdings after deregulation, interest of foreigners to enter the European market, deregulation of certain industries, and unsolved successor problems in Germany's "Mittelstand" as reason, cf. Müller-Stewens[178], pp. 16, 17. *Achleitner* discusses the market's perspectives in Achleitner[5], pp. 144–146.

34 *Pretzlitz* reports how the current economic development affects investment banks' M&A business franchise and perspectives, see Pretzlitz[190]. Müller-

Besides shrinking business volume, investment bankers fear margin pressure as a consequence of strong competition in a shrinking market[35]. The increasing sophistication of the big enterprises regarding investment banking products may reinforce such price deterioration, and strengthen expertise as a key factor of success for winning a mandate[36]. Increased customer sophistication, as well as tightening competition, may thus challenge established investment banking and commercial banking relationships[37].

The combination of current stagnation and good mid-term development perspectives make the competition for the M&A market look difficult while desirable to win. A better understanding of the business' key success factors may provide the basis for improving one's positioning in the M&A advisory business. It is one goal of this thesis to provide some empirical foundation for such endeavours.

2.2 Practical pitfalls

The role of the brand resp. reputation has been the subject of some debate, first of all in consumer goods industries, where providers realised that offering a product of superior functionality at a competitive price may not always be sufficient to win a consumer's choice[38].

Stewens[178], page 17, and Achleitner[5], pp. 83, 146 deal with the general link between economic and M&A development.

35 In fact, margins have already decreased, and a further decrease is strongly feared in connection with a further move from relationship towards transactional banking, see for example Müller-Stewens[178], page 35, Achleitner[5], pp. 73, 88, 94, 95, 153.

36 See for instance Hunt[121], pp. 106–108, Müller-Stewens[178], page 35, Achleitner[5], pp. 94, 95, 153.

37 The opportunities to cross-sell M&A in commercial banking relationships can in general be questioned, since the relationships to be cultivated for M&A (CEOs, CFOs, finance directors, etc.) differ significantly from those to be cultivated for commercial banking (treasury departments, etc.), cf. Hunt[121], page 107.

38 Apart from the companies themselves, many of the market research and marketing agencies have provided brand equity management systems. Some introduction to the basic ideas of such models, as well as the discussion of their shortcomings, can for instance be found in Sattler[201], pp. 670–676,

While there is usually agreement among top management that intangible assets, such as reputation or corporate knowledge, ought to be managed and controlled as any tangible asset a company owns, there are various issues that potentially endanger the successful implementation of best intentions. The most precarious of these issues shall be revisited in this section.

2.2.1 General issues

Although many companies show increased sensibility for brand management and marketing topics[39], a successful implementation of corresponding management practices faces a multitude of potential obstacles. Whereas some of these obstacles are home-grown (marketing-as-opposed-to-business ownership antagonism, misunderstanding of marketing's means and purpose, short-term-business focus), others are directly linked to the nature of objects that marketing deals with (difficulties in linking cause to effect, intangibility of objects to be monitored).

Marketing-as-opposed-to-business-ownership antagonism

Lacking direct business ownership, marketing functions often have a difficult standing in their companies[40]. Being disregarded for their "outsider-ignorance", the marketing function may not be considered a sparring partner for going to market, but an artificial appendix. As

---

[203], pp. 196–205, [204], pp. 634–636, Aaker[3], pp. 304–319, Bauer[19], pp. 15–21, Keller[141], pp. 344–367, Esch[87], pp. 954–965.

39 Cf. for example Yankelovich[240], pp. 7, 8, 13, 14–21, 28, or Aaker[2], pp. ix, x, 90. Recently conducted research by the *Chartered Institute of Marketing* in industrial goods industries showed that industrial marketers and their customers perceived branding and related issues of major importance for their overall business success. But, while such importance is considered high, "brand management [is] not in evidence, even in larger business-to-business organisations with more established brands. This is in marked contrast to consumer marketing, where brand management is often at the centre of the marketing role", see Sweeney[227].

40 *Lovelock* diagnoses dominating operations mentalities in most service businesses, which results in marketers' "lack of clout", which again limits their ability to shape the company's marketing strategies, see Lovelock[159], pp. 19, 20.

a result, marketing functions may find it hard to share and further develop their insights with the functions who "do the business".

Misunderstanding of marketing's means and purpose

The misunderstanding of marketing's means and purpose represents another major threat to the successful implementation of marketing strategies.

Mistakenly, marketing is often equated with advertising and brochure-printing[41], taken care of by some weird gurus who love colours and glossy paper, but who do not know what the business is really about. Dissociating themselves from any such practices, "product people"[42] may be taken in by the belief that doing the business right is just enough to get the right business.

If such beliefs prevail, then chances are high that marketing is not going to happen at all – for, marketing's aspirations go far beyond brochure printing or just doing the business right[43]; its aspirations consist in aligning the business functions for each product to the requirements of the market, in order to get demand side's attention and to be judged in a more favourable way than competitive offers, short: to establish comparative competitive advantages[44]. Put differently, marketing is the art of knowing more about the demand side's wants than competitors do, and of taking advantage of such knowledge by ensuring the development of adequate offers, identifying effective ways on how to insinuate potential customers of the product offer's superiority, and to make profit from this[45].

41 I. e., communication, see also Lovelock[159], pp. 19, 20. Similarly, *Kotler* points out that marketing is often mistakenly equated with selling, that is promotion, advertising, direct mail, sales calls, etc., cf. Kotler[147], page 3.

42 By using the term "product people", we adopt these people's notion that market and product orientation denote antagonisms – although, for successful go-to-market, product and market orientation should be complements rather than antagonisms.

43 Cf. for example Kotler[147], pp. 3, 11–13, Menon[171], page 27.

44 Cf. Backhaus[16], page 771.

45 Cf. Kaas[130], pp. 540, 541. Similar thoughts can be found in Kotler[147], pp. 10–14, where the *marketing* concept and the *societal marketing* concept are contrasted with others, such as the *selling* or the *production* concept, or Herrmann[114], page 15. A review and discussion of selected marketing definitions can be found in Backhaus[17], pp. 7–9.

Short-term business focus

Certain communication activities, such as event sponsorship or active management of public relations, as well as other market-oriented activities a company may undertake to improve its competitive positioning[46] show their results only with a time lag[47]. This causes basically two problems: first, commonly evaluated in the short rather than the medium or long term, decision-makers may feel tempted to skimp on activities whose benefits can only be seen in the longer term. Second, the impact of activities that show their effect only after time is difficult to measure.

Difficulties in linking cause to effect

The time lag problem gets serious when activities' effects get, in addition, overlaid by "accidental" occurrences, such as for example industry wigging due to some competitor's misbehaviour[48]. This dilemma of hard-to-identify cause-effect links does not only render fact-based decision-making[49] difficult, but it also puts marketers into difficulty when having to justify brand-building expenditures to other budget holders in the company, or to the company's shareholders.

Intangibility of objects to be monitored

Another issue about managing comparative competitive advantages is that some of them are hard to measure[50]. Brand image, corporate reputation, or the quality of employees constitute immaterial assets, such that they can neither be easily observed, nor measured directly

46 Such as for instance quality improvement programs

47 Cf. for example Aaker[2], pp. 174, 175, Aaker[3], page 316, Low[161], pp. 175, 187, Keller[141], page 31, Shocker[215], page 153. *Aaker* points out how long it takes to transform actual improved quality of a product into perceived quality – which is the only one among the two to impact sales figures –, see Aaker[2], page 101.

48 Cf. for example Sattler[203], pp. 194–196, Keller[141], pp. 221, 252.

49 E. g., regarding the composition of the marketing mix, cf. for example Sattler[203], page 194.

50 According to *Lovelock*, an additional problem for service businesses arises from the fact that most of them sell their products themselves and not through third parties. So in order to gain insights as to how they perform compared to competitors, they have to conduct expensive research and cannot rely on independent retail audits, see Lovelock[159], page 20.

in terms of dollars. This nurtures the temptation to skimp on certain activities, just because they are harder to observe[51].

2.2.2 Business-service-specific issues

Besides the above-mentioned general issues which companies have to overcome or deal with in order to successfully implement the marketing strategies, there are others which are mostly business-service-specific[52]. Most prominent among the latter are the following.

Marketing judged obsolete for institutional expert buyers

Institutional service providers may feel tempted to argue that, their clientele being well-informed experts, rethinking current marketing practices and potentially changing them would be in vain. To put it into easier words, the buyer is assumed to know anyway what he wants, and therefore marketing activities are perceived obsolete. But the truth of both of these statements should be questioned – the premise as well as the conclusion drawn from it.

As to the premise, one can doubt that institution-al buyers' expertise and knowhow be generally higher than the one of non-institutional consumers[53]. In the case of M&A advisory, the following may be used to support such position: first, the many novice or unexperienced buyers that enter the market in each M&A wave, which translates into a high share of buyers who lack significant prod-

---

51 Cf. for example Menon[171], pp. 29, 30. Once a company is dedicated to identifying and monitoring non-monetary factors that constitute comparative competitive advantages, it will often have to rely on input- rather than output-oriented measurement. To give an example, the dollar spending for advertising may have to serve as a substitute for the effect that such advertising achieves in the consumers' minds. But ideally, the dollar measure should be adjusted for effectiveness and efficiency. That marketing effectiveness depends strongly on what you do and how you do it, and not on how much you spend, is for example discussed in Keller[141], page 221, Aaker[3], page 186, Menon[171], page 28.

52 *Jackson* and *Cooper* present an overview of explanation heuristics for the dominance of production as opposed to marketing mentalities in the context of industrial businesses, cf. Jackson[123], pp. 113, 114.

53 Such position somewhat disagrees with parts of academic literature, such as Engelhardt[84], page 6, Plinke[187], page 174.

uct experience[54]. Second, the long buying cycles that apply, at least for the majority of its buyers, to the product, which deprive buyers of the possibility to really get familiar with the product[55]. Third, the complexity of the product – whether a buyer is an expert buyer or not, does not only depend on the buyer's knowledge regarding the product, but also on the assessibility of the product, which in the case of M&A advisory is highly immaterial and complex[55].

As to the conclusion. Even if buyers do have a lot of expertise and knowledge, there is evidence that, as competition becomes tighter[56], having the right market insights and adopting own behaviour accordingly may constitute the crucial competitive advantage to win a mandate, instead of losing it to competitors.

Professional ethos perceived contrary to marketing

Professional ethos and disdain of commercialism represent further barriers that have prevented many professional service providers from consciously thinking about, let alone from engaging into marketing programs.

While in some professions advertising and direct solicitation practices were prohibited by law[57], other professions – among them investment banking[58] – created and adopted codes that fostered marketing-averse resp. selling-averse attitudes, on their own. Until today, "few professionals like to think of themselves as businessmen"[59], and, as long as marketing gets equated with selling, such attitude may even be comprehensible. But when marketing is being understood to comprise the "organized activities and programs [...] designed to retain present clients and attract new clients by sensing, serving, and

54 Cf. Deiß[70], page 489.

55 See also paragraph 6.3.1, page 128.

56 Cf. for example Kotler[148], page 71, Müller-Stewens[178], page 35, Achleitner[5], pp. 72, 73.

57 *Kotler* and *Connor* mention accounting, actuarial and law as examples for professions in which "anything resembling selling activity" had been forbidden, see Kotler[148], page 72. Similarly, a historical review of professional association standards can be found in Lovelock[159], page 6, and [160], page 9.

58 Cf. the guidelines drafted by John P. Morgan at the beginning of the 20th century, see Achleitner[5], page 129.

59 See Kotler[148], page 71. Similarly, *Schade* discusses management consultants' hostile attitude towards marketing, see Schade[207], pp. 12–14.

satisfying their needs through delivery of appropriate services on a paid basis in a manner consistent with creditable professional goals and norms"[60], such neglect seems unforgivable – in particular from the perspective of increased competition in the market.

2.3 Theoretic interest

Being a service provided by businesses to other businesses, M&A advisory belongs to the category of *business services*[61]. Business services have not gained much attention in marketing theory yet, and the availability of empirical research on this class is very limited to date[62]. Thus, M&A advisory constitutes a subject of high academic interest, from a theoretic as well as an empirical research point of view. It is one goal of this thesis to revisit and further develop the research on the marketing for this product class – in part by comparing theory-based suggestions with empirical evidence.

To start, let us first revisit the most important specifics of the two major product classes which M&A advisory belongs to: *services* and *industrial goods*.

60 See Kotler[148], page 72.

61 Cf. Dawes[67], page 186. In *Stock* and *Zinszer*'s terms, "producer services", see Stock[226], page 1. M&A advisory is in fact the "purest" service that an investment bank provides to its corporate customers. Unlike many other investment banking services, it is not connected to the retail business (underwriting, where a broad access to the retail market is crucial to provide enough distribution power, may serve as a counterexample). Furthermore, the product result (the advice on whether and how to do a transaction) is highly immaterial.

62 Cf. Stock[226], page 13, Dawes[67], pp. 185–187. *Meffert* notes that investment core services have been hardly examined yet by academic literature, cf. Meffert[170], page 21.

2.3.1 Service specifics

Although literature has struggled a lot and failed so far to give a concise definition for services[63], there is intuitive evidence that services differ from other goods in a fundamental way. For the time being, *Meffert* and *Bruhn*'s working definition shall be used here, which characterises services as performance potentials, whose realisation requires the integration of external factors, where the goal of such realisation consists in beneficial effects on people or other objects[64]. From the most apparent specifics of services, peculiarities for the marketing of services can be derived. A brief review of select issues and their consequences[65], all of which apply in particular to

---

63 Cf. for example Jackson[123], Engelhardt[85], page 403, Stauss[223], pp. 82–85, Meffert[169], pp. 521, 522. The difficulties arising for a general definition can vastly be attributed to the wide range of products that services span, e. g. from standardised to highly individualised, from automated to person-bound products, as well as to the fuzziness of boundaries to other product classes (consider for example the construction of a highly individualised building, which comprises lots of service components, but also physical goods). This is why it makes sense to view services as one extreme of a continuum, as suggested by *Meffert*, see Meffert[169], page 525. A discussion of existing activity-oriented, process-oriented, result-oriented, resp. potential-oriented definition approaches can be found in Meffert[170], pp. 23–27.

64 Cf. Meffert[170], page 27. Following *Berry* in contrasting services from goods, *Lovelock* and *Wright* provide a simple but useful working definition for services, which characterises them as “an act or performance offered by one party to another”, see Lovelock[160], page 5.

65 A detailed discussion of most of these peculiarities can be found in Berry[25], pp. 24–27, Corsten[59], pp. 17–19, 24, Staffelbach[222], pp. 278, 283–284, Zeithaml[243], pp. 40–42, Meyer[173], pp. 197–203, Stauss[223], pp. 92–93, 97–98, Meffert[169], pp. 521–524, 528, 531–537, [170], pp. 59–66, Jacob[125], pp. 199–200, Lovelock[159], pp. 15–19, Keller[141], page 14. A good overview on which authors consider which service features (intangibility, inseparability, heterogeneity, perishability) constituent for services, can be found in Zeithaml[242], figure 1 on page 34. Service marketing specifics are then summarised in figure 2, page 35. Note that some of the issues discussed in literature are being left out, since one cannot consider them to be universally valid for services.
Besides, a restriction is made in that characteristics are being addressed from a *buyer*'s perspective. Other characteristics, which are mostly linked to problems the *provider* may face when marketing services, such as for instance matching demand levels without building excess capacity, the challenge of which results from services' perishability, are not being addressed.

the marketing situation of M&A advisory services, shall be given in the following.

- Sales before production[66] yields
  - Increased importance of performance potential signalling (e.g., signalling the superiority of production factors) at sales[67]
  - Increased importance of experience and credence qualities
- The immateriality of the product[68] results in
  - Particular importance of credence qualities (as opposed to experience qualities)[69]
  - Increased importance of tangible product substitutes (such as physical facilities, employees, price) when it comes to product choice and evaluation, in particular a strong link between brand-as-a-product and brand-as-an-organisation
- Higher potential for intra-provider quality variability, due to the integration of external factors – which the provider cannot completely control – in the production process[70], thus

66 That sales takes place before production results from the impossibility to stock services (such impossibility applies in particular to process-oriented services, where consumption happens in parallel to production) resp. the necessity to integrate external factors into their production (this necessity applies particularly to result-oriented services).

67 Performance signalling shall be expanded on in paragraph 5.2.2.

68 The immateriality applies at least to the major part of the product, cf. for example Meffert[169], page 522. It is worth pointing out that the product should not be confused with its effect or the process, both of which may be highly material.

69 Search qualities do not exist, while experience qualities are often of vague character due to the intangibility of the product, cf. also section 5.2, pp. 88–94.

70 In literature, this "intra-provider" quality variability is mostly attributed to differences between the individuals (motivation, qualification, mood, etc.) performing the service. Such argumentation would not hold for automated services, such as automated car wash, though, which means it cannot be considered universally constituent for services. In contrast, the point to be made here is that the outcome quality may vary due to differences in the

- Lower utility of (third party's) experience for the purchase decision[71]
- Difficulty for the provider to issue guarantees because of the buyer's influence on product quality[72].

Besides these specifics, other factors, such as the degree of interaction, individualisation, and automation, have a strong influence on the marketing of services from an information perspective[73]. But since they do not categorically apply to services, they shall be dealt with only later[74].

2.3.2 Industrial good specifics

Industrial goods constitute another product class which M&A advisory belongs to, and whose marketing peculiarities have been discussed a lot recently[75]. In contrast to services, concise definitions for industrial goods are straightforward. Industrial goods are goods or services which are provided by organisations to organisations[76].

---

quality of external factors provided by the user, including his level of care. Thus, to use *Lovelock* and *Wright*'s terms, this perspective addresses the "input" quality variability, cf. Lovelock[159], page 16.

71 Experience strategy is less reliable, cf. also figure 5.3 on page 93.

72 buyer's influence often cannot be separated from seller-controlled determinants of product quality. Besides, there may be difficult-to-separate external factors influencing the quality outcome.

73 An example on how different services may vary regarding such aspects, can be found in Meffert[170], page 45.

74 See chapter 6.

75 And, as *Wind* and *Thomas* note, "few empirical generalisations have emerged which can provide specific guidelines for action [...] due in part to the fragmented nature of much of the published organisational buying research, the lack of a replication tradition, and the relatively small and non-representative samples of most academic studies", see Wind[238], page 250.

76 Investment goods constituting a subclass that has attracted much of the scholars' attention in the German-speaking tradition. Investment goods being "services or goods, which are procured by organisations for production of further goods or services, and which do not consist in the distribution to the end consumer", see Backhaus[16], page 771 (similar or related definitions can for instance be found in Engelhardt[82], page 153, [83], page 146, [84], page 6, Plinke[187], page 172), M&A advisory does not fall into this category, since the organisation constitutes the end consumer of this service.

Accordingly, determinants and peculiarities of the marketing situation for industrial goods can be described as follows[77].

- Buyers are not individuals, but organisations, and the buy decision is often not made by a singular individual, but by a so-called *buying centre*[78]. The latter means in particular that, for the provider, contacting the right individuals of the buyer organisation at the right time with the right issues, is key[79]
- The most important role of the provider brand may consist in risk reduction[80]. Besides, the provider brand may be important for justification of choice toward third parties, within or outside the company. This constitutes some contrast to consumer goods brands, that may, besides functional benefits, offer emotional or self-expressive benefits[81].

---

77 A discussion of these specifics can be found in Engelhardt[82], page 154, [83], pp. 146–147, [84], pp. 6–7, Günter[104], page 109, Merbold[172], page 109, Plinke[187], pp. 173–174, Kleinaltenkamp[145], page 77, Backhaus[17], pp. 1–6, 9, Garbe[94], page 1109. As in the case of services, some of the issues discussed in these sources are being left out, since they do not apply categorically to all industrial goods, but only to specific subsets, as for instance investment goods or subclasses of them.

78 In contrast to many other industrial goods, cf. for instance Garbe[94], page 1117, the potential buyer-user antagonism within the buying centre remains, in the case of M&A advisory, limited, since the purchase department usually is not represented in it. Decision processes within the buying centre shall not constitute a subject of this thesis, but have for instance been researched by Lynn[165] in the context of professional services.

79 Cf. for instance Engelhardt[83], page 147, or Choffray[55], pp. 29, 30. *Sheth* points out that, for effective communication with the buying centre, it is no sufficient to know about individual differences, but that one must also know group decision making emerges from individual preferences in combination with other factors, as for instance decision or company specifics, see Sheth[214], pp. 53, 54. In Puto[191], pp. 89, 90, heuristics regarding such transition from individual to group decision making, are developed. *Wind* and *Thomas* discuss conceptual issues arising from this constellation, see Wind[238], pp. 240–242, 251–254. Decision-theoretic modelling that addresses the issue of a group's decision making in a simplified context can be found in Arora[13].

80 Cf. Sweeney[227].

81 To use *Farquhar*'s terms, cognitive evaluations may play a dominant role in buyer's brand evaluation, cf. Farquhar[88], page 27.
In the industrial context, self-expressive benefits might play some role in the

Besides these characteristics, which may be considered the only ones that apply universally to industrial goods, other characteristics have been discussed in literature, most importantly[82]:

- The sales process can often be characterised by interaction rather than one-sided action, and is usually complex and time-intensive
- Classic marketing instruments ought to be used differently (direct distribution, one-to-one marketing, importance of contraction process)
- Competitive landscape is often special (including alliances, long-lasting relationships, etc.), and it sometimes reflects strategic partnerships between supplier and buyer.

In fact, all of them hold for M&A advisory.

It is evident that services, as well as industrial goods, span a wide range of product categories. This is why there have been numerous endeavours to identify homogeneous subsets within them. As in the case of services, such approaches shall be recurred to in chapter 6.

It has thus been shown that the marketing of M&A advisory differs a lot from the marketing of other goods classes, such as for instance consumer goods. For the buyer, the immateriality of the product and the risk associated with its purchase, make it a product whose quality is difficult, but important to assess. It is one goal of this thesis to explore vehicles which the buyer usually bases his advisor choice on in such difficult choice situation.

---

sense that the choice of a highly renowned service provider might constitute one mean for a company to express its own quality standards towards other market participants, as well as its internal organisation.
The classification of benefits in the consumer goods context is taken from Aaker[3], pp. 95–105; other categorisation of benefits the consumer might associate with a brand can for instance be found in Bauer[19], pp. 2–7, Keller[141], pp. 99–100, Tomkins[230].

82 Most of the particularities reviewed can be found in Engelhardt[82], page 154, [83], pp. 146–148, [84], page 6, Plinke[187], pp. 173, 174, Merbold[172], page 109.

3 Basic concepts

This section shall provide a clarification of the most important concepts to be dealt with throughout the thesis.

3.1 Marketing concepts

First of all, general and marketing expressions shall be clarified. By this, the reader's confusion arising from the terms' possibly different usage in other contexts, shall be precluded.

Buyer

The term buyer shall denote an individual[1] or a company that is interested in buying the product that is subject of the context.

In particular, the term buyer will be used to denote a company that may want to buy M&A advice[2].

Experienced buyer, repeat buyer, switcher, first time buyer

The term experienced buyer shall denote a buyer who buys the product in question for repeat time, thus has already made experience with it before. Conversely, buyers buying a product for the first time shall be denoted as first time buyers.

Within experienced buyers, repeat buyers shall be differentiated from switchers. Repeat buyers are experienced buyers that buy from a provider from which they have already bought the product in ques-

1 The term "buyer" shall be used for both female and male buyers, but for simplicity reasons, the male forms of the pronomina shall be used. Similar propositions hold for the term "provider", "banker", "principal", "agent", etc.

2 Where most of the marketing theory uses the word consumer, the term buyer shall be used, in order to avoid a spontaneous mental association of the M&A advisory product buyer with a buyer of consumer goods.

tion before, while switchers buy from a provider from whom they have not bought the product in question before.

Company

If not specified differently, the term company shall denote a company, or the part of it, which is or may want to get involved into, or is subject of, an M&A transaction.

Comparison

The term comparison shall denote the efforts a buyer undertakes to compare the quality and utility of branded products offered to him, with the goal to make the optimal choice. Thus, comparison may in particular include information collection and processing.

Brand

The term brand shall denote a "name, term, sign, symbol, or design, or a combination of these intended to identify the goods or services of one seller or group of sellers and to differentiate them from those of competitors"[3].

As *Sweeney* notes, "in B2B terms the brand is commonly (but not always) the corporate name, and is often applied to entire ranges of products".

Brand asset

The term brand asset shall denote a physical or immaterial asset, such as for instance patents, employees, production equipment, etc., linked to or possessed by the brand.

Brand association

The term brand association shall denote anything linked in memory to a brand, thus anything that connects a person to the brand[4]. Such

3 See Kotler[147], page 597. Similar definitions can for instance be found in Kapferer[136], page 187, or Keller[141], page 2, Lovelock[160], page 166. A historical perspective on the utilisation of brands and branding is provided in Farquhar[88], page 24.

4 Cf. Kapferer[136], page 54, Aaker[2], page 109, [4], page 17, Keller[141], pp. 93–124. *Farquhar* differentiates between three types of associations:

associations may include user imagery, product attributes, usage situations, organisational associations, brand personality, symbols, etc.

3.2 Investment-banking-specific concepts

Acting on behalf of the companies involved, investment banks facilitate transactions on the market for corporate control. This section shall clarify the basic investment banking concepts to be dealt with throughout the thesis. This includes a review of the specific activities investment banks undertake in the course of an M&A project. Finally, the solicitation process, whose structure and content shall provide an important basis for the research of marketing and sales success factors in part III, shall be depicted.

3.2.1 Definitions

Investment bank

For the sake of simplicity, the term investment bank will be used to denote both an investment bank or the investment banking division of a universal bank.

M&A – mergers and acquisitions

The term M&A shall denote such transactions on the market for corporate control – the object of such transactions are ownership rights for whole companies, parts of companies, or shares of either of them[5] –, where

- A joint management of the merged business is established (in the case of mergers) or

affective responses, cognitive evaluations, and behavioural intentions, see Farquhar[88], pp. 27, 28.

5 Similar definitions can be found in Craven[62], page 1444, Müller-Stewens[178], page 1, Achleitner[5], page 137. A more detailed discussion of definition approaches and their peculiarities can be found in Jansen[127], pp. 30–33. *Picot* uses the broader Anglo-American definition, which includes – among others – alliances, IPOs, and restructuring, see Picot[186], pp. 15, 16.

- The buyer gains control over the acquired business's management and integrates the acquired business into his own combine of enterprises as subsidiary (in the case of acquisitions/divestments).

Note that this definition excludes transactions in which the buyer does not envision to manage the target, such as in the case of sleeping partnerships.

M&A advisory

The term M&A advisory shall denote the consultation service that an investment bank delivers to its corporate customer on M&A[6].

Buy side, sell side, take-over defense

Dependent on the role of the party which the investment bank serves, M&A advisory mandates can be categorised into

- **Buy side.** The investment bank advises a company on whether and how to act as a buyer on the market for corporate control
- **Sell side.** The investment bank advises a company on whether and how to act as a seller on the market for corporate control[7]
- **Take-over defense.** The investment bank advises a company whose management fears to be taken over by some other company, resp. a company that has already received a take-over bid, but that does not want to sell[8].

6 *Achleitner* acknowledges the usage of the term "M&A" also for several types of advice offered by various parties to the parties involved in an M&A transaction, see Achleitner[5], page 137, similarly Becker[22], page 198. In order to make a clear differentiation between the financial advice offered by investment banks, and the actual transaction on the market for corporate control, their service shall be denoted by "M&A advisory". Paragraph 3.2.2 gives a description of this service.

7 Thus, advising a company on a merger comprises both buy and sell side advice simultaneously.

8 Such take-over bid is then considered "hostile". The inhering difficulty of such task is discussed in Achleitner[5], page 207: while a defense is, for the shareholders of a company, only desirable if a take-over does destroy shareholder value, the target company's management's main motivation to appoint a take-over defense advisor may consist in the endeavour to preserve their own power. Thus, there is substantial risk that the management of a company may knowingly act against their shareholders' interests.

Merger, acquisition, divestment

Depending on which counterpart takes the initiative for a transaction and what the envisioned goal of such a transaction is, three types of M&A transactions resp. advisory mandates can be differentiated[9].

- **Acquisitions.** The term acquisitions shall denote such transactions on the market for corporate control where the initiative for the transaction lies by the company who wants to buy another company in order to gain control over it
- **Divestments.** The term divestments shall denote such transactions on the market for corporate control where the initiative lies by the company who wants to sell its business or parts of it to some other company that is then taking control over the sold business
- **Mergers.** The term mergers shall denote such transactions on the market for corporate control where a joint management of the newly created company is established. Analogously to acquisitions and divestments, one can differentiate between *acting counterpart* and *reacting counterpart*, dependent on which party takes the initiative for the transaction.

Thus, a transaction on the market for corporate control can be initiated by either buy or sell side[10], with or without support of external advisors. The target, in return, may appoint their own advisors to help them find and evaluate potential strategies.

Due to potentially conflicting interests of buy and sell side, a bank can only act on behalf of one of them in an acquisition[11].

9 Such typology takes into account the most common mandate types, and abstracts from less common types, such as demergers, management buyouts, etc.

10 A description of different modi operandi when the initiative lies by the seller, as well as a discussion of their suitability, can for instance be found in Müller-Stewens[178], pp. 41–44, or Achleitner[5], pp. 201–205.

11 An implication of this is that the advisory mandates theoretically acquirable by one bank amount to less than 100 percent of all mandates. They represent more than 50 percent, though, since there are many M&A projects where only one counterpart uses M&A advice, not to speak of the numerous M&A transaction that are not advised at all. This observation represents an important aspect in the assessment of conversion ratios along the purchase funnel, cf. part III.

Only in few cases, where the transaction counterparts are not conflicted, one investment bank may advise both of them at a time[12].

Bulge bracket and major bracket

Bulge bracket banks are the market leaders in terms of volume advised, and this position is currently held by Goldman Sachs, Morgan Stanley Dean Witter, and Merrill Lynch[13]. Major bracket banks are the banks positioned next in terms of transaction volume advised. As to the research reported in this thesis, J.P. Morgan Chase, UBS Warburg, Credit Suisse First Boston, Rothschild, Lazard LLC, Citibank[14], Dresdner Kleinwort Wasserstein, Deutsche Bank, and Lehman Brothers have been included in this bank segment[15].

3.2.2 Investment banks' tasks

Following this clarification of the most important investment-banking-specific terms, let us now depict what the contribution of an investment bank to an M&A project specifically consists in[16].

As shows figure 3.1, the focus of its service lies in advising and accompanying the customer through the execution of a transaction,

---

12 Such simultaneous advice may be given in the case of mergers, and it usually deals with integration issues, cf. for example Achleitner[5], pp. 47, 218.

13 Based on a 1998–2000 average, or a 1999–2001 average of advised volume. Cf. also Currie[64], page 50, Achleitner[5], page 15. The term "bulge bracket" is derived from the graphical position of the bank's name in newspaper advertisements on successfully executed transactions (so-called tombstones), cf. Achleitner[5], page 15.

14 Formerly known as Salomon Smith Barney.

15 Major bracket banks are banks that also enjoy a good reputation and serve a significant customer share, but which are not that omnipresent in the market (for instance, geographical restrictions) and do not enjoy that consistent a reputation in all market segments, as do bulge bracket banks, cf. Achleitner[5], page 16.

16 *Deiß* and *Achleitner* discuss how M&A projects may benefit form third party advisor's contributions in general, see Deiß[70], pp. 495, 496, Achleitner[5], pp. 147–149.

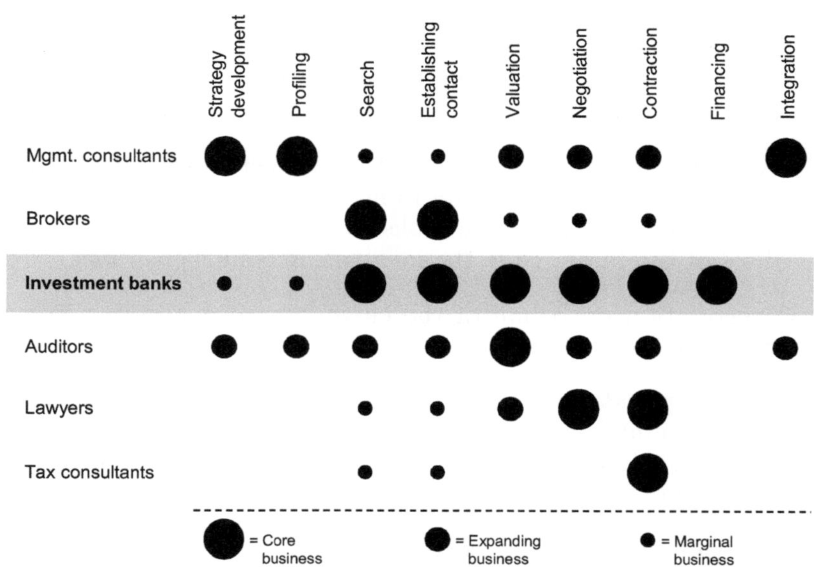

Figure 3.1: Self-explained task focus of M&A advisors
(Modified, after Deiß[70], *page 496)*

once general strategy and corresponding target profiles have been developed[17]. An investment bank's core tasks include[18]

- Identifying potential buyers/sellers that fit into the company's strategic context and satisfy the profile requirements[19]

---

17 A description of general steps of a merger or acquisition is provided in Craven[62], pp. 1449, 1452, 1453, and a detailed process flow can for instance be found in Picot[186], pp. 20–27. *Deiß* gives a description of the tasks that different M&A advisors perform during an M&A project, see Deiß[70], pp. 496–498.

18 A description resp. discussion of investment banks' tasks can for instance be found in Becker[22], page 198, Jacob[124], pp. 40–42, Deiß[70], page 498, Müller-Stewens[178], pp. 55–60, Achleitner[5], pp. 150–154, 187–225.

19 The results of such search are the so-called long resp. short lists.

- Establishing the contact between the potential M&A counterparts, once preliminary consent between the investment bank and its customer has been reached on who the most promising candidates are
- Valuation of the business which is subject to sale or purchase. In such valuations, a wide range of information is reflected – from general industry outlooks to very specific assets or liabilities of the target resp. the investment bank's customer
- Negotiation on behalf of the customer, resp. negotiation support for the customer
- Drafting and revising the contract to be closed between the M&A counterparts. This includes outlining the transaction's structure, in particular, whether an acquisition will be paid for by cash or by equity[20]
- Provide financing if needed[21].

While the first two activities – in which the investment bank acts as a market maker – make use of a bank's (superior) access to and connectivity with the market, the other ones make use of an investment bank's (specialised) knowledge and knowhow[22]. Once the negotiations are over, and a transaction has been agreed or rejected, an investment bank usually withdraws from the project.

20 A more detailed description of the degrees of freedom in a transaction's structure can be found in Achleitner[5], pp. 180–187.

21 This applies only to buy-side mandates. A comprehensive discussion of financing issues can be found in Achleitner[5], pp. 192–197. The big investment banks – including the investment banking arms of the universal banks – usually provide such financing – at least partially – themselves. This aspect shall not be focused on any further, because the provision of financing (1) hardly constitutes an exclusion criterion in the upper M&A advisory market, (2) may also be provided by other than the advising banks, and (3) does not constitute advice in the narrower sense itself.

22 The business's valuation constitutes the core of any M&A transaction. A description and discussion of the most common valuation tools can for instance be found in Jacob[124], pp. 64–105, Schröder[212], Jansen[127], pp. 170–199. Richter[194] provides a practical discussion of the topic, which incorporates real-life restrictions (such as the taxes a company has to pay when selling some of their business).

Dependent on the side which the investment bank advises, and dependent on the objective resp. desired outcome, specific approaches and techniques may be differentiated. It is outside the scope of this thesis to expand on the specifics of buy side, sell side, merger, and take-over defense advice any further. Therefore, the interested reader may be referred to Achleitner[5], Dietzsch-Doertenbach[74], Gerpott[96], Jacob[124], Klemm[146], and Müller-Stewens[178][23].

3.2.3 Solicitation for mandate

The understanding of the solicitation process constitutes an important prerequisite for the research of success factors in M&A advisory mandate acquisition. In the following, the solicitation process shall be revisited and broken down into self-contained phases – the latter of which will provide one basis for the research of key success factors in chapter 11.

Solicitation types

Solicitation types may be differentiated according to the degree of competition (exclusive vs. competitive solicitation) and to the party who takes the initiative for the M&A project (investment bank vs. advised company).

23 A description of buy-side strategies can in particular be found in Achleitner[5], pp. 190–192. Sell-side strategies are for instance assessed in Müller-Stewens[178], pp. 41–44, Achleitner[5], pp. 201–204. Dietzsch-Doertenbach[74], pp. 9–19 and Achleitner[5], pp. 217–225 assess merger mandate specifics and complement their findings by fictitious, resp. real-life examples. Literature on take-over defense has described the strategies in question a lot, see for example Jacob[124], pp. 54, 55, Gerpott[96], Achleitner[5], pp. 214–217, but has not that much discussed their suitability and feasibility (an exception provides the discussion of potential legal obstacles to some of the strategies in Klemm[146], pp. 4–6). One reason for this shortcoming may lie in the rare occurrence of hostile take-over bids due to the public's (in particular the European public's) traditional disregard for them, which made the advice on defense for long times widely obsolete. Besides explicit defense strategies in the case of an already pronounced take-over bid, there exist also precautionary measures a company may take in order to avoid becoming a take-over target, see for example Jacob[124], pp. 52–54, Achleitner[5], pp. 209–214.

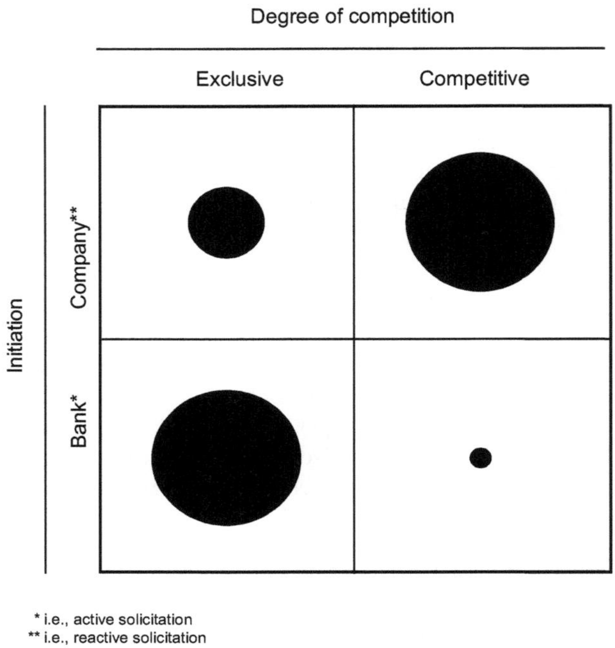

Figure 3.2: Solicitation types by initiative and degree of competition *(Size of circle symbolises estimated incidence according to literature)*

Figure 3.2 visualises these categorisations and provides an indication of their frequency of incidence, as suggested by literature[24].

Competitive vs. non-competitive solicitation.

Dependent on how many investment banks a company contacts to give their perspectives on a certain M&A project, two basic solicitation types can be differentiated.

24 See Deiß[70], pp. 492, 493, Achleitner[5], pp. 156, 157.

If only one investment bank is being contacted, such solicitation shall be called *exclusive* or *non-competitive.* Taking the company's perspective, one can alternatively speak of *exclusive* or *non-competitive selection.* Alternatively, solicitation may be *competitive*, i. e., a company may prefer to contact several banks and decide thereafter to which of them to award the mandate[25]. Competitive solicitation is frequently referred to as *beauty contest* by practitioners. Taking the company's perspective, the term *competitive selection* may alternatively be used to describe these circumstances.

Competitive solicitation may be of more or less formal character, dependent on whether soliciting banks give sales presentations, or whether the company discusses the transaction in question with several banks. Both sales presentation and discussion shall be referred to by the term *solicitation events.*

Active vs. reactive solicitation.

If an investment bank initiates an M&A project, solicitation shall be called *active*, while in the case where a company decides to make an M&A project and then looks for an advisor, solicitation shall be called *reactive.*

Active solicitation may have two different starting points. The first (deal drafting) takes a market, the second (strategic dialogue) takes a specific company's perspective.

- **Deal drafting**. An investment bank may screen a particular industry to identify M&A transaction opportunities, and draft a concept by which such transaction could be implemented. Presenting its ideas to one of the potential transaction counterparts, the investment bank may then solicit the M&A advisory mandate.

  Deal drafting is common in cases where an investment bank has not yet been able to establish a relationship (key account

25 A discussion of competitive as opposed to exclusive solicitation can for instance be found in Deiß[70], pp. 493, 494, Müller-Stewens[178], pp. 37, 38, Achleitner[5], page 157. If a transaction is big, a company may also choose several advisors, the group of which are then called the *syndicate.* In such cases, one bank among the syndicate members is usually appointed *lead advisor* by the company.

management) with a company which it considers generally attractive to serve, or when the transaction is considered attractive by the investment bank, but key account management for either of its counterparts is not worth the investments[26].

Traditionally, such approach has been taken by the Anglo-American investment banks in Europe, rather than the universal banks, due to the former's lack of relationships with many of the big corporates

- **Strategic dialogue.** The relationship with former customers resp. other promising, usually big, companies (key accounts), constitutes another strategy of active mandate acquisition. In such case, a senior banker acts as a company's sparring partner on a broader basis. By rendering outstanding service to the company, the banker may gain its trust and have better information than competitors on upcoming business opportunities.

It is evident that high pre-project expenditures[27], on the one hand, and uncertainty regarding the company's decision on whether or not to engage the advisor, on the other hand, constitute a source of financial risk for the investment bank[28].

Figure 3.3 on page 43 gives an overview over different types of mandates, according to the type of transaction and the role of the

26 Cf. also Berry[27], page 239, or Grönroos[101], page 408. *Grönroos* finds that "the main thing is [...] not whether a relational strategy is possible or not, but whether a firm finds it profitable and in other respects suitable to develop a relational strategy".

27 High specific investments are characteristic for contract goods in general, see for instance Kaas[132], pp. 73–75. A short review of the concept of "sunk costs" in connection with highly specific products can for instance be found in Williamson[234], page 522.

28 This problem is termed the *loose linkage* problem, see for instance Deiß[70], page 493. It should be noted that the compensation structure of M&A advisory – an investment bank is, apart from take-over-defenses, only paid for its service if a transaction does happen – contributes a lot to the loose linkage problem.

company that the investment bank advises. Mandates that may *actively* be acquired by an investment bank are highlighted.

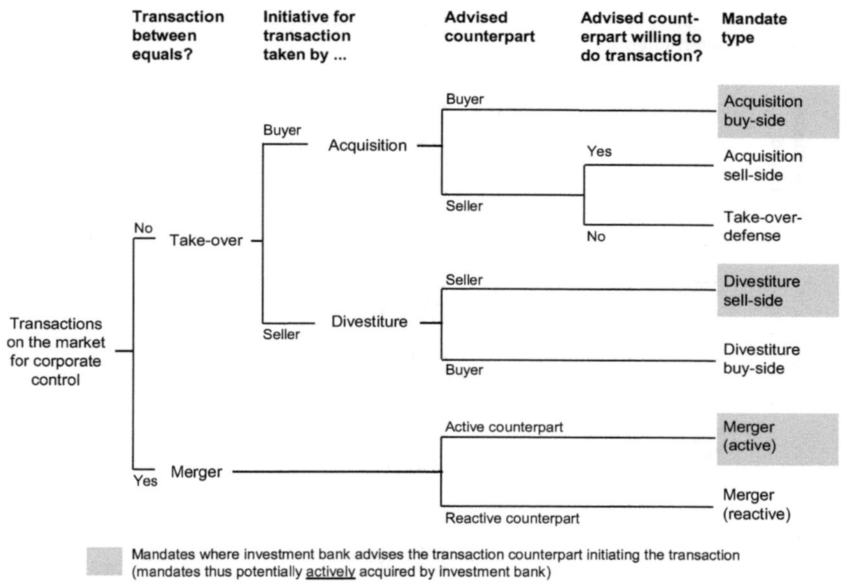

Figure 3.3: Types of M&A advisory mandates

Reactive solicitation

In order to have a clearer understanding of different banks' "advice for sale", a company may invite tender offers. Thereby, the company's choice decision emerges gradually, and, from a bank's perspective, it can be broken down into the following steps[29]:

29 The break-down is done in analogy to the "steps of movement toward purchase" suggested by *Lavidge* and *Steiner* in Lavidge[152]; similar thoughts are reflected in *McKinsey*'s purchase funnel. Since this thesis deals with industrial goods and concentrates on major providers, the lower steps (awareness, knowledge) do only play minor roles, since – as will also show the empirical findings on reputation – most buyers do have some opinion about the major investment banks. Thus research is focused on the higher funnel steps.

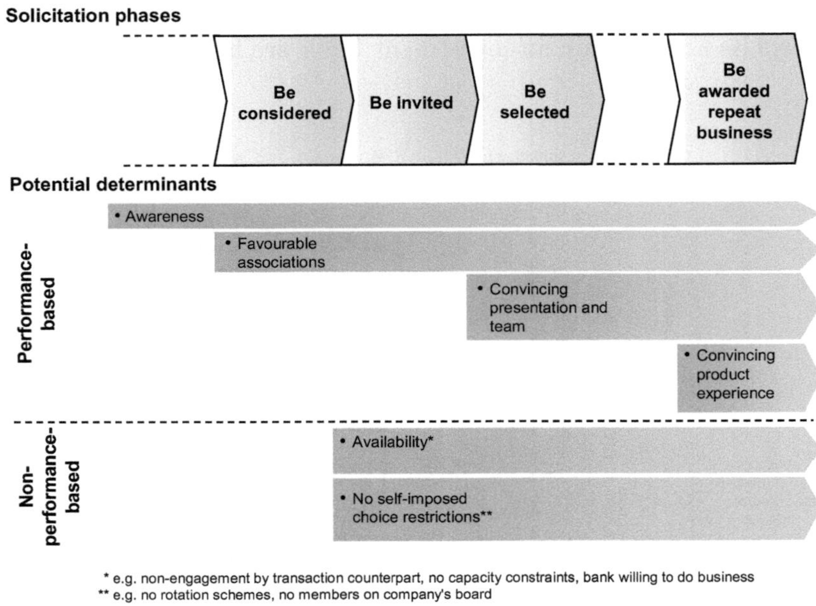

Figure 3.4: M&A advisory customer decision funnel

- **Be considered.** The most basic precondition for consideration is awareness[30]. Due to the companies' supposedly high involvement into the making of their investment bank choice decision and the upper end market concentration on the supply side[31], buyers will be aware of most suppliers, which suggests that awareness does not represent a major restriction

30 The purchase process of M&A advisory points at unaided (as opposed to aided) awareness as the relevant precondition, since the buyer does not get presented a set of brands from which to choose (as in many in-store consumer goods purchase situations).

31 Advice on transactions that surpass a critical size is requested only from the leading big banks. The research in this thesis shall be restricted to M&A projects where the transaction volume in question surmounted Euro 50 million (this hurdle is suggested by practitioners as the size where – against the background of cost-benefit reflections – the big banks only come into consideration as service providers, see Achleitner[5], page 154).

for consideration in the case of M&A advisory. But besides, favourable associations, which may have been built in direct or indirect ways, can be expected to play an important role for the buyer's decision whether or not consider a bank a suitable advisor candidate or not[32]. For products like M&A advisory, for which business relationships play an important role, one can expect that the set of companies that are considered potential supply candidates is largely composed of companies with which relationships are being maintained

- **Be invited** to present ideas on the transaction. This constitutes the next step towards mandate acquisition. Transaction and banks specifics may be expected to play an important role for the buyer's decision as to which of the considered banks he is going to invite for presentation

- **Be selected.** This constitutes the final step in mandate acquisition. The buyer's eventual choice may be influenced by many factors. Most prominently, the quality of the sales presentation and the investment banking team presented at the pitch may constitute determinants for selection. Still, the buyer's choice decision may be dominated by other than "pitch-specific" factors. In the end, a buyer of M&A advisory may, for instance, choose an investment bank for its excellent reputation rather than its sales presentation

- **Be awarded repeat business.** Convincing product experience constitutes a necessary precondition for being awarded repeat business[33]. Due to M&A advisory's low utility of search qualities[34], investment banks may gain considerable advan-

32 Cf. also Keller[141], pp. 51, 103.

33 Cf. for instance Lavidge[152], Oliver[181], Fornell[92], Bloemer[35], Anderson[9] and [10], Peter[183]. Researching the more specific shape of the satisfaction-loyalty graph, *Herrmann* and *Johnson* have, in the context of consumer goods, found differing differential impact of satisfaction on customer loyalty, dependent on the satisfaction level, cf. Herrmann[113].

34 Cf. paragraph 5.2.1.
Müller-Stewens, *Spickers*, and *Deiß* report that good service delivery can less and less be considered a guarantee for repeat business, though, see Müller-Stewens[178], page 51. This may be attributed to the market's increasing maturity.

tages from good service delivery for future solicitation[35]. Due to formal or informal agreements that a company has with other banks (e. g., a rotation scheme), though, strong-performing banks may not profit to the fullest extent from good previous performance[36].

One peculiarity of the M&A advisory business is that such prototype competitive selection rationale may get "distorted" by non-performance-based factors. The engagement of a bank by the potential transaction counterpart, or the bank's non-availability for other reasons[37], as well as the application of non-performance-based selection criteria[38] may effectuate a choice where the mandate is awarded to a bank that – without these restrictions – would only be the buyer's second or third choice.

Figure 3.4 summarises these thoughts. Purely performance-based choice determinants have been separated from such factors that may restrict or "distort" the company's purely performance-based choice.

Contents of the sales presentation

The sales presentation constitutes the most direct and specific vehicle of information exchange in a competitive selection process[39]. This is why its goals and contents shall be briefly revisited.

35 Although cumulative satisfaction, as opposed to transaction-specific satisfaction, can be considered the more adequate concept to explain repurchase intention, cf. for instance Herrmann[113], pp. 582, 583, Johnson[129], pp. 751, 752, one can expect transaction-specific satisfaction to well explain repurchase intention in the case of M&A advisory, due to its long purchase cycles and the high transaction-specific value at stake.

36 If an investment bank shows consistently a stronger performance than its competitors do, one would expect a company to change such agreements in the strong-performing investment bank's favour (if it is free to do so), so that a company's agreements with other investment banks may constitute restrictions to purely performance-driven choice only in the short-run.

37 E. g., bottle-neck in capacity, business not considered big/attractive enough from provider's point of view.

38 For instance rotation schemes, where the buyer rotates mandates among an evoked set of banks, or the bank's presence on the company's board.

39 Cf. paragraph 5.2.1. An interesting observation is that the presentation is one of the few assets under ad hoc control of the bank, i. e., a factor that does not need to be built long-term in advance, as for instance reputation.

The presentation takes place after a company has got into contact with an investment bank[40]. Presenting to the company, an investment bank thus wants to demonstrate its superior aptitude to advise on the transaction. Accordingly, such presentation comprises the following elements[41]:

- General information indicating the bank's performance potential
  - Investment bank's track record, i. e., reference transactions (in general, in the industry, resp. in the geography)
  - Investment bank's league table ranking (in general, in the industry, resp. in the geography)
- Project-specific information illustrating the bank's performance potential
  - Perspectives on the transaction
    - Perspective on the transaction background, comprising an assessment of the buyer's[42] industry and geography
    - Recap of M&A goals and further discussion of the specific transaction in question, including for instance first-draft short lists, proposals on deal structure, or rough value estimates
  - Perspectives on the project organisation and deliverables
    - Preliminary project schedule, including proposed activities and end products
    - Specification of investment bank's project team
    - Fees.

40 In the case of active solicitation, it is the bank that approaches the company, in reactive solicitation, it is the company that approaches the bank.

41 Cf. also Müller-Stewens[178], page 51, Achleitner[5], pp. 157, 158. *Müller-Stewens*, *Spickers*, and *Deiß* observe that, nowadays, the buyers of M&A advisory expect the project-specific part of the presentation to be comprehensive, while formerly the presentation focus was on league tables and track record to indicate the bank's general performance potential.

42 Buyer denotes the company that wants to buy advice.

Dealing with the information that a company may use to base its M&A advisor choice on, chapters 5 and 8 are going to recur to the sales process concept and tools discussed in this section.

Part II

Theoretic foundations and preliminary conclusions

4 Risk and its explanatory power

What are the determinants of whether and how a buyer will engage into comparison when he has to make a purchase? – One important driver may be provided by the risk associated with the purchase decision, some measure of which is the decision-dependent variance in value (personal welfare resp. corporate welfare[1], or both). If the potential impact of the buyer's choice decision on welfare is big, and when, in addition, he can assume a wide variance of outcome depending on the decision he makes, he will know that his decision matters a lot. The buyer will thus be motivated (or pressured) to engage into comparison.

Knowing that choice matters is not enough to make a good choice. If the buyer knew for instance that the decision-dependent variance in value was huge, but he could not differentiate the product offers from each other, then making a choice would be pure gambling. If, on the other hand, he had the knowledge that information collection and processing would help him to meaningfully differentiate the values of different offers, he would have to decide whether such activities are worth the cost. That is, he would have to compare the expected benefits with the expected costs of information search, in order to determine how overall expected value could be optimised. Thereby, the availability and exploitability of information for the choice does not only depend on characteristics of the product itself, such as whether it is highly immaterial or not, but also on the buyer's situation, for example on his knowhow and experience (allowing him to process collected information in a meaningful way, or not)[2]. In cases where a product's quality is difficult to assess before purchase, guarantees given by the provider (and the perceived reliability regarding their settlement) could provide an important means of risk relief, on the availability of which the buyer could base his choice.

1 In the case of corporate decision-making.

2 For consumer goods, *Bettman* did a lot of research on the topic of prior-purchase information collection and processing in dependence of the buyer's experience and familiarity with the product, see for example Bettman[29] or [31].

These preliminary thoughts give motivation to explore the theories on risk and information, in order to assess the marketing of M&A advisory accordingly.

4.1 The concept of risk

When making his purchase decision, the buyer usually cannot be completely sure about the selected product's quality and thus its consequences on his, resp. in the case of industrial goods, his personal and the company's welfare. As *Bauer* noted, "consumer behavior involves risk in the sense that any action of a consumer will produce consequences which he cannot anticipate with anything approximating certainty, and some of which at least are likely to be unpleasant"[3].

Research on risk-taking in choice decisions and on perceived risk's explanatory power for buyer behaviour have constituted a subject of research for the past 40 years. This section shall revisit selected aspects that are important for the discussion of risk-taking in the case of the M&A advisor choice[4].

4.1.1 Perceived risk

Risk can impact a buyer's behaviour only in the way and to the extent that it is perceived by the buyer. Thus, when risk's explanatory power is being researched, the concept of perceived risk, and not the one of "objective" or "actual" risk, is the one of relevance. Looking at an identical purchase situation, two different buyers may have quite a different perception of the risk associated with this purchase decision, as well as risk appetite. The forces at work, which the differences in perception and appetite can be attributed to, are

3 See Bauer[20], page 24. *Bauer* was the first to address the risk aspect in the field of consumer research.

4 Comprehensive overviews on the perceived risk concept and its measurement can be found in Dowling[77] and Ross[200]. In addition, Stem[224] gives a overview on the subject.

buyer-specifics, such as erroneous or lacking knowledge[5], the buyer's familiarity with the product, personality traits, or wealth position[6].

4.1.2 Risk components

Risk arises from basically two aspects the buyer has to deal with when making his choice decision:

- **Uncertainty** about the product's quality. At sales, the buyer usually does not completely know the quality of the products he considers for selection[7]
- **Consequences** of the product's quality[8] on his personal or, in the case of industrial goods, his company's (and his personal) welfare.

If any of the two was absent, the buyer could directly infer his post-purchase welfare from his choice decision[9], thus no risk would be

5 Restricted rationality is, for instance discussed in Alchian[7], page 66, or Picot[184], page 179.

6 Dowling[77], pp. 196, 197, gives an overview over the most prominent research conducted in the field of personality-related risk scales; *Cunningham* and *Cox* were among the pioneers to research personality traits in connection with risk perception, see Cunningham[63], pp. 97–107, Cox[60]. *Tversky* and *Kahneman* have devoted some of their research to the phenomenon of reference-dependent loss aversion, see Kahneman[135], an important subject of prospect theory. Besides, they identified "certainty effect", "reflection effect", "isolation effect", and "probabilistic insurance" as phenomena that may affect a buyer's risk notion, see Kahneman[133], as well as "the decision maker's conception of the acts, outcomes, and contingencies associated with a particular choice", which they termed "decision frames" see Kahneman[134], page 453. Taking up, besides others, thoughts from *Kahneman* and *Tversky*, *Puto* et al. find empirical evidence that decision frames, as well as source loyalty, have mediating effects on risk perception and appetite in industrial buying behaviour, see Puto[191]. A compact review of reference dependence and loss aversion, and their implications on value function shape, can for instance be found in Herrmann[112], pp. 6–8.

7 Cf. figure 4.1.

8 Cf. for instance Cunningham[63], pp. 82–84.

9 Provided he could perfectly assess the cause-effect chain between choice and consequences in the case that he had complete certainty about product quality. If, on the other hand, the product's quality did not affect the buyer's welfare, then his welfare would not depend on the choice.

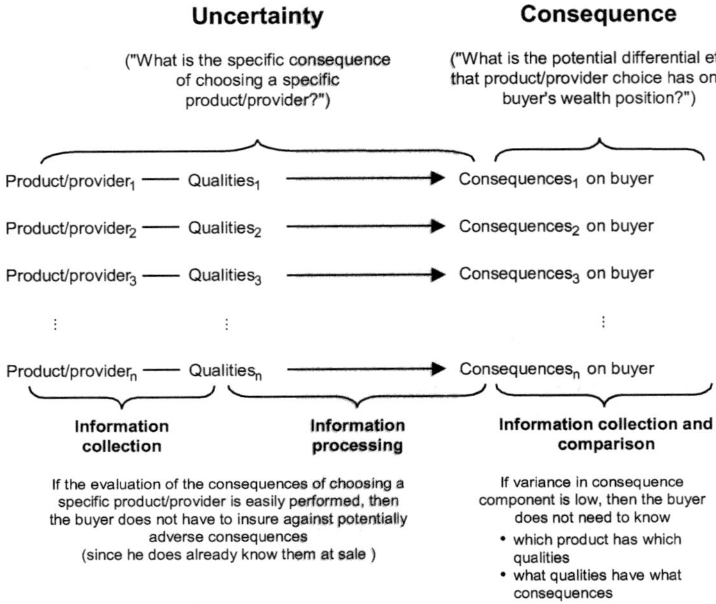

Figure 4.1: Risk components

associated with the choice decision. More general, risk can be considered the multiplicative resultant of uncertainty and consequences[10]. Figure 4.1 illustrates these observations.

It is an immediate consequence of paragraph 4.1.1 that, when risk is being researched for explanatory purposes, *perceived* uncertainty, and *perceived* consequences, are the concepts of relevance.

---

10 As *Dowling* notes, there are "theoretical and practical arguments" for a multiplicative relationship, in particular "(1) that the absence of either variable would eliminate risk, and (2) the influence of a non-salient adverse consequence on overall perceived risk is reduced", see Dowling[77], pp. 199, 200. Still, empirical analyses on the buyer's risk perception have so far found evidence for an additive rather than a multiplicative relationship, see Bettman[30], pp. 381–384, cf. Dowling[77], pp. 198, 199, Ross[200], page 3.

Assessing the uncertainty component of risk

What are measures that can be applied to assess the uncertainty component of risk? – The more difficult it is for the buyer to assess a product's quality (or rather: the more difficult he perceives this task to be), and its consequences for his welfare, the higher the uncertainty associated with his choice decision. Figure 4.1 hints at two potential sources for uncertainty, namely unavailability of information, and difficulty to process it. The more difficult it is to obtain and/or process information on product quality, the higher the uncertainty component of risk. These considerations shall be taken up in sections 4.2 and 5.1.

Assessing the consequence component of risk

When do consequences of purchase matter a lot? – For sure when the value level (relative to the current wealth level) is high, i. e. when the expected value arising from the choice decision has a huge impact on the buyer's wealth position[11]. It deserves special mentioning that the stronger the irreversibility of a purchase decision's consequences on the buyer, the higher this value level[12]. But a huge lever in wealth position would not really matter if all purchase decisions yielded the same outcome. That is, in order to assess the consequence component of risk, the variability of outcome needs to be taken into

11 In this sense, expected value denotes the mean of all potential values. Note that *Arnthorsson* et al.'s definition of quality, which follows *Zeithaml*, is directly linked to the value for the buyer. Defining quality as "the value or pay-off that a consumer obtains from purchase and consumption of the product", see Arnthorsson[12], page 217, inspectability of quality requires the buyer to know both: the product's attributes *and* the impact of these attributes on his welfare. In the terms used here, the determination of quality comprises the assessment of certain product features' attributes (termed "information collection" in figure 4.1), while the determination of a product's value for the buyer requires an additional cognitive process, which is symbolised in figure 4.1 by the arrows linking quality to consequences ("information processing").

12 In this context, the reader's attention may be drawn to the observation that the consequence component of risk has not necessarily much to do with purchase price. Even if a product was for free, the purchase decision could bear a potential for negative consequences on the buyer's welfare. Thus, the purchase price constitutes, so to say, only a cost component that the buyer faces at any case.

consideration[13]. Since the distribution of consequences can look very differently from case to case[14], and since the adverse consequences a buyer may be willing to bear in case of adverse selection also depend on his specifics, in particular on his wealth position (i. e. what losses he *could* sensibly bear) and his risk appetite (i. e. what losses he is *prepared to take*)[15], risk theory usually uses value-at-risk measures[16], which capture the worst outcome within a certain confidence level.

To summarise, the following may be considered useful for assessing the consequence component of the risk associated with a purchase decision:

- Value level (expected value, possibly assessed in relation to current wealth position)
- Degree of irreversibility of consequences
- Variability of outcome (for instance standard deviation, possibly assessed in relation to expected value)

13 Best in relation to expected value. That way, expected value measures the average lever of product purchase on wealth position, while variability relative to mean – measured for instance by the standard deviation – assesses the differential effect that different purchase decisions may have on this lever. – It was already suggested by *Cox* that consequence component of risk be conceptualised by "level and amount" of consequences, as well as "level and amount" of "consequences variance", see Cox[61], in particular figure 24.1 on pp. 632–634.

14 And can, in particular, deviate from normal distribution, think for instance of fat-tailed distributions or asymmetrical distributions.

15 For this reason, *Bettman* asked experimentees to tell him for which brands the quality fell below a level that was acceptable for them, and calculated from this the percentage of acceptable brands to assess the riskiness of product choice, see Bettman[28].

16 *Value-at-risk* is a term borrowed from risk theory and finds, besides others, its application in economic capital calculations or in the evaluation of a potential credit customers' credit-worthiness, cf. for instance Kaplanski[138]. It describes the stake at risk within a certain probability, e. g., with a probability of bigger than 1 percent. This means that, provided one can assume a specific shape of the loss distribution (for instance, normal distribution), value-at-risk can easily be calculated from the distribution's parameters, such as for instance its variance. As to calculating economic capital, a bank's rating is related to the ability to sustain losses by means of the capital it keeps. The lower the probability for losses that surmount the bank's capability to survive without bankruptcy, the higher the bank's rating.

- Value-at-risk (possibly assessed in relation to expected value or current wealth position).

Figure 4.2 illustrates the instruments by means of which the consequence component of risk may be assessed.

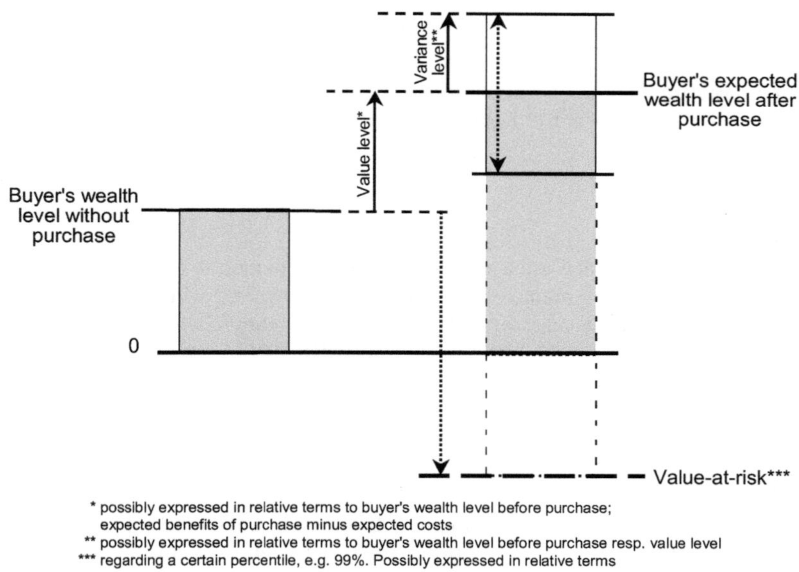

Figure 4.2: Measures for the consequence component of risk

4.1.3 Corporate and personal risk

One peculiarity of the risk associated with corporate purchase decisions arises from the fact that employees do not only strive for corporate, but also for personal welfare.

Although one can assume a positive relationship between corporate and personal welfare dependent on the outcome of the purchase decision, the importance of the two may vary from case to case.

While, for instance, an individual's career (thus, also welfare) may strongly depend on the outcome of a specific project, this project may only play a marginal role for the company's welfare. This means that personal welfare and company welfare are, on the one hand, positively correlated (this is one reason why companies work[17]), but their relative importance may, on the other hand, vary from decision to decision[18].

In the following, the risk that addresses the buy decision's impact on company welfare shall be termed *corporate risk*, while the risk related to personal welfare shall be called *personal risk*. The idea of differentiating between these two types of risk goes back to *Bauer*, who suggested there be two types of risk, namely "company risk" and "buyer risk"[19].

---

17 The means by which such correspondence of personal and company goals, termed differently: management (agent) and owner (principal) goals, is being achieved, constitutes one of the fields of agency theory, see for instance Eisenhardt[79], page 59, Elschen[80], pp. 1010, 1011. Agency theory shall be briefly revisited in chapter 5.

18 In the field of consumer goods, literature has dealt a lot with other risk types, such as for instance psychological as opposed to performance risk, see Wilding[233], Ross[199]. Roselius[198], Jacoby[126], Lutz[163], Zikmund[245], and Kaplan[137] have, among others, differentiated between other types of risk, most prominently between financial risk, physical or hazard risk, time risk, ego risk, opportunity risk; *Lovelock* and *Wright* provide a risk typology for services, see Lovelock[160], page 73. While such risk type considerations have helped to make explicit about what a buyer cares most when making his purchase choice, the arithmetical combination of different types of risk to derive "overall risk" has proved very difficult, basically because their relationship to overall perceived risk varies from person to person, cf. for instance Dowling[77], page 200, Ross[200], page 8. When a product fails, a person usually faces all types of losses, such as money loss, time loss, ego loss, etc. A second ambition of risk type research has consisted in linking reliever types to risk types. To date, this kind of research has also shown equivocal results, cf. Ross[200], pp. 9, 10, Derbaix[72], pp. 25, 33–35.

19 See Bauer[20]. The differentiation between the two only regained attention some time later, when researches started dealing with industrial markets. *Newall* for instance operationalises overall risk by means of a buyer- and company-specific component, cf. Newall[180], pp. 168, 169. Similarly, *Choffray* and *Johnston* differentiate between consequences on organisational and individual level, cf. Choffray[56], pp. 334–337.

Thus, in order to understand the risk perceived and the amount of effort undertaken by a company to optimise a choice decision, it may be insufficient to look at the situation from a corporate point of view, but it may be necessary to look (in addition) at the importance of the decision from the personal point of view for each of the individuals that form the buying centre.

Positive correlations between personal and corporate risk seem highly sensible, but a strong variation in the strength of this relationship can be expected. In particular, this relationship can be expected to be relatively strong for persons that occupy top positions, and lower for employees occupying positions in the lower hierarchy.

4.1.4 Underlying risk and transfer lever

To conclude this section on basic risk concepts, the concepts of underlying risk and transfer lever shall be introduced, which up to date have not been discussed by literature. These concepts apply to any purchase decision that is embedded into a further-reaching value chain, thus to any purchase decision of derived nature (in the sense of the underlying, further-reaching goal of activity)[20]. As to the risk considerations regarding such a purchase decision, the embedded transaction shall be called the *primary* transaction, while the further-reaching value chain shall be called the *underlying* transaction, which in itself holds risk. Now, the bigger the risk associated with the underlying transaction, and the more impact the primary transaction supposedly has on the underlying transaction, the more it matters to make the right primary decision – put differently, the bigger the primary's transaction's consequence component of risk. That is, it is proposed that the primary transaction's consequence component is influenced by

- **The (perceived) riskiness of the underlying transaction** on the one hand and

20 Note that nearly any purchase decision is embedded into some further-reaching value chain. But often, such embedment is not of strongly exclusive character: for instance, alternatives in the further-reaching value chain may be taken if the purchase turns out to be of bad quality, or a second purchase may be made.

- **The (perceived) impact or importance that the primary transaction has for the outcome of the underlying transaction**, on the other.

The former of these two risk drivers shall be termed the *underlying risk*, and the latter the *transfer lever*[21].

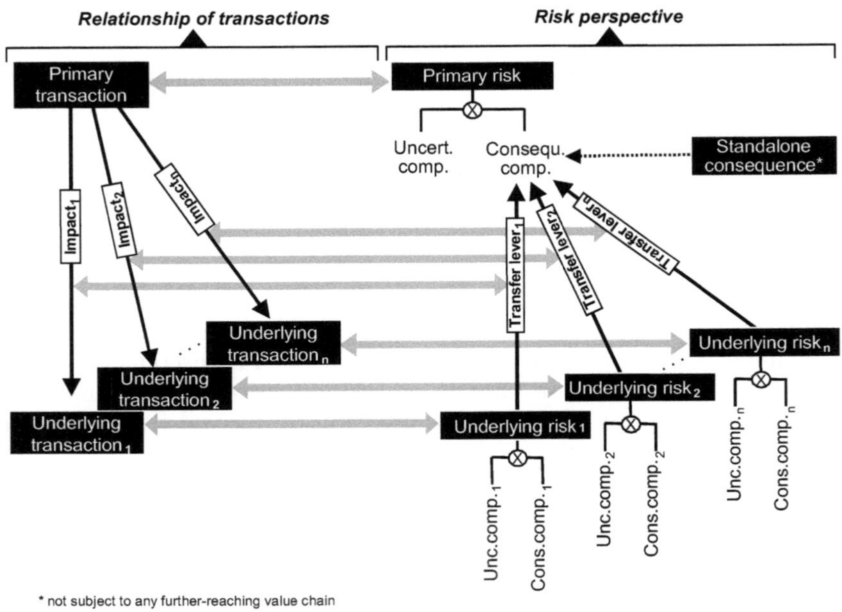

Figure 4.3: Underlying risk and transfer lever

Both underlying risk and transfer lever can be expected to have positive impact on the consequence component of risk associated with the primary transaction[22]. More specifically, the multiplicative resultant

21 Note that a primary transaction may have several underlying transactions, and that the primary transactions' respective transfer levers may be differently strong, while a significant purpose of the primary transaction may not at all be explainable by any further reaching value chains, i. e., it may have stand-alone character.

22 It is evident that the underlying transaction and the involvement of the advisor should *not* affect the uncertainty component of risk associated with the

of the two can be expected to be most meaningful for the explanation of the consequence component of risk associated with the primary transaction, at least as long as the primary transaction does not have a significant stand-alone purpose, nor embedment into other underlying transactions. In particular, if any of the two risk drivers was nil[23], and if the sole point of making the primary transaction consisted in the one underlying transaction, the primary transaction's consequence component of risk can also be expected to be nil, and thus primary risk as well. Figure 4.3 illustrates these relationships.

To give two examples, the M&A transaction constitutes the underlying transaction for M&A advisor choice, which is thus going to be termed the primary transaction.

Suppose you travelled a lot from A to B, and always had the choice between two airlines. Now for one specific day, it would be of crucial importance for you to personally be at B at least 30 minutes after scheduled arrival time, since you would very much like to be present at the auction of a carpet that you had always wanted to buy – that is, your welfare would strongly depend on being able to bid for and buy this carpet. Then the risk associated with the carpet purchase, i. e., the underlying transaction, would transfer to your choice of the airline, the primary transaction[24]. As a result, associated with choosing the airline would be higher for this specific instance than usually for you.

---

primary transaction. That is, while the risk associated with the underlying transaction may be huge, and the advisor's involvement, thus his influence on the outcome of the underlying transaction, may be high, one cannot make any conclusions as to how uncertain the buyer feels about the advice for purchase's quality. The buyer will just know that his choice matters, but it is another question how difficult he perceives the choice decision to be.

23 I. e., no risk associated with the underlying transaction, or no involvement of the advisor into the underlying transaction. The argumentation here is analogous to the one of uncertainty and consequence component of risk.

24 Transfer lever in this case is high, since there is no alternative solution left once the chosen plane is late. Suppose on the other hand, you had a friend at B who could bid for you in case you are not able to make it to B in time. Then the impact of your airline choice on the carpet purchase would decrease, since flying there would only constitute one of several options. That way, risk associated with choosing the airline would decrease as well, compared to the example discussed.

4.2 Risk reduction methods

A variety of topics have been researched in connection with risk perception[25]. By dealing with activities the buyer may perform in order to reduce risk, this section shall provide a basis for a better understanding of M&A advisory's marketing from an information perspective.

4.2.1 Thresholds

Let us start this section by revisiting the threshold concept, which aims at explaining why the risk associated with a purchase decision may influence the buyer's behaviour in possibly different ways, dependent on its level and the buyer specifics[26].

Nearly all our activities involve a certain amount of risk, but at many occasions, we do not care about this risk, because we can tolerate it. Moreover, if the product fails to exceed a certain risk level, we will even try to increase risk, for instance by looking for more risky alternatives[27]. This threshold, which has been researched a lot by psychologists, is individual-specific, and called *minimum tolerable risk threshold*[28].

---

25 An overview of such topics and their findings – in particular the explanatory power that risk has for opinion leadership, new product adoption, and the relation between risk perception and other personality traits – can be found in Ross[200], pp. 4–11, Dowling[77], page 196. Most of this research, which has mainly been conducted in the field of consumer goods, has not shown clear results to date.

26 Major thoughts to the topic have been contributed by Coombs[57] and Deering[69]. Empirical research on the topic has been contributed recently by *Dowling* and *Staelin*, cf. Dowling[78]. A review of the threshold concept can be found in Dowling[77], pp. 203, 204. Already *Cox* speculated there might be situations in which perceived risk falls significantly short of "ideal risk" ("underrisky situations"), and others, where perceived risk "exceeds desirable and tolerable risk" ("overrisky situations"), cf. Cox[61], pp. 629, 630.

27 If risk is low, the utility of variety seeking may dominate the utility of risk decrease by means of loyalty, cf. for instance Herrmann[113], pp. 587, 588.

28 This terminology adopts *Dowling*'s denotation of maximum and minimum risk threshold, see Dowling[77], page 203.

Conversely, there is a level of risk which we do not want to take on, and which – as long as the risk associated with a purchase decision exceeds such critical size – we will try to reduce to a level acceptable to us, or, in case we cannot do so, try to avoid to make the purchase at all. This risk threshold is called the *maximum tolerable risk threshold.* The maximum tolerable level of risk is – besides psychological factors –, influenced by the buyer's current wealth position, in particular, his ability to suffer a monetary loss ("wealth proposition")[29].

Only when perceived risk falls between minimum and maximum tolerable risk, a buyer will engage in his normal shopping behaviour (which may comprise further risk reduction activities).

4.2.2 Uncertainty and consequence relievers

The strategies a buyer may pursue in order to reduce the perceived risk associated with a buy decision are many-fold[30].

The strategies can, among others, be categorised by the risk component they relief. While *uncertainty relievers* help to lower the uncertainty as to what quality and value to expect, *consequence relievers* focus on relieving the losses ex post, once consequences have already turned out to be adverse[31]. If a consequence reliever was perfect for a whole product category, there would be no need for uncertainty relief[32]. Conversely, if an uncertainty reliever was perfect,

29 See Dowling[77], pp. 203, 204. *Dowling* and *Staelin* base their research of information search behaviour in the field of consumer research on these thresholds and find that, besides information availability and utility, the maximum tolerable risk level influences search behaviour significantly. Similarly to *Kahneman* and *Tversky*, see Kahneman[135], they also find that the person's current wealth position and his ability to suffer a monetary loss influence the level of acceptable risk positively, see Dowling[78].

30 *Roselius* was among the first to explore the perceived suitability of strategies in connection with risk types, see Roselius[198].

31 Cf. for instance Ross[200], page 2. More efforts, from a theoretic as well as a decision maker's point of view, are usually made to explore the opportunity of reducing the uncertainty component, see for instance Ross[200], page 7, Gemünden[95], page 79.

32 Because, in the case of product default, the buyer would be covered for all his losses.

Reliever type	Examples
Uncertainty relievers	• Intrinsic product cues • Expert tests • Former experience with the product performance • Assessment of production potential • Certificates • Track record • Market share • Reputation
Consequence relievers	• Money-back guarantee • Insurance

Figure 4.4: Examples for uncertainty and consequence relievers

the future consequences of the purchase would already be perfectly known by the buyer at sales. This means, that uncertainty and consequence relievers are equally apt to decrease risk, which can be considered the multiplicative resultant of the uncertainty and consequence component of risk[33].

Figure 4.4 classifies select reliever strategies[34] according to this aspect.

4.2.3 Mode of action risk reliever typology

Comparing different providers' product offers and claims, what can a buyer rely on? Put into information-theoretic terms, when do the

33 Cf. Ross[200], page 2.

34 Many of them are taken from Roselius[198], pp. 57, 58.

signals sent out by different providers promise a good chance that they actually do differentiate their senders as to expected product quality resp. to low losses for the buyer[35]?

Important thoughts on the topic have been provided by *Spence*, who argues that, from a market's point of view, a signal is *effective* if it is "unprofitable for sellers of low quality products to imitate it. That is, high quality sellers must have lower costs for signaling activities"[36]. It is evident that such signals promise a strong positive link between product quality and the attribute, or more basically, the availability, of the signal[37].

---

35 The giving away of information by the informed party to the uninformed party is called "signalling". The review of such signals, which the uninformed party undertakes, is called "screening", see for instance Kaas[130], pp. 540, 541. Provided a sales situation where the buyer has to make his choice between different offers whose quality he does not know, providers may engage into signalling, in order to convince the buyer of the superiority of their product. This means that signalling and screening can be considered "opposite sides of the same coin", cf. Spence[219], page 592. The importance of signalling and screening differs by the market-specific provider-buyer relationship: in buyer markets, signalling will be relatively more important than in seller markets; and, conversely, screening will be relatively more important in seller markets than in buyer markets. Not only is signalling costly (for the provider), but so is screening (for the buyer).

36 Cf. Spence[219], page 592. Within signals, *Spence* differentiates between *contingent contracts* and *exogenously costly signals*. Whereas the former work because buyers create by means of ex post quality assessment a negative correlation between signalling costs and quality, the basis for the latter is an (expected) negative correlation between the cost of acquiring certain capabilities (which are sunk, thus expenses the signaler has really incurred) and product quality, cf. Spence[219], pp. 593–597. *Spence*'s discussion focuses on extrinsic cues that promise the buyer to decrease uncertainty about the product quality offered by the senders of the signal. This signal typology shall be complemented by signals that work due to an intrinsic relation with the product, and by mechanisms that help the buyer to decrease potential losses in case of adverse selection, that is, relievers that focus on consequence relief.

37 Questioning the effectiveness of advertising (interpreted as a signal sent out by the advertiser to potential buyers), *von Ungern Sternberg* and *von Weizsäcker* take up these considerations, see Ungern[231], page 619. Stating that advertising is equally expensive for low as for high quality provider, they extend *Spence*'s considerations from *cost* to *utility* considerations; similar thoughts in the same context can be found in Tolle[229], page 930. Such

Spence's thoughts may be built on and extended to a typology of four risk relievers a buyer may look for, in order to decrease risk. Figure 4.5 provides a summary of this mode of action reliever typology, which shall be developed in the following, and gives the main reason for which these reliever types work.

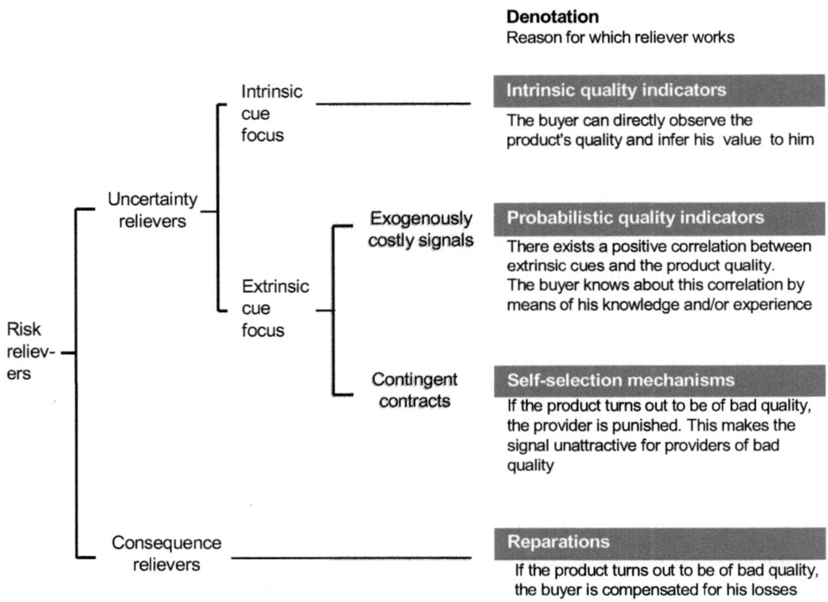

Figure 4.5: Mode of action-based reliever typology

Intrinsic quality indicators

If the signal screened by the buyer allows him to directly infer the product's quality, one speaks of an intrinsic relationship between

extension seems both justified and useful, since it are utility considerations rather than pure cost considerations that determine rational beings' decision processes. Thus, any signal that promises high quality senders higher utility (income minus costs) than low quality senders, can be considered an effective one.

the signal and the product quality[38]. A simple example for such a relationship provides the purchase of a dress, where the buyer can directly infer from the product's trim and fabric the value of the product to him. Another example provides a consumer product manufacturer's purchase of a chemical. From the chemical's composition, given in terms of chemical formulas and their ratios by the supplier, the buyer may immediately infer what value to expect, and would not take on much uncertainty, respectively risk[39]. The availability and utility of this type of signals depends most notably, first, on the inspectability of crucial product features and, second, on the buyer's ability to evaluate the impact of these features' attributes on his welfare.

By providing an intrinsic, thus highly reliable link between the value to expect and the product inspected, these signals are highly useful for uncertainty reduction – provided they are available and processable at decent cost.

Probabilistic quality indicators

These are signals of the type that *Spence* calls "exogenously costly"[40]. A correlation between them and product quality provides the basis for their effectiveness, and the buyer knows about such correlation by means of experience or heuristics. Diplomas certifying the provider's employees' education, from which the buyer may infer their superior

38 Difficulty of pre-purchase quality inspection, as defined by *Arnthorsson* et al., refers to the availability and processability of intrinsic cues, namely "the difficulty of assessing or verifying the quality of a product prior to purchasing it [...]. Inspection is defined as the consumer's effort to physically examine, assess, and verify the quality of the product at the point of purchase [...] Pre-purchase quality inspection, then, involves examining the product in an effort to determine (before purchasing) how well the product will deliver on the benefits the consumer expects from it", see Arnthorsson[12], page 217.

39 To use the terms that are going to be introduced in paragraph 5.1.1, the uncertainty component of risk would in such case mainly consist in uncertainty of compliance, rather than quality uncertainty. Put differently, the buyer may have to enforce his claims against the supplier legally in case the chemical turns, upon delivery, out to be of another than the promised composition, but it should be easy for him to infer from the chemical's composition its value to him.

40 See Spence[219], pp. 593–597.

aptitude to deliver the service in question, may serve as an example for signals that work on this basis.

Spence's terminology pinpoints that the provider incurs real costs to build such signals, so that "market equilibria are inefficient by the standard of the world of perfect information"[41] – all the more, as the correlation between the signal and product quality is only positive, but not equal to one. No risk is shifted from the buyer to the provider, and the signal contributes to the reduction of the uncertainty component of risk.

Self-selection mechanisms

These are the signals that *Spence* calls "contingent contracts". The main reason for which these signals work lies in their provider's commitment to being punished if he fails to deliver the promised product quality. Thus, these signals express and premise the provider's will and capability to deliver the promised product quality, and have self-selection character. As an example, a provider may commit himself to pay a fee (to the buyer or a third party) in case of bad product delivery. Then the only providers willing to accept such conditions are the ones that are able and willing to deliver high quality products, provided they act fully rationally. Similarly, reputation can be considered a vehicle through which self-selection may become effective. On bad product delivery, the buyer may damage the provider's reputation by means of bad word-of-mouth. Facing such a threat, only providers that have the willingness and ability to deliver high quality will enter into a specific type of contract. Self-selection mechanisms are "decision situations generat[ed] by the A with which he is going to confront B, so that the A is able to deduce B's characteristic from B's choice. Thereby, B is absolutely aware that he is going to disclose himself by means of his choice decision. But the choice decision is of such a high economic relevance for B, that it lies in his self-interest not to lie"[42].

As *Spence* notes, "the equilibrium in this type of situation is, in terms of resource allocation, indistinguishable from an equilibrium with perfect symmetric information. Thus, no seller uncertainty,

41 See Spence[219], page 596. *Spence* discusses for this reason in how far an over-investment in such signals could cause inefficiencies.

42 See Spremann[221], page 578.

contingent contracts are efficient signaling mechanisms. There are penalties, but no one pays them"[43].

In contrast to the first two types of signals, self-selection mechanisms are linked to the ex post quality assessment of a product. By threatening to reduce the provider's welfare in the case where the product turns out to be defective, they set incentives for the provider to deliver his best[44]. But as such, they help the buyer to determine product quality ex ante, thus to reduce uncertainty regarding the product quality.

Self-selection mechanisms help the buyer to identify the provider delivering best quality, rather than that they compensate him for losses. Thus, in cases where product quality turns out to be unsatisfactory ex post, self-selection mechanisms do not provide reparation to the buyer, but the buyer can only lower the provider's wealth position. This is different for the fourth type of reliever, which is going to be discussed next.

Reparations

The fourth type of risk reliever offers the buyer compensation in case the product turns out to be defective. An insurance that covers all the losses incurred by the buyer in cases where the product turns out to be defective, provides an example for such a mechanism.

Thus, unlike the first three risk reliever types, this type decreases the consequence component of risk. As in the case of self-selection mechanisms, the actual costs of reparation do not need to be incurred – at least as long as one abstracts from the costs of setting up contracts, as well as monitoring costs and costs of inforcement[45].

43 See Spence[219], page 596. Note however, that such argumentation premises fully rational behaviour.

44 *Spremann* discusses reputation as a pledge given by the agent to his principal, and infers as a necessary precondition for such transaction design the existence of some wealth position of the agent that can be damaged by the principal, see Spremann[220], page 619. It should be added that, if there is no such "natural pledge" as reputation, a pledge can be created by means of a contract for instance, as in the case of penalty payment agreements.

45 Such view is, of course, simplistic. As *Williamson* notes, "[t]here is growing awareness that the [comparative] limitations of the courts are more severe than the legal centralism tradition admits [...]. Accordingly, the study of

Since high quality suppliers do incur lower reparation costs[46], this signal is effective in *Spence*'s sense. It is important to note though, that this risk reliever's primary mode of action does not lie in this effectiveness (which would mean the reliever acted as an uncertainty decreaser), but – in the perfect case where the buyer is compensated for any loss in the case of adverse selection, thus choice of a defective product – in its nihilisation of consequences for the buyer.

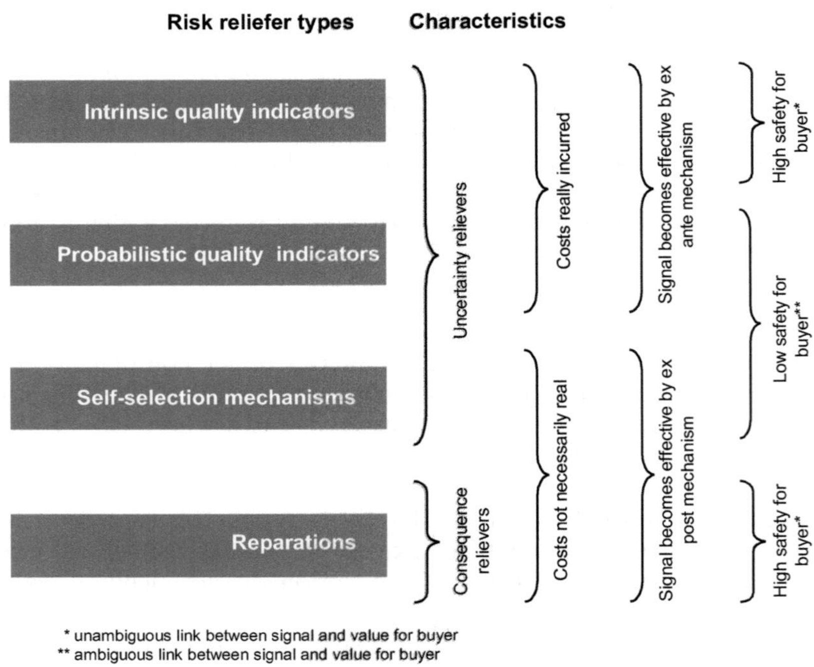

Figure 4.6: Mode of action-based reliever characteristics

contract is appropriately extended from legal rules to include an assessment of alternative governance structures, of which the courts are only one", see Williamson[234], page 537. Such costs would not only comprise the costs associated with setting up insurance contracts, but also the costs incurred in making contracts enforceable.

46 Themselves or indirectly through third party insurers, which they have to pay a lower fee to than bad quality providers.

Figure 4.6 summarises the most important characteristics of the four reliever types discussed in the previous paragraphs.

Risk relievers should be thought of as spanning a continuum, the constitutional prototypes of which have been discussed in the previous paragraphs. Intrinsic cues, certificates of qualification, penalty payments to third parties, and insurances provide examples for these four prototypes of risk relievers.

Many other relievers, though, are affiliated with more than one mode of action prototype. Reputation, for instance, constitutes an example for a self-selection mechanism, because the provider puts his reputation at stake if he fails to deliver the promised product quality. On the other hand, one can expect a positive correlation between reputation and expected quality, thus, reputation can be considered an extrinsic cue, and constitutes in addition an example for the second reliever type[47].

To give another example, variable compensation punishes, on the one hand, the provider upon bad product delivery, but on the other hand, it may compensate the buyer for some of his losses – although, probably, by far not all of them. Thus, variable compensation provides an example for the third and fourth reliever type.

Or, the experience a buyer has made with a certain product brand, may be based on intrinsic cues that can be assessed only ex post[48]. Then, on the one hand, the buyer of the product will usually know a lot more about the quality to expect at the next purchase occasion than a buyer who lacks such experience. On the other hand, there is some chance that the quality of the product for sale deviates from the quality of the product experienced, so that the link is not as direct as it is in the case of intrinsic cues that are directly observable at sale – thus, there is a positive, but only probabilistic link between quality experienced and quality for sale.

47 In particular, when one takes into account that companies may undertake reputation building communication initiatives, which means they do incur costs, it is evident that reputation cannot unequivocally and exclusively be assigned to the third reliever type.

48 An example for cases where such cues are important are products that do not exist at purchase (for instance slightly individualised contract goods), but that are observable ex post.

Figure 4.7 shows examples for relievers by means of which the risk a buyer faces can be reduced. The examples have been ordered on a continuum, spanned by the four reliever prototypes.

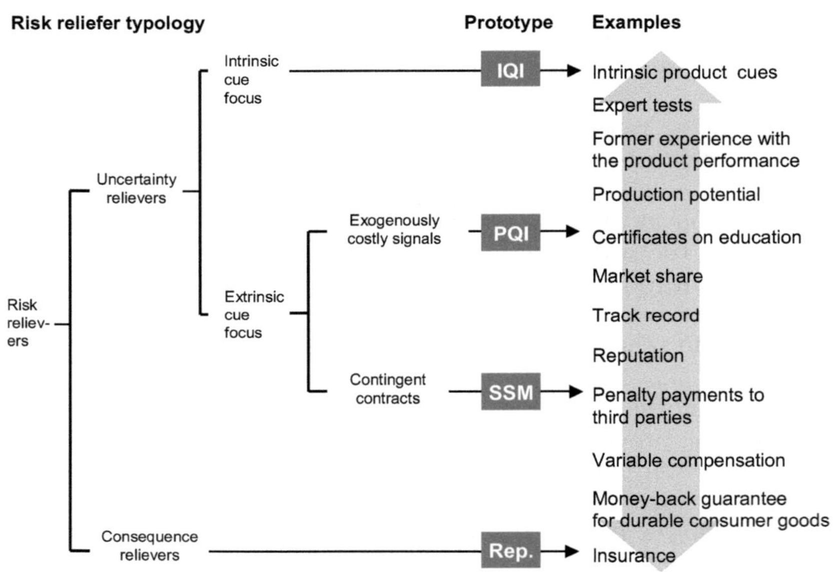

Figure 4.7: Examples for mode of action-based risk relievers

It is evident that, if intrinsic quality indicators or reparations are available, a customer does hardly care about probabilistic quality indicators or self-selection mechanisms, since the former offer him by far a higher safety[49]. But then, it is also clear that for products, where neither of them is available, resp. offered, the relative importance of probabilistic quality indicators and self-selection mechanisms increases. These thoughts apply in particular to M&A advisory.

49 Cf. also figure 4.6.

4.2.4 Inherent risk and handled risk

If risk reduction methods are being applied by the buyer, then the explanation of his product choice has to take into account these intermediary activities undertaken by the buyer. That is, handled, rather than inherent risk, is the explanatory concept of relevance, since it most precisely pictures the risk a buyer perceives when making his choice decision at sales[50].

Bettman was the first to make a distinction between *inherent risk* and *handled risk*, where inherent risk is "the latent risk a product class holds for the consumer – the innate to arouse", and handled risk is "the amount of conflict the product class is able to arouse when the buyer chooses a brand from a product class in his usual buying situation". Consequently, "handled risk to a first approximation represents the end results of the action of information and risk reduction processes on inherent risk"[51].

Thus, inherent risk could be assessed by looking at the "anonymous"[52] value distribution of the product alternatives for sale to the customer. Handled risk, in contrast, would take into account the information a buyer has about certain brands[53], and would, for instance, reflect that the buyer makes his choice only among an evoked set of brands whose quality he has already experienced for several times.

Figure 4.8 illustrates the inherent and handled risk concept for some product class, for which inherent risk lies above the maximum

50 The assessment of the M&A advisor choice from a risk perspective will use two measures for handled uncertainty: intermediary handled uncertainty before potential solicitation events, and finally handled uncertainty after solicitation events, cf. section 7.2.

51 See Bettman[28], page 184. *Bettman* researches then on which factors inherent risk and handled risk depend most, and identifies importance of the brand-choice for the product class and size of set of unacceptable brands as drivers for the former, and inherent risk and amount and usefulness of information for certain brands (the latter in an inverse way) as drivers for handled risk.

52 I. e., value to the buyer dependent on the choice decision is known, but it is not known which brand is linked to which value.

53 I. e., the buyer may know for certain brands what quality range to expect.

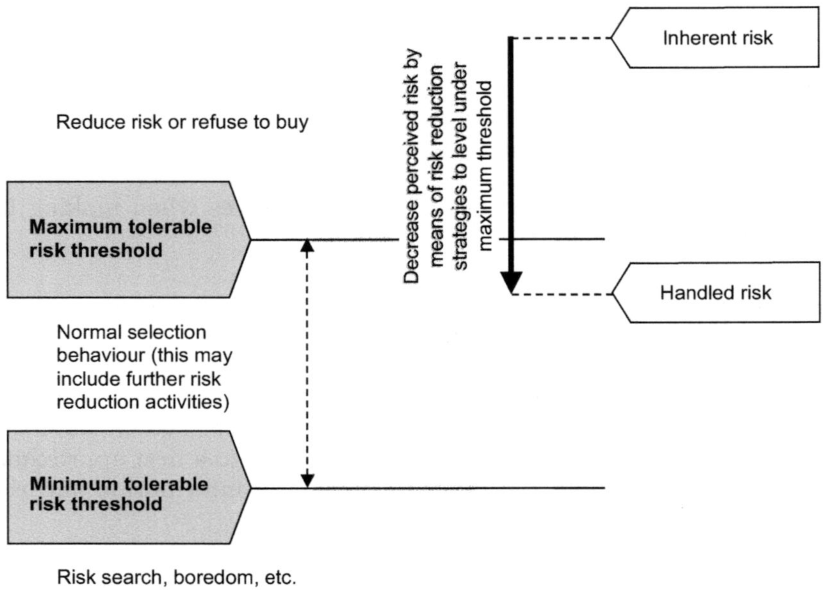

Figure 4.8: Risk thresholds and implied buyer behaviour

threshold level[54], and thus links the concept of inherent and handled risk to the one of thresholds and their implications on buyer behaviour, as discussed in paragraph 4.2.1.

This chapter has developed the most basic concepts by means of which the risk associated with choosing an M&A advisor can be assessed and relieved. Narrowing the risk reliever focus down to the ones of highest relevance in the context of the M&A advisor choice[55]

54 The inherent risk associated with a purchase does neither have to lie above maximum, nor above minimum tolerable level. For illustration purposes, though, some product class whose inherent risk is huge has been chosen, which means that inherent risk first has to be decreased to some level below maximum tolerable level, before a purchase decision can be made at all.

55 Relievers that are available to date for the buyer. Part III will take a more comprehensive perspective by discussing whether banks could and/or should offer additional reliever mechanisms.

– namely uncertainty relievers, and, in particular, probabilistic quality indicators –, the next chapter shall review and discuss the concepts of information and information asymmetries, which play the most prominent role in this reliever field.

5 Information and its utility

5.1 The concept of information

If there was no informational imperfection, then there would be no uncertainty, and thus no risk. The reason for which information provides the most prominent vehicle by means of which uncertainty of outcome can be decreased, is that uncertainty is caused by the lack of information. This section wants to highlight the different types of uncertainty a buyer may face at purchase. The theories that are going to be used for this purpose, are principal agent theory and information economics.

5.1.1 Types of uncertainty

In his famous article "The Market for Lemons", *Akerlof* has modelled an anonymous market in which cars are sold[1]. One important specific of the market considered by *Akerlof* consists in the inability of buyers to assess product quality of the goods for sale ex ante; buyers only have the notion of some probability by which they are going to buy a good car as opposed to a bad one, a so-called lemon. The situation changes once buyers have made their purchase and are able to use their cars. Buyers (now car owners) gain a clearer opinion on whether they have bought a good car or a lemon. When it comes to reselling the car, lemon owners are more motivated to do so, than are owners of good cars. Thus, in the used car market, probability to be presented a lemon is higher than in the primary market. Buyers of used cars are, again, not able to distinguish qualities ex ante, while expecting a higher probability of being presented a lemon for sale than in the primary market. Thus, owners of good cars who want to resell can only do so at a price below the fair price for a good car, and, even worse, a price that, for arbitrage reasons, is even lower than the one in the primary market. Being faced with

---

1 See Akerlof[6].

such unattractive price conditions, resellers of good cars are driven out of the used car market, and the market becomes a lemon market.

The problem illustrated by *Akerlof*, the so-called problem of *adverse selection*, has constituted an important topic of research. It arises from the fact that sellers of high quality products are unable to demonstrate they do sell superior products, or can do so only at prohibitive costs[2]. Besides, there are other types of uncertainty which a buyer may have to face. A systematisation of such different types of uncertainty shall be reviewed in the next paragraphs[3].

Exogenous and endogenous uncertainty

First of all, uncertainty can be differentiated whether both seller and buyer face them, or whether there is some informational asymmetry between them. In the latter case, principal agent theory calls the better informed party the *agent*, whereas the worse informed is called the *principal*, where the agent usually operates on behalf of the principal[4].

Uncertainty which both seller and buyer face, is called *exogenous uncertainty* or external uncertainty, while uncertainty that arises from asymmetrical information distribution is called *endogenous uncertainty* or market uncertainty[5]. Endogenous uncertainty thus constitutes the uncertainty type of relevance from an information-economic perspective, and plays a highly important role in the company's selection of the M&A advisor.

2 *Hartmann-Wendels* discusses the types of market equilibria which hidden characteristics may yield, dependent on the cost of revealing them: "pooling", where each seller gets the same price, as opposed to what he calls the "signalling equilibrium". The former may occur when there are few sellers of bad quality, and when the cost of signalling (the good quality) offset the welfare loss arising from adverse selection. The latter may occur in any other case, see Hartmann-Wendels[108], page 730.

3 This review largely follows Alchian[7] and Spremann[221], which incorporates ideas from Arrow[14], Spence[218], Klein[143], Holström[118], Harris[107].

4 In this thesis' considerations, the buyer takes the role of the principal, whereas the seller (the investment bank) takes the role of the agent.

5 See for instance Hopf[120], pp. 313, 314, Spremann[221], pp. 564, 565, Kaas[131], pp. 886, 887, Fischer[90], page 451. Put differently, exogenous or external uncertainty is "uncertainty that also would exist if buyer and seller constituted one party", see Schmidt[211], page 422.

The weather for the crop farmer and for the wholesaler, the future negotiation behaviour of the transaction counterpart, as well as of competitors, for a company and its advising bank, constitute examples for exogenous uncertainty.

As to endogenous uncertainty, it makes sense to further differentiate different types. This shall be done in the following.

Uncertainty of compliance and remedies

Spremann uses two dimensions by means of which endogenous uncertainty can be differentiated:

- Whether, after selection, the hidden characteristic can deliberately be influenced by the better informed party or not
- Whether the attribute of the (at sales hidden) characteristic can be assessed from ex post[6].

The type of uncertainty whose attribute can still be influenced by the agent shall be termed *uncertainty of compliance*[7]. The complementary type of uncertainty is usually termed *quality uncertainty*[8].

As to the first uncertainty type, it can, by means of the second criterion, further be differentiated into *holdup* and *moral hazard*[9]. While in the case of holdup, the agent's opportunistic behaviour becomes obvious from ex post, moral hazard is even difficult to be

6 See Spremann[221], pp. 564–566.

7 At its core is a potential goal conflict between agent and principal: in order to maximise his profits, the agent may not behave in the way that simultaneously maximises the principal's profits. These thoughts already hint at mechanisms that align agent's to principal's interest as potential remedies, which shall be discussed in the following paragraph.

8 See for instance Hartmann-Wendels[108], page 715, Spremann[221], page 563.

9 *Spremann* differentiates also in the case of quality uncertainty according to whether the hidden characteristics can be observed ex post – at least in indirect ways – or not, and restricts his considerations to characteristics that get known from ex post, see Spremann[221], page 566. The systematisation given does without such differentiation for quality uncertainty, since self-selection mechanisms and signals may be considered equally apt to reveal characteristics, which without these remedies would remain revealed for ever.

detected from ex post[10]. Holdup originates from the agent's hidden intention at sales, which at some point after sales becomes evident to the buyer. The incompleteness of contracts and sunk costs incurred by the principal[11] provide the agent with the means to act opportunistically[12]. Moral hazard is given opportunity by the fact that the resources under the control of the agent are plastic, that is, the way in which he handles them is not exactly determined, so that "there is a wide range of discretionary, legitimate decisions within which the [agent] may choose"[13] – put differently, when task programmability is low[14]. If further (1) the principal is not able to observe the agent's behaviour at decent cost, and (2a) the quality of output cannot be observed or (2b) can be observed, but is also strongly subject to external effects, whose influence on the quality cannot analytically be separated, then it is difficult for the principal to determine the agent's behaviour from ex post[15].

Principal agent theory focuses on researching the conditions under which moral hazard and holdup are likely to emerge, and researches remedies by means of which their potential threat can be decreased already ex ante[16].

---

10 See Spremann[221], pp. 564–566. Similar definitions can for instance be found in Schmidt[211], page 424, Eisenhardt[79], page 61, Richter[196], page 584, Kaas[130], page 543.

11 I. e., costs that are non-recoverable if the principal terminates his exchange with the agent.

12 This insight goes back to Marshall[168], pp. 453, 454. Sunk costs as important prerequisite for holdup are, for instance, also discussed in Alchian[7], page 67, Spremann[221], page 570, or Richter[196], page 584.

13 See Alchian[7], page 69.

14 Where "task programmability" denotes "the degree to which appropriate behaviour by the agent can be specified in advance", see Eisenhardt[79], page 62. Thus, high programmability presumes non-plasticity.

15 Cf. Spremann[221], pp. 571, 572, or Picot[185], page 374. *Alchian* and *Woodward* formulate the same idea in saying that high plasticity and high monitoring costs yield high probability for moral hazard, see Alchian[7], page 69.

16 As *Fischer* et al. note, principal agent theory "deals with the efficient ex ante formation of cooperations" see Fischer[90], page 452. Similar thoughts can be found in Eisenhardt[79], pp. 59, 60, Picot[185], pp. 370–375. Or, as *Elschen* notes, the subject of agency theory consists in "principal agent relationships, where (1) there is potential for goal conflict between principal and agent, (2) result forecast is precarious, and (3) an assessment of the agent by the principal is not always possible", see Elschen[80], page 1004.

The remedy most frequently discussed for moral hazard consists in *incentive systems*, by means of which the agent's interests get better aligned to his principal's interests. One problem associated with such incentive systems is that incitement goes hand in hand with risk shifting, which in the case of risk-averse agents may thus constitute a severe barrier to implementation[17]. Besides, a variety of other designs that help to align the agent's to the principal's interest, have been discussed, such as[18]

- **Monitoring**. The utility of monitoring depends in particular on monitoring costs, which represent a welfare loss compared to a world of perfect information
- **Taking hostages**. Most prominently among these, reputation can be considered "valuable to the agent. Reputation is not transferable on others, but it can be damaged by others (the principal) by bad word-of-mouth [...] The agent's reputation enables [the principal] to threaten the agent with punishment, which induces him to great carefulness"[19]. An incentive system may be considered as taking money as a hostage
- **Guarantees**[20]. If directly issued by the agent, this requires that the agent is willing to take on risk, and when he is ready to do so, he is likely to demand a risk premium. Guarantees

17 This is why the subject of agency theory has often been identified as the problem of "risk sharing, incentive formation, and control", see Fischer[90], page 453; similar thoughts can be found in Hartmann-Wendels[108], page 715, Eisenhardt[79], page 58. *Eisenhardt* reviews the impact of certain factors, such as the existence of information systems, outcome uncertainty, the distribution of risk appetite between agent and principal, goal conflict between agent and principal, task programmability, outcome measurability, length of agency relationship, on the implementation of behaviour-based as opposed to output-based contracts, see Eisenhardt[79], pp. 61–63. A similar, though less extensive, review can be found in Elschen[80], pp. 1008, 1009.

18 Cf. for example Schmidt[211], pp. 428, 429, Spremann[220], pp. 616–621, Kaas[130], page 545, [131], Backhaus[16], pp. 782, 783, Schade[206], pp. 19–22, Jacob[125], pp. 204, 205, pp. 212–215, page 889, Richter[195], pp. 112–117.

19 See Spremann[220], pp. 619, 620. The consideration of reputation as "hostage in the customer's control" goes back to *Schelling*, see Schelling[209], pp. 135, 136.

20 Limitations of guarantees are for instance discussed in Shapiro[213], page 662.

are best applicable to products which have a high degree of reversibility.

It is worth a note that any such design offered by the agent puts the principal into the agent role, thus offers him the opportunity for holdup or moral hazard[21]. Another issue that deserves special mentioning is the accruement of so-called agency costs associated with the designs chosen: monitoring costs, bonding costs, and residual loss (opportunity costs)[22].

Both observations hold similarly for holdup remedies, whose most important representatives shall be dealt with next.

Holdup differs from moral hazard in that the agent knows that his action is going to be known from ex post. Thus, in cases where the agent does not care about his action being known ex post, some of the moral hazard remedies, like reputation, may only be of limited efficiency. Since, further, holdup consists in (mis-)interpreting contractual gaps to one's own profit, *authority* is the design that promises the highest effectiveness for its avoidance[23]. Additionally or alternatively, some of the designs discussed above, may be chosen, as well as the following

- **Third party arbitration**. A clear disadvantage of this remedy are the high costs associated with its implementation
- **Business relationships**. These may induce the agent to act responsibly in the longer-term in order to keep the relationship going, rather than to agitate opportunistically in the short-term. In contrast to third party arbitration, no costs are being incurred.

Quality uncertainty and its remedies

Besides uncertainty of compliance, whose remedies have been discussed in the previous paragraphs, a buyer may face quality un-

21 See for instance Tolle[229] page 934. This gives motivation for research like the one conducted by *Emons*, who researches the double-sided moral hazard problem for goods whose quality cannot be observed, but for which guarantees are offered, see Emons[81].

22 This differentiation goes back to *Jensen* and *Meckling*, see Jensen[128], in particular pp. 308, 309.

23 See Alchian[7], pp. 68–70.

certainty when having to make his purchase decision. Quality uncertainty effectuates from hidden characteristics, i. e., characteristics known by the agent, but not by the principal; it arises from the fact that "the provider knows more about the technology, functionality, and quality of his product" than does the potential buyer[24]. As illustrated by *Akerlof*'s lemon market, quality uncertainty may lead to adverse selection, which denotes "the process of market displacement of the qualitatively better by the qualitatively worse, which takes place due to the imperfect quality knowledge of the demand side"[25]. Consequently, remedies to prevent adverse selection are mechanisms that reveal the hidden characteristics with preferably high reliability: "self-selection mechanisms" and "signalling"[26]. This section shall not expand on self-selection mechanisms and signalling any further, since section 4.2.3 has already excessively done so[27].

Figure 5.1 revisits this paragraph's findings, by pinpointing the most prominent distinguishing features of uncertainty types.

5.1.2 Uncertainty of compliance in M&A advisory

In markets that are characterised by a strong supply side concentration, buyers have a high awareness of (and often also a strong opinion

24 See Kaas[130], page 542.

25 See Fischer[90], page 448. Or, as *Eisenhardt* puts it – stressing more the role of the agent as opposed to the principal –, "adverse selection refers to the misrepresentation of ability by the agent. The argument here is that the agent may claim to have certain skills or abilities when he or she is hired [...] and the principal cannot completely verify these skills [...] at the time of hiring", see Eisenhardt[79], page 61.

26 These are the inner mechanisms of the risk relievers illustrated in figure 4.5 on page 66. As shows the example of variable compensation, though, while they are commonly discussed as relievers of quality uncertainty, they may also contribute to avoid holdup or moral hazard, by inciting the agent to act with great carefulness. Screening and signalling as actions performed by the market participants in order to exchange information, are for instance discussed in Spence[218], pp. 355–358, [219], page 592, Hopf[120], page 317, Kaas[130], page 541, Fischer[90], page 448, Tolle[229], page 928.

27 This section has, among others, provided a comprehensive review of commonalities and differences between self-selection mechanisms and probabilistic quality indicators.

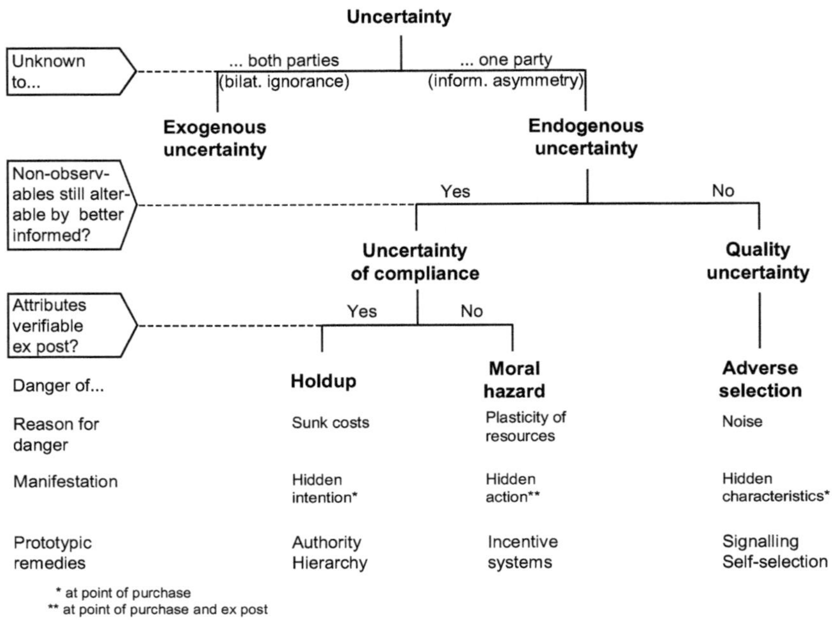

Figure 5.1: Uncertainty types

about) the different suppliers in question[28]. Further, if the market is strongly relationship-driven, a high share of the total customer-specific "pay-off" may be incurred only in the later phases of the customer life cycle, which means that a premature termination of a relationship, e. g. due to the customer's dissatisfaction, is highly undesirable from the provider's perspective[29]. All the more, since in business relationships the role of principal and agent switches repeatedly between buyer and seller[30], and welfare optimisation can

28 I. e., the market is far from being an anonymous market.

29 The concepts of reputation and relationship shall be revisited in section 5.3.

30 Cf. for instance Schmidt[211], where the information distribution between buyer and provider in the course of mutual interaction for industrial products where sales takes place before production, is discussed. *Kaas* discusses this issue in the context of contract goods with interactive production, see Kaas[131], pp. 889–891.

only be achieved if trust partially replaces monitoring[31]. Besides, chances even are that repeated moral hazard gets revealed[32]. Thus, both moral hazard and holdup do not seem compelling strategies to take by a provider, since it sets much of their future pay-off at risk – not only with their specific customer, but also in the market.

All of these characteristics apply to the market of M&A advisory: market concentration is the effective case in the "upper", high-volume market segment, and banks usually market their advice in relationships, which usually require significant "upfront" investments. Thus, uncertainty of compliance can be expected *not* to represent a major issue in the choice of an M&A advisor. Put differently, buyers can expect investment banks to be "naturally interested" in delivering their best.

Thus, as to the uncertainty component of risk associated with the M&A advisor choice, buyers can be expected to be mostly concerned about quality uncertainty, rather than about the banks' uncertainty of compliance.

5.1.3 Cost, benefit, and utility of information

When will a buyer search for information, and what will he be ready to "pay" for it, also in non-financial terms? – If the buyer acts with full rationality, it is desirable for him to collect and process information, as long as the incremental utility of such information, i. e., incremental benefits minus incremental costs, associated with collecting and processing it, is positive[33]. The fact that the usefulness

---

31 Thus decreasing agency costs, cf. paragraph 5.1.1 on page 82. Cf. also Diller[75], pp. 217–219, on suitability of cooperation as opposed to competition or egoism, dependent on time horizon and other relationship characteristics, or Ganesan[93], on long term orientation of relationships as function of mutual dependence and mutual trust.

32 "[I]t seems reasonable that when principals and agents engage in a long-term relationship, it is likely that the principal will learn about the agent, and so will be able to assess behaviour more readily", see Eisenhardt[79], page 63.

33 See for instance Nelson[179] pp. 313, 314. The cost of information is for instance discussed in Hopf[120], pp. 314, 318, Kaas[130], pp. 542, 543. Taking a broader perspective, information costs can be considered one type of transaction costs, cf. for instance Picot[184], page 178, Bössmann[36], pp. 107, 108.

of information can only be completely determined once its content is known, explains the fact why we sometimes eagerly search for information, and then, once we have obtained it, realise we could have done without it. This is called the "paradox of information"[34]. Fortunately, this does not happen so frequently, since we often do have quite a good idea of the searched information's potential value to us, by virtue of experience or heuristics[35].

It is thus evident that the research of information search behaviour has to take into account both the cost and value of the information to the buyer.

In the next chapter, a natural typology of information shall be developed, which shall provide the basis for a qualitative assessment of its availability (costs) and processability (value)[36]. In an intermediary step, the way by which certain product characteristics affect the utility of the discussed information types, shall be examined[37]. Eventually, these findings shall be used to formulate hypotheses on the marketing of M&A advisory from a risk-information perspective[38].

5.2 Natural information typology

Although there have been quite some controversies about the interpretation of information-economic concepts[39], literature has lacked

---

34 It is immediately evident that one can attribute information search inefficiencies to this paradox – without even having to assume that the buyer acts irrationally.

35 See for instance Spence[218], page 359.

36 This is done in section 5.2.

37 See chapter 6.

38 This shall be done in chapters 7 and 8.

39 To give an example, source and cognitive origin, let alone reference and affinity, have not been discussed as dimensions which any piece of information can be simultaneously characterised by, and conclusions on the utility by the means of such assessments, have only fragmentarily been drawn. This can be illustrated by *Backhaus*' criticism about *Schade* and *Schott*'s definition of quasi credence goods in Backhaus[16] on page 786. *Backhaus* argues that

a systematisation of information that differentiates such aspects explicitly, respectively reconciles them. Since, furthermore, the availability and usefulness of information also depends on such natural specifics, a first draft that categorises information accordingly seems desirable. This section shall draft such a typology by using the characteristics displayed in figure 5.2.

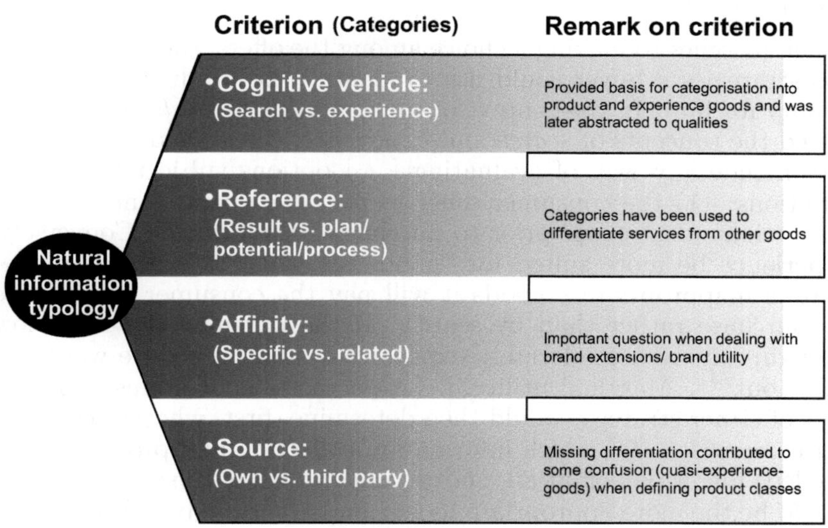

Figure 5.2: Characteristics used to differentiate information types

The characteristics depicted shall be used to assess information's utility for an *ex ante quality assessment* of a product for sale. Thus, this section is going to be concerned with information's utility for uncertainty decrease, dependent on these characteristics.

---

other market participants' experience could serve as a replacement for own experience, thus giving quasi credence goods the properties of experience goods. While this is true, the important question then is: how useful is such replacement, and in dependence of what criteria?

5.2.1 Cognitive vehicle

Information can be differentiated by its cognitive origin, which addresses in particular whether product features can be evaluated before or after purchase, or not at all. The search, experience, and credence framework, introduced by *Nelson*, and refined by *Darby* and *Karni*, provides guidance for such a typology.

Categorisation

When it comes to making a choice among the offers, there are numerous strategies a buyer could use to identify the product of superior quality for him. In the context of consumer goods, *Nelson* has introduced the concepts of *search* and *experience*, where he defines search "to include any way of evaluating [...] options subject to two restrictions: (1) the consumer must inspect the option, and (2) that inspections must occur prior to purchasing the brand." Conversely, experience be more suited for "goods for which this search procedure is inappropriate – goods it will pay the consumer to evaluate by purchase rather than by search. If the purchase price[40] is low enough, any even moderately expensive search procedure would be ruled out"[41]. Marginal utility, i.e. expected benefit minus expected cost of either strategy, would then determine, first, whether continuing comparison (for which information collection and processing are needed) might pay off at all, and, second, which of the two strategies would be the more appropriate to use, and accordingly classify goods as search goods or experience goods[42].

Darby and *Karni*[43] abstracted the concept of search and experience from goods to product qualities, and extended this classification

40 The discussion in paragraph 4.1.2 shows that value to the business and potential loss, captured by a value-at-risk measure, are more appropriate determinants than purchase price. A product that is for free might not be sampled unless value-at-risk is low enough!

41 See Nelson[179], page 312.

42 As criticised by *Arnthorsson* et al., see Arnthorsson[12], page 217, the way by which *Nelson* himself assigned goods to the search and experience goods categories – namely by looking at their non-merchandise receipts to merchandise receipts ratio – is highly questionable. But it is *Nelson*'s merit to have established the distinction between quality inspection ex ante and quality inspection ex post.

43 See Darby[66], pp. 68–69.

by the category of *credence* qualities, whose crucial characteristic is that they "cannot be evaluated in normal use. Instead the assessment of their value requires additional costly information"[44]. Thus, credence qualities cannot be assessed appropriately by the user, neither before (search), nor after (experience) consumption[45].

Some observations ought to be made to the theory so far. Whether a good is a search or experience good is – when *Nelson*'s definition is being strictly applied – not an attribute belonging to the product per se, but is also dependent on buyer specifics[46]. In particular, the more product-specific knowhow a buyer has developed, the more he will be able to infer from the product's observable features its value to him.

Applying an origination-oriented perspective[47], one can differentiate search type information from experience type information.

- **Search type.** Search type information is information that is collected by means of inspection at or before sales. That way, search type information can either refer to the product itself or a surrogate[48], such as production factors or employees that are going to be involved into the production of the product.

  The trim of a dress, the plans of a house to be built, the documents certifying certain qualifications of the provider's employees, the project schedule with milestones as depicted in a

44 See Darby[66], page 69.

45 Heart surgery provides an example for a product that is dominated by credence qualities.

46 Cf. also Stigler[225], page 216, Ford[91], page 240. Buyer-specific differences in search cost or number of envisioned repeat purchases could make a product a search good for one buyer, while it may be an experience or credence good for another.

47 Which means that information shall be categorised according to the way it originated, rather than the way it may be accessed. To give an example, an expert user's usage experience depicted in a magazine is experience type, but the way in which this information can be accessed is by search (namely by reading the magazine).

48 For the concept of surrogates, cf. for example Backhaus[16], pp. 782–784, Kleinaltenkamp[144], pp. 819–822, [145], page 84, Stauss[223], pp. 92–93, Jacob[125], page 207, Günter[103], page 148.

sales presentation by a bank when trying to gain the M&A advisory mandate, all constitute examples for information that is "search type" to the buyer

- **Experience type.** Experience type information is information collected ex post by means of product experience. As search type information, experience type information may refer to the product itself or some surrogate, such as production factors or the production process.

  To give some examples, the taste of an apple, the cleanliness of the car after car-wash, the ex-post assessment of the smoothness of interaction between the customer and the banking team during an M&A project, constitute information that is "experience type" to the buyer.

Discussion

In general, the utility of information for uncertainty decrease strongly depends on a reliable link between the information in question and the product for purchase. Differentiating search from experience type information, the following observations can be made regarding this link:

- **Search type information.** If the product itself is being searched, then the exploitability[49] of search type information depends strongly on a reliable link between specific product features and the product's value for the buyer. While such deduction may be trivial for certain products and their features, it may require a significant amount of technical knowledge for others. And, as discussed earlier, the relationship between the searched feature and the product's value may be of intrinsic or extrinsic character, where the former promises a closer link between the two[50]. In the latter case, the object actually searched would tend to be a surrogate for the product rather than the

49 The term *exploitability* shall hint at a situation where costs to access the information are close to zero, thus information is available. So the question of utility reduces itself mainly to the question of what the expected benefit of using the information is.

50 Cf. figure 4.5 on page 66, figure 4.6 on page 70.

product itself. But also in cases where the product itself is not searchable, a high reliability between a searched surrogate, such as for instance a product plan, or the production factors, may exist. Such a strong link between searched surrogate and product quality is given when the surrogate has a low degree of plasticity, and when its degree of task programmability is high[51].

An example for search where there is a highly reliable link between the searched surrogate and product quality, thus low quality uncertainty, is provided by the plan for a house, specifying size and materials, as drafted by the architect (product plan)[52]

- **Experience type information.** As to the exploitability of experience type information, it is not enough that a product's value to the buyer is ascertainable ex post. If one cannot infer from the value of an already used resp. consumed product the value of the next product (of the same provider) one is going to buy, such knowledge is no good to serve the purpose of an ex ante quality assessment of the product for sale. That is, as a necessary condition, the product's quality must not strongly vary from purchase occasion to purchase occasion. This prerequisite shall be termed low *inter-buying-occasion quality variability*, short, low *IQV*.

  If the quality does vary a lot, the exploitability of experience type information is restricted, and it will be a better strategy to search the product (or surrogates) in its concrete peculiarity at sales, if this is feasible. One important point to note here is that IQV needs not be product-category-specific, but can also be provider-specific: there may be products for which certain providers are capable of keeping product quality constant

51 Note that, in contrast to paragraph 5.1.1, task programmability and factor plasticity are now being reviewed from a quality uncertainty, rather than an uncertainty of compliance perspective.

52 As to quality uncertainty, such plan may, though, fall short in specifying the timeliness of delivery, which may constitute an important quality feature of the house. As to uncertainty of compliance, the buyer may face costs to legally reinforce the promise, and he may even have to deal with holdup.

– these providers in fact being high-quality providers *because* they are able to do this –, whereas others are not, rendering the utility assessment of experience type information even more complicated. Non-automated services may serve as a typical example for the latter.

Thus, there are basically three reasons for which the utility of experience type information may be high. First, a high degree of task programmability, that is, low IQV by means of low plasticity of production factors. Second, if task programmability is low, as for instance in non-automated services, the inter-buying-occasion identity of the production factors. For non-automated services, such identity would man that the buyer re-engages an individual he has already made experience with before.

These two prerequisites, low plasticity of production factors, or identity of production factors, may be considered "intrinsic" utility increasers for experience type information. The third utility increaser is different in this respect. It is proposed that if individuals vary, and if task programmability is low, then a corporation's credibility for employing equally suited individuals, may compensate the lack of intrinsic utility increasers. Such credibility is reflected in the corporation's reputation.

Finally, the more consistent the experience with a product or company is over time, the more there will be the notion of a heritage. Such heritage might be an important asset when it comes to selling goods whose production stretches over a long time period, and where a buyer wants to get reassured about a company's stability over time[53].

Examples for products with low IQV include shampoos or the car wash provided by a fuel station's cleaning machine, while for products with non-automated production, experience type information may be more of a limited value, in particular when

53 German private health insurance might serve as a typical example: a consistent long-term track-record is an important prerequisite for success; the buyer extrapolates consistency in the past to consistency in the future.

the person performing the production is not the same. Examples for the latter comprise the styling by the hairdresser, or the advice given by an investment bank on transactions.

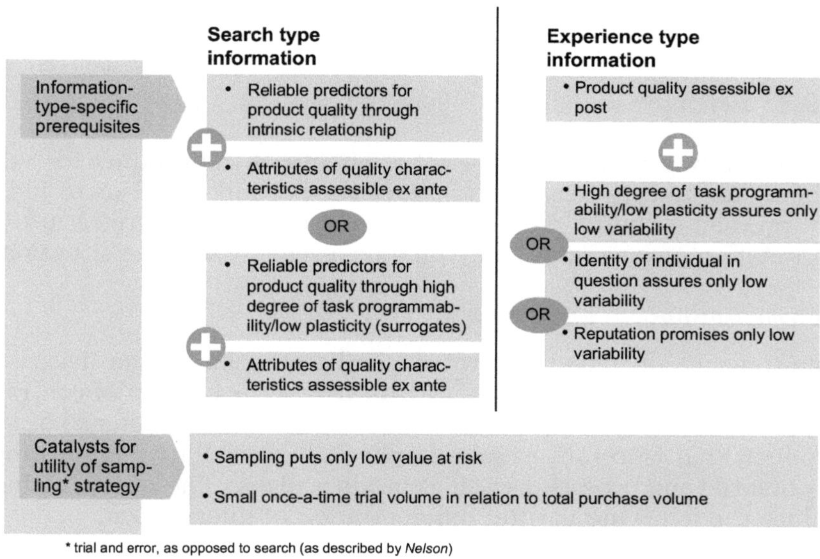

Figure 5.3: Utility drivers for search and experience

Factors that foster the utility of search or experience type information for quality assessment should be differentiated from factors that foster the utility of search (inspection) as opposed to experience strategy (sampling) in *Nelson*'s sense[54]. Experience strategy, as opposed to search strategy, is attractive when the relative value at stake, which may be lost in case of bad product quality, is small, and when a once-a-time purchase is small compared to the total purchase volume in question. Thus, while these thoughts clearly imply that M&A advisor choice should not be optimised by means of a

54 See Nelson[179], page 312: "[...] there will be goods for which [a] search procedure is inappropriate – goods it will pay the consumer to evaluate by purchase rather than by search. If the purchase price is low enough, any even moderately expensive search procedure would be ruled out".

sampling strategy, experience type information, referring to former interactions or projects with the banks in question, may be used to evaluate the quality of the product offers for sale.

Figure 5.3 summarises this paragraph's most important observations.

5.2.2 Reference

When the buyer wants to assess the quality of the product for sale, he may not always be able to inspect the product itself, or to judge the product's quality by means of experience. The buyer's use of information on surrogates may provide a remedy in these situations.

Categorisation

The concepts of potential, process, and result, have been discussed a lot in the context of services[55]. But also in the context of contract goods[56], they play an important role, since the non-existence of the product, that is, result, at sales implies a higher relative importance of potential and process, as well as product plans. These observations induce the following natural differentiation of information.

- **Result.** As discussed in section 5.2.1, the buyer could potentially use search or experience type information on the product itself in order to assess its quality[57]. In other words, he may look for information on the *result* of the production process.

  The trim of a dress and the cleanliness of the car after car-wash provide examples for information that refers to the result

55 Cf. for instance Corsten[59], page 17, Bruhn[45], page 22, Staffelbach[222], pp. 278, 278, Meyer[173], pp. 197, 198. See also the introductory remarks in paragraph 2.3.1 on page 26.

56 Contract goods are "performance promises, whose most important characteristic is their non-existence at sales", see Schade[206], page 19 – thus, M&A advisory belongs to this product class. A similar, but somewhat narrower definition can be found in Kaas[131], page 884.

57 In the case of search type information, the product itself may not yet exist at sales, but some of its components may already exist and be searchable. This shows that inspectability of the product itself spans a continuum.

- **Plan, potential, or process.** In cases where the buyer encounters difficulty in obtaining or evaluating information on the result, he may take a step back and look for surrogate type of information – namely information on plan, potential, or process.

  The buyer could for example search a *product plan* describing the approach and its targeted result, as common in the professional services industry (letter of intent and sales presentation[58]), or by inspecting the production factors themselves, such as machinery, people, corporate knowhow, which reflect a provider's *production potential.* Furthermore, the *process* by which the result is being generated, may serve as a surrogate for the result. In the case of services, the process may offer a higher degree of materiality than the actual product, and may in particular serve as a surrogate when product quality is even difficult to judge from ex post, as for goods dominated by credence qualities.

  The perceived newness of the surgeon's equipment, the banker's perceived knowledge of the industry, and the management's satisfaction with the interaction with the investment banking team during an M&A project, may all serve as examples for surrogate type information.

Discussion

For a surrogate to be exploitable, it needs not only be inspectable or ascertainable ex post, but it is crucial that there exists a reliable link between the surrogate and the product as such. This takes us back to the question of whether the surrogate is implastic with respect to the result, whether the production task in question is programmable, or whether, in particular, there exist cause-effect-chains between the surrogate and the result[59].

58 Cf. paragraph 3.2.3 on page 47.

59 Note that, in lack of anything better, inspection may be drawn to assessing "surrogates of the surrogate". To give an example, when assessing the provider's employees (that is, when production factors already serve as a surrogate for the product in question), the attire worn by the staff of the provider company or the company building may be used as a surrogate for

Furthermore, in cases where output quality is strongly influenced by external factors that lie outside the provider's power, and where the effects of such external factors on output quality are hard to measure, the assessment of input quality will be relatively more important than in other cases[60]. In the extreme, when it takes the buyer lots of effort to integrate his own factors into the production process, one could even think that the expected smoothness of the production process may be traded off with expected output quality by the buyer when he makes his purchase choice[61].

Figure 5.4 summarises the findings on the exploitability of information dependent on its reference, and also provides some thoughts on when non-result type information will play a relatively important role.

5.2.3 Affinity

Following the discussion of plan, potential, and process as surrogates for the result in the previous paragraph, this paragraph wants to discuss another surrogate a buyer may assess to make his purchase decision: related products provided by the provider in question. Both customised products of the same class, as well as related product classes can be considered related products. While product individualisation has attracted scholars' interest in the research of marketing-homogenous product subclasses[62], related product classes

the employees' competence (which, of course, cannot be considered a superior strategy to assess product quality).

60 For, in cases where the buyer cannot do this, he will not know whether to attribute the quality outcome to the provider or to accident; see also Spremann[220], page 615. In such cases, the law of large numbers may provide a remedy; but an important prerequisite to make this law applicable is the availability of a multiplicity of experience type information. Note that these observations abstract from the reasons due to which the provider's level and quality of input in the production process (intention vs. incompetence) could vary.

61 As *Lovelock* puts it, "although purchasers are interested primarily in the final output, the manner in which they are treated during the process of service delivery can also have an important impact on their satisfaction", see Lovelock[159], page 4.

62 Such systematisation shall be dealt with in chapter 6, page 118 and following pages.

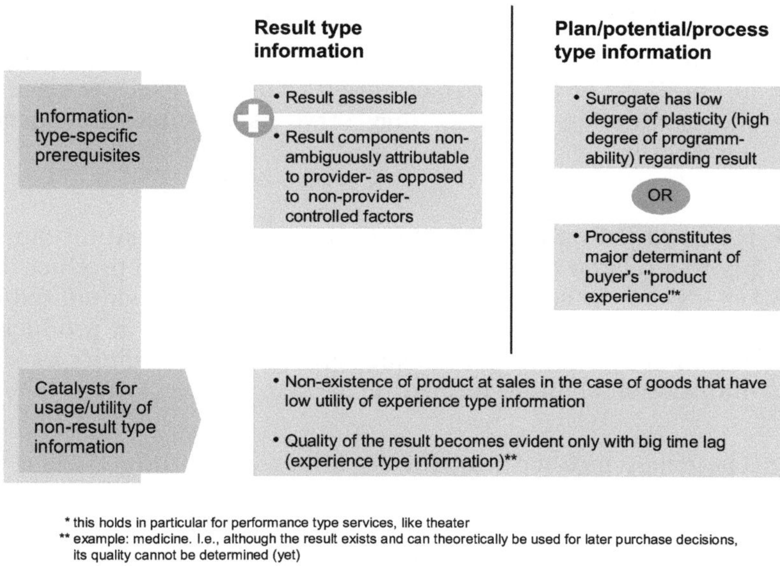

Figure 5.4: Utility drivers for result and plan/potential/process

have constituted an important subject in the discussion of brand extensions[63].

Categorisation

Accordingly, the following types of information may be distinguished:

- **Specific information.** Information can refer to the product in its concrete specification, as for instance in cases where the product can be inspected at sales, or in cases where the buyer repurchases a certain product in the very same design in which he has already purchased it before, thus has already made experience with it. The affinity of such information shall be called specific.

63 See for instance Aaker[2], pp. 220, 233, Keller[141], page 52, Sattler[202], Vasek[232].

The cloth composition of the dress for sale, the perceived know-how of the banker who is going to lead the team on the project in question, or the satisfaction with the previous car-wash by the provider in question, may serve as examples for specific information

- **Related information.** Alternatively, the information can apply to a related product, such as an individualised product that belongs to the same category – but has been individualised according to someone else's specifications –, or as a product of a related category by the same provider. The affinity of such information shall be termed related.

  The experience with a provider's hair care product when the buyer has to choose a skin care product, or the investment bank's IPO track record in the industry when a company is looking for an M&A advisor, provide examples for related information (related product class). The experience made with an investment bank during the past M&A project when it comes to choosing the M&A advisor for a new M&A project, represents also related information, in so far as M&A advisory's customisation varies – both by buyer and by transaction –, but it is of course more closely related to the product for sale, than information on the bank's IPO business.

Discussion

The importance of related experience becomes particularly apparent in markets where highly individualised goods are sold, that is, where products differ from buyer to buyer, maybe even from transaction to transaction, so that specific experience may hardly be available[64]. Conversely, one should note that product individualisation is no sufficient to infer the non-existence of specific experience: for highly individualised products specific experience may be available, namely in the case of repeat purchase[65]. And, for non-individualised prod-

64 Cf. for example Günter[103], pp. 145–146.

65 If customisation is only buyer-specific and not transaction-specific, as is the case of component supply business, cf. also page 118.

ucts, specific experience may not be available, namely if the provider is new to the market.

Most products though – no matter what their degree of individualisation – will have some common aspects, be it similar components in the case of electronic systems, be it a considerable overlap in the chosen approach in the case of corporate bank advice. This shows that specific and related information span a continuum.

When will a buyer feel comfortable to rely on related information? – Certainly if there is some rationale to believe that high quality providers of the related product can equally well produce the product in question[66]. As long as functional benefits dominate the value of the product to the buyer, one should believe such inference seems justified as long as the related product and the product in question show a high congruence in production factors and/or process[67]. In order to be able to use related information as a decision basis at all, the buyer must, moreover, be aware that the related product and the product in question are provided by the same company[68]. Often, this awareness is being supported by the implementation of umbrella brands, as common in the investment banking industry. But branding on its own will not do the job to establish the buyer's belief that different product classes of the same provider offer the same (functional) benefit, as illustrates a look at the corporate banking industry, which shows that the banks believed to be leading in commercial banking are not the ones believed to be leading in the investment banking area, although many a bank offers both services under the same brand name (the corporate brand)[69].

---

66 *Von Weizsäcker* and *von Ungern-Sternberg* provide such a heuristic in Ungern-Sternberg[231], page 614.

67 This fits to *Aaker*'s observation that emotional and self-expressive benefits stretch further in the context of brand extensions than do others, see Aaker[2], page 220.

68 While in consumer goods industries, there are many companies who have chosen to take the multi-brand (example: Procter & Gamble) as opposed to the corporate brand approach, this seems by far less common in the service and the business-to-business industry. This may be explained by the companies' deliberate effort to foster the transfer of goodwill between classes of products whose quality is more difficult to assess.

69 Different banks' "spikes" are for instance discussed in Currie[65], page 93. Also within investment banking, there are products of lower and higher de-

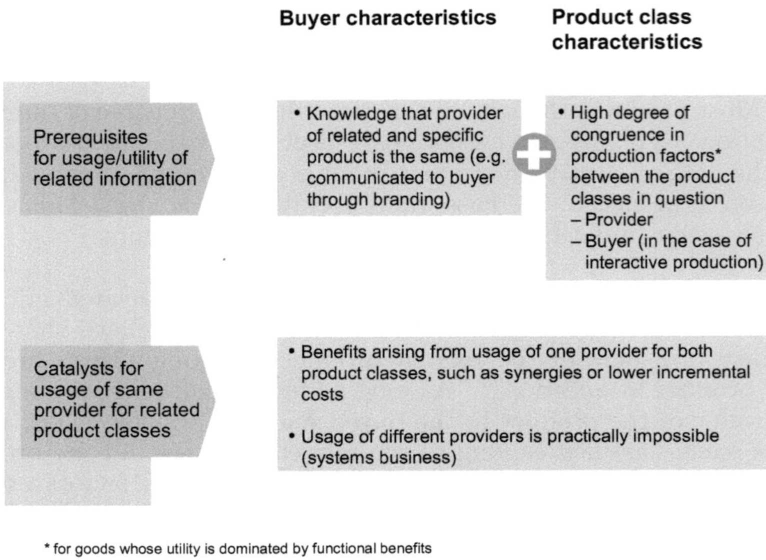

Figure 5.5: Utility drivers for related information

The prerequisites for the use of related information as vehicle to decrease uncertainty should be differentiated from catalysts that foster the actual usage (of the product, not just of the information) of the same provider for different product classes. The latter include potential synergies arising from the usage of the same provider, or prohibitive costs associated with the use of different providers. Systems business may serve as an example for the latter.

Figure 5.5 depicts the main ideas discussed in the previous paragraphs. Since specific information represents the naturally preferred information type, the figure restricts itself to reviewing the prerequisites for the utility of related information.

---

gree of relationship with each other. While M&A advisory is quite related to the IPO business, it is not so related to proprietary trading.

5.2.4 Source

Information can further be distinguished according to its source, that is, according to whether the information has been collected and processed by the buyer himself, or by others.

Categorisation

Besides resolving some of the confusion that has arisen in the discussion of goods categorisations[70], tackling the source issue also helps to explicitly think about the mechanisms that help to increase the utility of information.

- **Own information.** The buyer himself can make efforts to search the product resp. surrogates, or he may have knowledge on them by virtue of his own experience
- **Third party information.** Additionally or alternatively, search may be conducted by a third party, such as an expert magazine in the case of shampoos[71]. Or, product-usage-based experience may stem from others, such as peers in the case of M&A advisory, and the buyer may search this information from third parties and use it to assess the quality of the banks soliciting the mandate.

Discussion

The perceived viability of third party information will strongly depend on the credibility and perceived competence of the third party source[72]. Although in general the reliability of own information may

---

70 An explicit differentiation taking different sources into account solves *Backhaus'* criticism, discussed in footnote 39 on page 87.

71 While the buyer may for instance be able to determine the effects of the shampoo regarding the cleanliness and odour of his hair by means of own experience, he may not be able to detect substances that may damage his health in the longer term.

72 Cf. for instance Stock[226], page 2, Cox[61], page 626, for a first review of empirical validations of this proposition. *Gierl*, *Stich*, and *Strohmayr* have found empirical evidence for this relationship in an experiment simulating the the market of hearing aids, cf. Gierl[99]. When analysing affective and cognitive antecedents of attitudes toward advertisements, *Lutz* found that recipients also try to evaluate the credibility of the source, see Lutz[164], page 49.

be judged superior over third party information[73] due to strong similarity of buyer situation and preconditions, as well as the consistency of the point of reference[74], there may well be cases in which a buyer will feel more comfortable to rely on third party than on own information, for instance in cases where he expects other, more experienced buyers to have developed a stronger expertise regarding the quality assessment of the product than himself. In particular, third party search will play a more important role for products where there is special knowhow required in order to collect and process information, than for products where search can be conducted by oneself at low cost[75]. Last but not least, third party information can only be used if third party sources are accessible – in particular, willing to share their information.

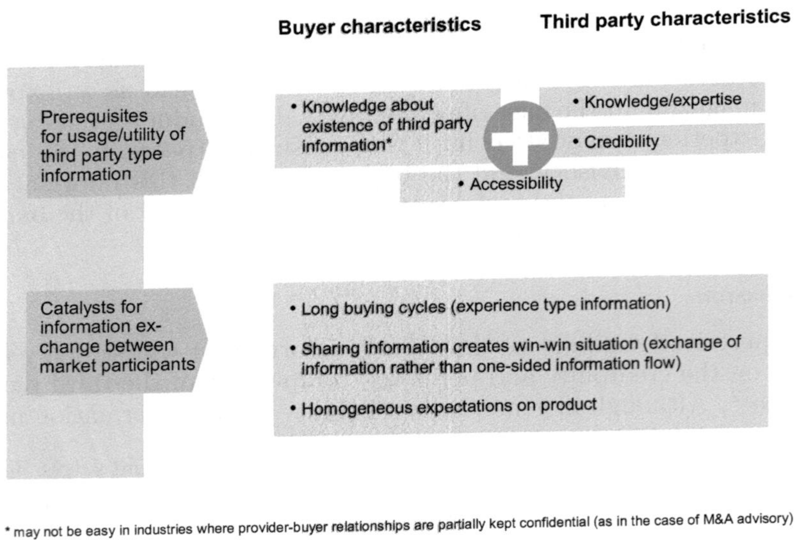

Figure 5.6: Utility drivers for third party information

73 Cf. Cox[61], pp. 607, 608.

74 Cf. page 53.

75 The assessment of contractual elements of insurance contracts (e. g., protection against the inability to work) by independent magazines, may serve as an example for such products.

To conclude, it should be noted that certain markets benefit the accessibility of third party information, while others do not. An example for the former is provided by the consumer goods market for household appliances. In contrast, strongly competitive markets, where buyers and suppliers form informal vertical alliances, and where sharing of experience may endanger a company's competitive position, are an example for the latter.

Figure 5.6 summarises the most important findings on the exploitability of information, dependent on its source. Since own information would usually constitute the preferred type of information, the figure restricts itself to reviewing prerequisites for the utility of third party information. This summary has been complemented by a list of factors that foster information exchange between market participants.

5.3 Reputation, relationship, information search

This chapter shall be ended by a review of three concepts that are of central importance for the marketing of industrial services: reputation, relationship, and information search.

5.3.1 Reputation

Reputation has constituted an important subject of discussion, but has hardly been defined by the scholars dealing with it. One of the rare exceptions represents *Herbig*, who defined reputation as "the estimation of the consistency over time of an attribute of an entity"[76]. *Herbig* further observes that reputation be "an aggregate composite of all previous transactions over the life of the entity, a historical notion, and [that it] requires consistency of an entity's actions over a prolonged time". While one has to acknowledge that this definition addresses important aspects of reputation – such as consistency –, it may be criticised for being too transaction-focused from the perspec-

76 See Herbig[111], page 23.

tive that non-transaction-related behaviour may significantly affect a company's reputation.

In part following *Herbig*, let us in the following use the working definition that reputation be the estimation of consistency of the quality or character of an individual or group by a collective, where the term "collective" shall denote the group of individuals that hold an opinion about the individual or group in question.

Correspondingly, an individual's assessment of A's public reputation captures the aggregate of what this individual thinks that others think about A, and can thus be supposed to be widely based on third party information.

The more individuals hold similar opinions about A, the more consistent public reputation assessments across individuals are going to be. This consistency of opinions shall be referred to by the expression of A having a *strong* reputation, while the term (very) *high quality* reputation shall express that A is (highly) appreciated among those that hold an opinion about him[77]. Finally, if a reputation is both (very) strong and of (very) high quality, it shall be called a *good*, respectively *excellent* reputation.

Reputation originates from a multitude of sources, e.g., from marketer-controlled sources, from word-of-mouth, from information communicated by third-party sources, from the association of the company with some particular person, place, or event[78].

Reputation plays an important role when buyers want to assess the quality of a product for sale, and when such quality is difficult to search[79]. In particular, if the perceived risk associated with the

77 Analogously, the terms *weak* and *low quality* reputation shall be used, where A may represent an individual or group. Similarly, one could use the term *broad* reputation to indicate that many individuals have an opinion about A, while *narrow* reputation may be used to denote the opposite.

78 Cf. for instance Herbig[111], pp. 23, 24. This aspect has also been frequently discussed in the context of brand image (which can be considered the product-wise correspondence of reputation), see for instance Kotler[147], page 597, Aaker[2], pp. 109, 110, Krishnan[150], Keller[141], pp. 92, 93.

79 Cf. for instance Kreps[149]. As *Shapiro* notes, "[t]he idea of reputation makes sense only in an imperfect information world", see Shapiro[213], page 865.

purchase is high, and own search and experience type information do not yield solid guidance as to which provider to choose, a buyer may strongly orient his decision at the provider's reputation[80].

An important peculiarity of reputation lies in its ability to provide clues on future provider behaviour via a two-fold mechanism. On the one hand, reputation provides a probabilistic quality indicator[81]. On the other hand, it is a "hostage" in the hand of the customer, that is, it provides the buyer with the means to punish the provider if his purchase turns out to be unsatisfactory, and, this way, can be considered a mechanism that helps self-selection taking place[82]. Thus, reputation can be considered a valuable asset that (1) needs to be built in the first place and (2) brings returns when being maintained, but may be destroyed in the second. This is the reason for which reputation if often referred to as "goodwill"[83].

5.3.2 Benefits of a good reputation

But one would take by far too narrow a perspective if one looked at reputation only from a risk relief perspective – its role goes far beyond.

80 See also Yoon[241], pp. 216, 218. As *Yoon* et al. summarise, the importance of reputation "increases under conditions of imperfect information. When performance information is not perfectly diffused among the customers, the marketer's reputation is used as a guideline to form expectations of quality", all the more when "information search costs are high", see Yoon[241], page 218. One may want to add that reputation may be able to "retain" and "extract" what may be difficult to assess by means of experience. To illustrate this by the example of M&A advisory, a bank's reputation can be supposed to also subsume the stock market's appreciations of the mergers or acquisitions advised by the bank, whereas the value of a specific merger or acquisition is difficult to assess for the M&A advisory buyer even ex post. The law of large numbers, and the multiplicity of perspectives, provide the designs that facilitate the utility of reputation.

81 See section 4.2.3 on pages 67 and following. That way, reputation helps "predicting the actions" of companies, see Herbig[111], page 23. Similar thoughts can be found in Shapiro[213], page 659, Yoon[241], page 215.

82 Cf. pages 68, 81.

83 See for instance Ungern-Sternberg[231], page 613, Shapiro[213], page 659, Merbold[172], page 110.

Most prominently, an intermediary's[84] reputation may constitute a device the customer might want to use to save costs of signalling himself. This is explained by the following. The damage of reputation is much more of a threat for an investment bank, since the bank continuously agitates on the market for corporate control, than it is for a company, who may agitate on this market only once (and whose most important market is its customer market). That is, the credibility that an investment bank has gained over time in a market may serve as a substitute for their principal's lack of credibility resp. track record[85]. Thus, a company dealing with M&A may not only look for a highly renowned M&A advisor in order to lower its own uncertainty associated with the advisor choice, but also in order to offer its potential transaction counterpart reassurance about its own intention to fairly agitate on the market of corporate control. This

84 In the case of M&A advisory, the bank's reputation.

85 For financial intermediaries, *Booth* and *Smith* were the first to give this raison d'être for financial intermediaries, see Booth[38], pp. 266, 267. Applying such rationale to the IPO market, *Carter* and *Dark* found empirical evidence for the hypothesis that underpricing of IPOs is less likely to happen when the underwriter has a good reputation than if it has not (although they admit that an alternative reason for the negative correlation between underpricing and reputation may also lie in the renowned banks' aptitude to choose low risk IPOs, see pp. 360, 361), see Carter[53]. Similar results, modelling equity markets that are characterised by strong information asymmetries, have been reported by *Chemmanur* and *Fulghieri*, see Chemmanur[54]. Other raisons d'être for financial intermediaries that do not take on risk themselves (and are thus intermediaries in the "broader sense", cf. Bitz[33], pp. 430–432, whose task focus consists in information and intermediation), can for instance be found in Benston[24], Leland[157], Campbell[50], Millon[174], Breuer[41], Jacob[124], pp. 23–30, Achleitner[5], pp. 37–57, Dibelius[73], pp. 34, 43–48. Most prominently, reasons consist in the intermediaries' ability to help their customers to economise transaction costs – for instance through higher efficiency and effectiveness of information search –, transformation and repackaging of assets, and market making.
To get back to the lemons problem in the car market, car dealers provide a certifying device for analogous reasons. One part of the game is that they, unlike the private user, are better able to assess a car's quality without using it, see Akerlof[6], page 496. The other one, though, is that they – unlike the private person, who may want to agitate on the market for used cars only once or twice as seller, – are anticipated to stay in the market, and thus have a reputation to lose, cf. the ideas formulated in Spence[218], page 355. For the sake of future business opportunities, it lies thus in the self-interest of the dealer to offer cars at fair prices.

is being achieved by means of borrowing on the bank's reputation, which offers higher signalling effectiveness.

Further, reputation may be used as a device for choice justification. Justification pressure is presumably particularly high when the stake at risk is high, when product quality is difficult to assess, and when choice makers act as agents for principals[86].

These initial thoughts already illustrate that a good corporate reputation offers a multitude of advantages to both provider and buyer[87]. In order to embrace the role of reputation[88], the following paragraphs shall briefly review the advantages of branding in general, as well as the competitive advantages gained by having a good or excellent reputation[88] in particular.

Benefits for the buyer

Most of the advantages a buyer gains from branding arise from the reduction of search costs. More specifically, benefits for the buyer consist in

- Shorthand devices and means of simplification for choice decision[89], lowering search costs externally and internally
  - Risk reduction[90]
  - Easy recognition if repurchase in the case of product satisfaction is intended, resp. when repurchase is not intended in the case of dissatisfaction[91]
- Facility of choice justification in the case of popular brands[92]

86 All of which apply in the case of M&A advisory. As to principals, decision makers may have to justify their choice towards colleagues and shareholders.

87 A deeper discussion of the topic in the brand image context can be found in Aaker[3], pp. 1–36, 201–205, Keller[141], page 123.

88 Or, in a more general context, of the brand image.

89 See Bauer[19], page 7, Keller[141], page 7, Esch[86], pp. 11, 12. See also Stigler[225], page 224.

90 See Aaker[2], page 215, Keller[141], page 8, Sweeney[227].

91 See for example Bauer[19], pp. 7, 8. In fact, reputation or brand image can even be thought of as a hostage given to the consumer, which in case of dissatisfaction may be harmed, cf. also page 81.

92 as being expressed by the legendary "You can't get fired for buying IBM", cf. Aaker[2], page 48, Bauer[19], page 9, Sweeney[227].

- Device to economise signalling costs in the case of intermediation.

Benefits for the provider

Benefits for the brand-holder[93] are many-fold, ranging from distribution cost advantages to lower vulnerability in the case of crises[94]. Most prominently, a good brand image resp. corporate reputation offer the brand holder the following[95].

- Lower distribution costs and higher reach, in the customer as well as the talent market, in particular
  - Higher willingness of customers to search for the preferred brand, translating among others into farther geographic reach
  - Better access to the talent market
- Increased efficiency and effectiveness when entering new markets, in particular
  - Easier access to third parties, while being prevented from losing business to them (e. g., in the case of service cooperations[96])

93 In fact, the brand-holder encounters advantages in all the markets he acts on, such as the customer, the public, or the talent market. Due to this thesis' focus on provider-customer interaction, considerations are restricted to the customer market, but some aspects of the talent market are included, since access to talent provides, due to production's high degree of non-automation, an important prerequisite for customer success in the case of professional services.

94 This review is restricted to advantages that may apply to professional service providers, that is, advantages such as superior retailer access or channel usage adoption by the customer to get the preferred brand, are being left out.

95 A discussion of most of the following advantages can be found in Farquhar[88], pp. 25, 26, Aaker[2], pp. 66–69, Caminiti[49], Yoon[241], page 217, Keller[140], page 9, [141], pp. 5–7, 53–68, 123, Herbig[111], page 23, Shocker[215], page 155, Bauer[19], pp. 7–15, Sattler[203], page 192, Sweeney[227]. The rest (reaffirmation issues, easier access to parties while preventing the brand holder from losing business to them) have been identified in interviews with McKinsey & Company's M&A practice experts.

96 An example in the case of M&A advisory would consist in the investment bank's cooperation with a second investment bank, auditors, lawyers, and

- Transfer potential, including licensing opportunities, and easier access to related product categories and new geographies[97]
- Higher acceptance of product innovations by customers
- Faster market penetration

- Reaffirmation, for customers as well as employees, in particular
  - Higher stability of customer relationships (by reassuring customers on the quality of the provider they have a relationship with)
  - Reassurance of employees regarding the quality of their employer
  - Higher ease for employees (in particular junior employees) to act confidently vis-à-vis their clients, thanks to being backed by a prestigious corporate name
- Higher predictability of demand and stronger stability of cashflows by means of higher customer loyalty, in particular
  - Larger margins and more inelastic responses to price increases
  - Ability to choose (attractive) customers oneself rather than depend on the customers to choose the company
  - Lower vulnerability in times of crisis, and in particular a higher willingness by buyers to forgive the company onetime faults[98]
  - Market entry barriers for potential competitors
- Increased effectiveness in voicing own opinion, in particular

---

management consultants in the course of a project, whose tasks are overlapping with the investment bank's tasks (see figure 3.1 on page 37). A strong reputation may prevent the bank from losing business to the other parties involved, and may also facilitate the establishment of contact, for instance when an investment bank looks for some lawyer on behalf of its customer for the purpose of contraction support.

97 *Aaker* discusses the chances of success for such strategies in Aaker[2], pp. 206–237. *Keller* discusses advantages and disadvantages of brand extensions in Keller[141], pp. 455–469.

98 This does not mean that crises need not be managed actively, see for example Aaker[2], pp. 176–179.

– Increased communication efficiency and effectiveness[99]
– Opportunity for opinion leadership in own market[100].

5.3.3 Relationship

Business relationships are "interaction processes between two or more persons that are motivated by the economic goals of two organisations"[101]. Thus, while being motivated by objective goals between two companies, the quality of relationships strongly depends on individuals, their capabilities and personality traits, and their way and organisation of interaction[102].

For relationships to successfully develop, they must be of mutual benefit for both organisations[103]. In their research on buyer-seller relationships across different types of industries, *Cannon* and *Perreault* have identified six "connectors" by means of which relationships can be established and by means of which benefits to the parties involved may be generated: information exchange, operational linkages, legal bonds, cooperative norms, adaptations by sellers, and adaptations by buyers[104]. Using this categorisation, investment banking relationships clearly fall into relationships whose dominant connector is information exchange. For commercial banking relationships, in

---

99 I. e., the buyer is more attentive when receiving and processing communication messages, thanks to his familiarity with the brand, cf. also Merbold[172], page 111.

100 E. g., in the case of investment banking, pull of public opinion towards own industry assessments.

101 See Diller[75], page 211. Note that the additional characteristic "once an initial transaction has been made between the two organisations" is being done without, since this would constitute a major restriction in the case of M&A advisory, where strategic dialogues (cf. paragraph 3.2.3) may be initiated without any such initial transaction.

102 *Diller* and *Kusterer* differentiate four relationship components: objective component, organisational component, hierarchical component, and interpersonal/emotional component, see Diller[75], pp. 214–216.

103 Cf. for instance Berry[27], page 239. Mutual benefits of relationships, such as increased probabilities to be awarded business, higher customer retention rates for the supplier, and social rapport, easier customisation for the buyer, are for instance discussed in Diller[75], pp. 212, 213, Maister[166], pp. 25–27, Berry[27], page 237, Bitner[32], pp. 249, 250.

104 See Cannon[51].

contrast, legal bonds, cooperative norms, and information exchange may be considered to play a significant role.

Since, typically, relationships are associated with upfront investments[105], they can, similarly to reputation, be considered devices by means of which "goodwill" may be built[106]. One important difference, though, is that relationship goodwill is specific to *one* buyer, whereas reputational goodwill stretches over all (potential) buyers. The connection between the two is provided by the observation that the total of a provider's relationship goodwill may feed his reputation goodwill by virtue of information exchange between market participants.

Seen from an information type perspective, relationships offer the buyer the opportunity to observe "with his own eyes" the capabilities and behaviour of a potential supplier[107]. For this reason, and for relationships' goodwill character, one can expect relationships to play an important role in the first step of the customer decision funnel, that is, consideration.

While practitioners have long come to realise the importance of relationships[108], in particular due to its supposedly rewarding impact on customer retention, which represents a strong lever for over-

105 For instance in the phase where no transactions are being made yet, as in the case of strategic dialogue, cf. page 42.

106 This is why some authors have emphasised the opportunity of trust-building that relationships offer. *Bitner* for instance writes that the essence of a mutually beneficial relationship consists primarily in "keeping promises", see Bitner[32], page 246. The same thought has been voiced by *Kleinaltenkamp*, who observes that relationships offer the supplier the opportunity to build goodwill, see Kleinaltenkamp[144], page 820. *Herrmann* and *Johnson* note that relationships foster mutual moral obligation between their partners, cf. Herrmann[113], page 586.

107 As such, relationship may be contrasted with reputation, in whose formation third party sources play an important role, and which in some cases even might exclusively originate from third party sources.

108 A recent survey conducted by the Chartered Institute of Marketing showed that industrial sellers attributed highest importance to their customer relationships going forward, cf. Reed[192], page 12.

all profitability in many industries[109], the subject of relationship antecedents continues to constitute a subject of interest in academia[110].

5.3.4 Information search

It has already been proposed that a buyer may perform information search (and evaluation) in order to decrease the uncertainty component of risk. In the context of industrial goods, information search may thus be contrasted with "source loyalty", which denotes a company's sticking with a specific provider without re-assessing different providers' capabilities through information search[111].

Much of the empirical research conducted in industrial markets has dealt with goods that are tangible and characterised by a continuous transaction flow, rather than by few, highly discrete transactions (as in the case of M&A advisory)[112]. Thus, first, by not being induced to re-consider potential alternatives at discrete sales occasions, it may be much less "natural" for buyers of such prod-

109 See for instance Buchanan[46], page 523, Berry[27], Reichheld[193].

110 The interested reader may be referred to Williamson[236], Jackson[122], Heide[110], Keep[139].

111 Cf. Luffman[162]. Note that in this sense, loyalty does not only mean sticking with the current provider, but also not even searching additional information on the provider or alternative choices. In the context of business-to-business markets, source loyalty had for a long time been discussed as potential risk reliever, extending propositions by *Roselius* for consumer markets, cf. Roselius[198], page 58.

112 For instance machine tools, freight transport services, industrial components, capital equipment, air conditioning systems, computer terminals etc., cf. Choffray[56], Wind[237], Newall[180], Luffman[162], Leigh[154]. Exceptions provide Stock[226], Dawes[67], and Brossard[43], that have dealt with professional services, consultancy services, and company investments abroad, respectively. They have, though, not directly focused on information search as such: *Stock* and *Zinszer* have found that service factors are more important selection criteria than are cost factors for the choice of the professional service provider. *Dawes* et al. have found that personal information sources were by far most important for the consultant choice. These results are in line with results reported by *Brossard*, who found that personal, internal sources were most critical for the selection of investments abroad.

ucts to reconsider the choices made[113]. Second, the value at stake, and value at stake over price, are comparatively low for most of the products researched, compared to M&A advisory, and most of the goods considered constitute tangibles rather than services.

The vast majority of these empirical studies have found that industrial buyers' information search activities increase with increasing risk associated with a buy decision[114], and that "source loyalty" is not considered to provide risk relief.

113 As *Luffman* reports, occasions at which choice is then being reconsidered, are mostly provided by regular reviews, dissatisfaction with current suppliers, endeavour to broaden the base of supply, incapability of in-suppliers, introduction of a new component, and active supplier initiative, cf. Luffman[162], page 99, rather than a specific sales situation.

114 Cf. for instance Cardozo[52], Lehmann[155], Grönhaug[100], Hakansson[105], Newall[180], Dempsey[71], Wind[237], Choffray[56], Leigh[154], Anderson[8]. *Gemünden*, who conducted a meta-analysis on the relationship between perceived risk and information search across consumer and industrial markets, using 100 empirical findings, could not find empirical evidence for a positive relationship in general, see Gemünden[95]. One explanation for this non-confirmation may be provided by the frequent occurrence of critically low risk thresholds in the consumer goods industry, cf. page 62.

6 Product classifications in the light of risk and information

Characteristics that categorically apply to services and industrial goods, respectively, and their implications on the marketing of these goods, have already been reviewed in the introductory part of this thesis[1].

The variety within these product classes being high, scholars have undertaken efforts to segment them further, in order to obtain a more powerful assessment of specific subclasses' marketing peculiarities[2]. This chapter wants to review such further characteristics, that, without categorically applying to all subclasses of services or industrial goods, respectively, have equally high impact on their marketing. By linking classification parameters to the risk and information concepts developed in the previous chapters, it shall discuss how these product characteristics affect the risk associated with product purchase and the utility of information types[3].

---

1 See section 2.3.

2 The first generation classification approaches which are based on the usage purpose, as for instance the one suggested by *Copeland*, see Copeland[58], pp. 130–155, shall not be expanded on, since usage purpose does not translate into marketing specifics. Similarly, provider-oriented segmentations (for an overview see for example Plinke[187], pp. 174, 175, or Kleinaltenkamp[145], pp. 79, 80) that focus on determining buyer segments of strategic importance, shall not be extended any further. – In contrast, this thesis aims at finding out how providers should act in order to win the mandates they want to win. Thus, its task consists first of all in taking a buyer's perspective to analyse his perception of the marketing situation, in order to derive, in a second step, promising marketing activities.

3 And thus their marketing. Thereby, one should keep in mind that buying behaviour is also affected by other than purely risk- and information-related factors, such as individual and organisational characteristics, and characteristics of the buying situation, see for instance Sheth[214], page 51, Wind[238], pp. 243, 245, Moriarty[176], page 138. But it also ought to be highlighted that the majority of these factors are somehow linked to the concept of risk, see for example Newall[180], pp. 168, 169. For instance do personality traits have impact on the risk perceptions, and so do many characteristics of the buying situation, as for instance the buying volume.

6.1 Review of characteristics

The review will be done in two parts. The first will deal with the most established classification approaches for industrial goods and services. In the second, the characteristics employed by these approaches shall be complemented by selected parameters that, in addition, have constituted popular subjects of marketing scholars' debate.

6.1.1 Select approaches

Most of the classifications that are going to be sketched could be applied to any type of goods. This is why classifications for industrial goods and classifications for services shall not be differentiated from each other, which means that potentially important characteristics within both classes shall be discussed simultaneously[4].

Kutschker (1972)

One of the earliest segmentations that assesses different buying situations from the buyer's point of view was provided by *Kutschker* in 1972[5], and uses three dimensions to determine the risk the buyer perceives when selecting the provider[6]:

---

4 As, for industrial goods, *Engelhardt* and *Witte* note, there has not been any integrated approach that reflects all factors of relevance and gives satisfactory and concrete recommendations on the marketing strategies. Rather, approaches have been built on select criteria, thus stressing and capturing partial aspects of the whole to analyse the marketing situation, see Engelhardt[84], pp. 14, 15. This holds similarly for services.

5 See Kutschker[151].

6 Note that these three criteria, used stand-alone, are such that very different situations might still be comprised in one segment: on the one extreme, a product may be pretty standardised, any supplier may have a lot of expertise in producing it, and the product may be generally well-known in the market, with the exception of the buyer in question. On the other extreme, a product may be new in the whole market, neither other buyers nor the buyer in question having experience with it, and even suppliers may not be experienced in producing it. Then, assuming that value to the buyer and organisational change were the same for both situations, in both cases the newness of problem definition to the buyer in question is high. But in

- The newness of the problem definition to the buyer[7]
- The organisational change when using the product, and
- The value of the product for the user[8].

Note that the attributes of the first and third dimension do not solely depend on the product class, but may also depend on the buyer, or the buyer and the transaction[9], respectively.

As shall be seen in the next section, this is one of the few approaches that, from a risk perspective, deals more with assessing the consequence than the uncertainty component of risk.

Backhaus (1992/1999)

The segmentation approach suggested by *Backhaus*[10] differentiates between three business types,

- Product business, installation business, and systems business.

The first two of them are self-contained, that is they do not entail limitations regarding future buying decisions. Product business is, in addition, characterised by a high degree of standardisation and production occurring before sales. In contrast, installation business

the first case, the (handled) risk involved in the buy decision is likely to be only small, while in the second case, it is likely to be high. This shows that the three given dimensions are no sufficient to describe the risk and potential remedies (risk relievers) in an exhaustive way (it is proposed that the given example constitutes a stronger argument for the insufficiency of *Kutschker*'s dimensions than the argument given by *Engelhardt* and *Witte* in Engelhardt[84], page 10, who claim that the segmentation would ignore the urgency of supply – which, alternatively, could well be subsumed under the dimension "value of the product for the user", increasing value in case of high urgency, and decreasing it in case of low urgency.

7 This dimension is somewhat similar to the "buygrid" framework introduced by *Robinson* et al., which categorises purchase tasks into new buy, modified rebuy, and straight rebuy, cf. Robinson[197], pp. 28–85. Their systematisation, though, is not so clear-cut, in that it also implicitly uses other criteria in parallel, such as for instance purchase frequency.

8 In the case of M&A advisory, user and buyer are widely identical.

9 In terms of size or volume.

10 See Backhaus[16].

can be characterised by a high degree of individualisation, and sales occurring before production. The third class, systems business, is ambiguous regarding the degree of individualisation and the chronology of sales and production[11]. But in contrast to the first two classes, it does not constitute a self-contained purchase process, but rather a sequence of purchase processes that show an internal connection – as it is typical for an electronic systems purchase, where the purchase of one component sets (for compatibility reasons) restrictions to following purchases.

Since the classification defines three types of businesses by means of three dimensions, namely degree of individualisation, (non-)existence at sales, self-containment, the impact on risk is many-fold. To deal with this segmentation in a more easy-to-grasp way, *Backhaus*' classification shall be unfolded into a three-dimensional one, which means products shall be characterised by their

- Degree of individualisation[12]
- (Non-)existence at sales[13], and
- Self-containment (systems business vs. others).

Later, *Backhaus* has extended his approach by the class of component supply business[14]. Component supply business is characterised by buyer-specific individualisation of the product, which in an identical individualised design is repeatedly supplied to the customer. Using the three dimensions of individualisation, (non-)existence at sales, and self-containment, which have been identified to be constituents for the other three product classes, component supply can be characterised by a high degree of buyer-specific individualisation and the absence of self-containment. Contrary to systems business, the sequence of purchase processes associated with the initial purchase are

11 Although according to *Backhaus*, it tends towards a high degree of individualisation, see Backhaus[16] pp. 780–781.

12 Note that such individualisation may not only be buyer-specific, but in addition transaction-specific, as in the case of M&A advisory.

13 This aspect is particular important for contract goods, cf. footnote 56 on page 94. *Kaas* discusses their marketing and production from such a principal-agent perspective in Kaas[131].

14 See Backhaus[17], pp. 669–754.

identical repurchases, which means in particular that individualisation is exclusively buyer- and not transaction-specific[15]. Eventually, the product does not exist at sales.

Engelhardt/Kleinaltenkamp/Reckenfelderbäumer (1993)

The two-dimensional segmentation approach suggested by *Engelhardt* et al.[16] classifies investment goods according to

- The degree of immateriality of their result, and
- The degree of integrativity of their production process.

Note that, while the degree of immateriality applies to the result, the degree of integrativity refers to the production process.

Meffert (1994)

Splitting the integrativity dimension into interaction and individualisation, *Meffert*[17] has extended *Engelhardt* et al.'s segmentation approach to the following three-dimensional classification by

- The degree of immateriality of the result
- The degree of interaction during production, and
- The degree of individualisation.

While the degree of immateriality applies to the result, the degree of interaction most strongly refers to the production process. In contrast, individualisation is considered a relevant discriminator for all: potential, production process, and result.

15 *Backhaus* discusses in the context of component supply business also the advantages and necessity of business relationships, see Backhaus[17], pp. 674–676. This aspect is explicitly taken up in *Kleinaltenkamp*'s approach, which shall be reviewed on page 120.

16 See Engelhardt[85].

17 See Meffert[169], pp. 522–526. It is worth noting that, in taking different (re-) purchase situations into account when giving reasons for the independence between the newly generated dimensions (see Meffert[169], pp. 525, 526), this classification already slightly deviates from a purely product-specific assessment of the marketing situation.

Kleinaltenkamp (1994)

Synthesising existing (buyer- as well as provider-oriented) approaches, *Kleinaltenkamp*'s segmentation approach[18] uses three dimensions

- The degree of individualisation of the solution
- The intensity of the provider-buyer relationship, and
- The degree of immateriality of the result.

Among these, the second dimension has not been used in any other categorisation discussed so far, but it should also be noted, that – while clearly being strongly influenced by product class characteristics (and implied industry structure) – it may also depend on buyer or provider characteristics[19].

6.1.2 Further classification parameters

Besides the criteria used in these segmentation approaches, other potential product subclass characteristics have been discussed to assess the marketing situation of services and industrial goods, respectively. The most prominent among them[20] shall be reviewed in this paragraph.

Product complexity

Let for the considerations at hand complexity be defined in the system-theoretic sense – thus number of elements, number of relations, and changes of any of them over time, as suggested by *Benkenstein* and *Güthoff*[21]. Looking at services, these translate into number

18 See Kleinaltenkamp[145].

19 As to *Kleinaltenkamp*'s claim (see Kleinaltenkamp[145], pp. 83, 84) to have integrated all aspects of *Kutschker*'s classification approach, it may be questioned: *Kutschker*'s classification will – in contrast to all other classifications – be found to address many product characteristics that affect the consequence component, rather than the uncertainty component of risk, cf. paragraphs 6.2.1, 6.3.1.

20 See for instance Meffert[169], page 45.

21 See Benkenstein[23], pp. 1498, 1499.

of components, number of persons involved, heterogeneity of components, and length of production[22].

Degree of automation

The degree of automation describes in how far a service or industrial good is produced by means of machinery, or by people. While people are more flexible and creative to develop customer-tailored solutions, their performance is not as stable and uniform as the one of machinery[23].

Discrete transactions vs. continuity services

Another important differentiation concerns the frequency and mode in which the service is delivered. Continuity services comprise services like bank account management and insurance, while M&A advisory provides an example for a discrete transaction business.

Purchase frequency

While clearly being strongly influenced by product characteristics, purchase frequency does also depend on buyer characteristics. More specifically, purchase frequency possibly varies strongly from product class to product class, but some of its variance may also be accounted for by buyer characteristics, such as usage purpose and usage habits.

22 *Benkenstein* and *Güthoff* add the degree of product individuality as a fifth criterion, arguing high individuality would not only increase perceived complexity, but also cause lack of information, which again would increase perceived complexity. But since degree of individuality has already been dealt with separately, and since the fit of the individuality criterion in the complexity dimension can be questioned (the determination of its peculiarity, for which a comparison between all systems would be needed, goes beyond the system-theoretic way of assessing a system's structure and should thus be separated out), number of elements, number of relations, and changes of any of them over time, shall be considered the sole complexity drivers.

23 Cf. for instance Lovelock[160], page 70, or Woratschek[239], page 36. People's performance may not only vary among each other, but a person's performance may also vary from day to day.

6.2 Parameters' impact on the consequence component of risk

Following the previous section's review of parameters by means of which product (sub-)classes may be distinguished from each other, their impact, if any, on the consequence component of risk associated with their purchase, shall now be discussed.

6.2.1 Product characteristics affecting the consequence component of risk

The following represent product characteristics directly impacting the consequence component of risk.

- **Production's degree of interaction.** The degree of interaction during production affects the consequence component in so far, as a higher variance in outcome can be assumed. This increase in variance is mostly caused by different buyers' different capabilities to deliver the external factor – e. g., information – as needed, and by the subsequent potential variety as to how the provider can integrate the delivered external factors into the production process[24]
- **Production's degree of non-automation.** People being more flexible and creative than machines in developing customer-tailored solutions, their performance is not as stable and uniform as the one of machinery. To put it into other words, chances are that the quality of the product varies from specimen to specimen. Quality and value variability being higher, value-at-risk increases as well
- **Product complexity.** Higher complexity causes higher variability of outcome, thus also higher value-at-risk[25]
- **Transaction's degree of self-containment.** By comprising a series of purchases that extend over a time period, the

24 See also Kleinaltenkamp[144], page 810.

25 The underlying rationale here is, that, the more things need to be done/put together during production, the higher the chances for failure.

potential variance of outcome increases, thus also the value-at-risk[26]. Furthermore, since the first purchase decision restricts the choice in subsequent purchase decisions, the degree of irreversibility increases

- **Organisational change when using the product.** The degree of organisational change when using the product has implications on the degree of irreversibility of the outcome. The more organisational change involved, the more difficult it is to reverse the consequences
- **Value of the product to the user.** The value of the product for the user assesses, of course, the value level. Provided same variance relative to the value level, higher value levels translate into a higher variability of consequences in absolute terms.

6.2.2 Product characteristics not affecting the consequence component of risk

Conversely, as also illustrated by figure 6.1, *no* reasons have been found for which the following characteristics should impact the consequence component of risk in a systematic way:

- Result's degree of immateriality
- Result's degree of individualisation
- Product's non-existence at sales[27]
- Continuity services vs. discrete transactions
- Purchase frequency
- Newness of the problem definition to the buyer
- Intensity of the provider-buyer relationship.

26 The farther experience type information stretches, the higher the probability for interim product quality change.

27 From a principal agent perspective, it may be argued that contract goods are characterised by a higher variability of product quality, due to offering the agent opportunities for moral hazard and holdup. Since the approach at hand concentrates on quality uncertainty for the reasons exposed in paragraph 5.1.2, this aspect is being abstracted from.

While this paragraph has aimed at determining the range and extent by which the buyer's welfare may get affected through different product choices, the following section will deal with the question how easily the buyer, by means of information collection and evaluation, may determine the specific consequences that a specific buy decision has on his welfare.

p = product class specific t = transaction specific ● = high impact
b = buyer specific pr = provider specific ○ = no impact

	Characteristic	Characteristic's impact on potential consequence for the buyer: Value level	Vari-ance	Value-at-risk	Irrever-sibility
p	Result's degree of immateriality	○	○	○	○
p	Result's degree of individualisation*	○	○	○	○
p (pr)	Production's degree of interaction	○	●	◐	○
p	Production's degree of non-automation	○	●	◐	○
p	Product complexity	○	◐	◐	○
p	Product's non-existence at sales (contract good)	○	○	○	○
p	Discrete transactions vs. continuity services	○	○	○	○
p t	Transaction's degree of self-containment	○	◐	◐	●
p t b	Value of the product to the user	●	○	○	○
p b	Organisational change when using the product	○	◐	◐	◐
p b	Purchase frequency	○	○	○	○
b	Newness of the problem definition to the buyer	○	○	○	○
b pr	Intensity of the provider-buyer relationship	○	○	○	○

* buyer-specific or both, buyer- and transaction-specific

Figure 6.1: Characteristics' impact on the consequence component of risk

6.3 Parameters' impact on the uncertainty component of risk

The utility of information in dependence on its cognitive origin, reference, affinity, and source[28], shall now be used to highlight certain

28 See section 5.2.

product characteristics' impact on the buyer's ability to decrease the uncertainty of quality by means of information collection and evaluation.

6.3.1 Product characteristics affecting the utility of information for quality uncertainty decrease

Similarly to the previous section, the characteristics influencing the utility of certain information types for uncertainty decrease shall first be dealt with. Two aspects are important in such consideration. First, information must be available (information must exist, or the buyer must be able to generate it). Second, information must be processable (evaluable), that is, information must yield (comparatively) reliable conclusions on the value of the product for sale to the buyer[29].

The following characteristics have been found to increase uncertainty, respectively to make uncertainty relief by means of information search a comparatively difficult task:

- **Result's degree of immateriality.** The product result being immaterial (as in the case of M&A advisory), search type information on the result is not available. Besides, experience type result information is more difficult to process[30]
- **Result's degree of individualisation.** Individualisation decreases the availability of specific experience type information[31]. The buyer may thus have to rely on related experience type information, which is more difficult to evaluate regarding the quality of the (then only related) product for sale

29 Section 5.2 has discussed prerequisites for such reliability, dependent on natural information characteristics. Some of the conclusions to be drawn can be found in Kutschker[151], Berry[25], Zeithaml[242] and [243], Corsten[59], Staffelbach[222], Engelhardt[84] and [85], Plinke[187], Meyer[173], Lovelock[159] and [160], Kleinaltenkamp[144] and [145], Backhaus[16] and [17], Meffert[169], Woratschek[239], Benkenstein[23].

30 Cf. for instance Engelhardt[85], page 418.

31 This holds for result as well as process, plan, or potential type information. Dependent on whether individualisation is buyer-, or buyer- and transaction-specific, specific experience may be available or not.

- **Production's degree of interaction.** A high degree of interaction during production restricts the availability of specific result type information to some time after sales, that is, the product for sale is not searchable. When looking for result type information, the buyer thus has to evaluate experience type information. But since the quality of the outcome also depends on the buyer's ability and willingness to deliver the factors necessary for production, such information tends to be related. More specifically, its evaluation tends to require adjustment for effects of external factors on product quality. This holds in particular for third party type information, since the buyer usually will not know much about the quality of the external factors that were integrated by others[32].

  Besides, when interaction constitutes a major component in the buyer's product experience, the buyer may orient his purchase decision relatively more at process- as opposed to result-oriented experience type information[33]

- **Production's degree of non-automation.** If production is strongly non-automated, it depends more on the capabilities of the individuals involved in it. In particular in cases where special skills are required for production, the potential for IQV is thus high. This means that experience type information cannot that easily be generalised across the whole corporation and across purchase occasions. Put differently, experience type information's utility is supposedly more determined by the question of identity of individuals performing the production[34], than it is for goods with automated production. More specifically, experience type information will decrease in utility if the person to which this experience type information refers

32 For example, peers. There is the implicit assumption that external factors are somewhat buyer-specific. This assumption should not constitute a major restriction though, since, if it was not, the provider would probably prefer to deliver and integrate these factors himself, since they also constitute sources of uncertainty for him.

33 As *Lovelock* notes, "the greater the degree of physical involvement by the customer in the service process, the more likely service personnel, equipment, and facilities are to form an important part of the service experience", see Lovelock[159], page 38.

34 Cf. page 92 of paragraph 5.2.1.

to is not the same as the one in question to perform the production of the product for sale

- **Product complexity.** Complexity affects the utility of search by rendering both the information collection and the information processing task more difficult – information collection getting costly due to the multiplicity of the task, information processing getting costly and more difficult due to the multiplicity of potential relations and scenarios to be processed, not to forget a high potential for error accumulation in information evaluation[35]. Such argumentation needs not necessarily hold for experience type information, since there are complex products whose performance may be easily assessed from ex post

- **Product's non-existence at sales.** If the product does not exist at sales, it is not searchable. Thus, surrogate type search information, as well as experience type information, increase in relative importance for the assessment of the product for sale's quality[27]

- **Discrete transactions (vs. continuity services).** As *Lovelock* notes, "firms in industries that sell discrete transactions have to work a little harder to establish relationships"[36]. But this means also that it is somewhat harder for the buyer to collect own information on the product if transactions occur only discretely[37]. In a nutshell, the availability of own specific result type information may be more limited

- **Transaction's degree of self-containment.** If transactions are self-contained, it is easier to evaluate the consequences

35 *Cannon* and *Perreault* state that complex supply needs make it more difficult for a buying firm to evaluate purchase choices a priori or even be certain about a supplier's performance ex post, cf. Cannon[51], page 444.

36 See Lovelock[159], page 197.

37 To provide a surrogate, providers may establish relationships and maintain them also in times where no product is sold – as in the case of M&A advisory – thus aiming at drawing the potential buyer's attention to their production potential on a continuous basis, cf. the discussion on strategic dialogue in paragraph 3.2.3 on page 42. But this means that the information provided is potential- rather than result-based.

arising from a specific product choice, since they do not affect (in particular, restrict the choice at) future purchase decisions. Conversely, if transactions have only a low degree of self-containment, the processing of both search and experience type information to assess product quality and the whole dimension of its consequences for the buyer, is more difficult

- **Purchase frequency.** The lengthier buying cycles, and the lower purchase frequency, the lower the buyer's familiarity with the product in question, and the higher the difficulty to evaluate both search and experience type information[38]. Furthermore, the longer buying cycles are, the lower are the chances that own specific experience information is available, and the lower the reliability of such information for quality assessment of the product for sale[39]

- **Newness of the problem definition to the buyer.** This criterion is somewhat related to the previous one. If newness of the problem definition is high, then the buyer has not made much experience with the problem and suitable solutions himself, which means that availability and processability of own experience type information is low. In addition, the evaluation of own search type information is comparatively difficult due to comparatively low product familiarty[40]

- **Intensity of the buyer-provider relationship.** If buyer and provider have no or only a weak relationship, then it is more difficult for the buyer to gather own specific information, in particular information on potential.

---

38 For instance, *Arnthorsson* et al. found empirical evidence that familiarity with the product class has influence on the utility, resp. processability of cues (or, as they term it, on "difficulty of pre-purchase quality inspection", where inspection denotes "the consumer's effort to physically examine, assess and verify the quality of a product at the time of purchase", and difficulty denotes the "difficulty of inspecting quality without help of extrinsic cues"), see Arnthorsson[12], pp. 217, 218.

39 Due to time lag. This means, utility of own specific experience type information decreases, since chances for interim quality change increase.

40 Both observations hold for both specific and related information. Since, if related solutions (and thus related problems) were not new to the buyer, then the problem definition in question would not be that new either.

Characteristic (and attribute whose impact is assessed)	Impact on information utility*: Availability	Impact on information utility*: Processability	Comment (● = high impact ○ = no impact)
Result's degree of immateriality (high)	●	◑	• Difficulty to obtain and process result type information
Result's degree of individualisation (high)	◑	●	• Lower availability of specific experience type information** • Higher difficulty to process experience type information
Production's degree of interaction (high)	◑	◑	• Non-availability of specific search result type information • Higher difficulty to process experience result type information, in particular from third parties
Production's degr. of non-autom. (high)	◑	●	• Lower availability of experience type information reflecting the individual in question's production skills • Higher difficulty to process information reflecting experience with other individuals
Product complexity (high)	◑	◑	• Availability of search type information questionable due to multitude of information required • Processability of search type information more difficult (time/knowhow required; risk of error accumulation)
Product's non-existence at sales	●	○	• Non-availability of search result type information
Discrete transactions (vs. contin. serv.)	◑	○	• Availability of own type information limited to discrete occasions
Transaction's degree of self-cont. (low)	○	◑	• Long-term impact of product choice multi-faceted, thus more difficult to evaluate
Value of the product to the user (high)	○	○	
Organis. change when using prod. (high)	○	○	
Purchase frequency (low)	◑	●	• Less occasions to collect own type information • Higher difficulty to process information due to lower familiarity
Newness of problem def. to buyer (high)	◑	●	• Only restricted availability of own experience type information • Higher difficulty to process information due to less familiarity
Intensity of buyer-provider relat. (low)	●	○	• Less occasions to collect own type information (search, exp.)

* for purpose of decreasing quality uncertainty   ** if transaction-specific: non-availability of specific experience

Figure 6.2: Characteristics' impact on information utility

Since relationships usually also do include a variety of transactions, the absence of a relationship in industries where provider-buyer relationships are common, such as in the case of investment banking advisory services, hints also at the non-availability of own result type information[41].

6.3.2 Product characteristics not affecting the utility of information for quality uncertainty decrease

To close the discussion of how product characteristics may affect the availability and processability of certain information types, characteristics that have no systematical effect shall be enumerated.

41 The intensity of the provider-buyer relationship can be expected to increase if specific information on the product is difficult to obtain (potential and processes serve then as surrogates), and when the interaction during production is high (economies of scope in interaction).

- Value of the product to the user
- Organisational change when using the product.

Figure 6.2 visualises this section's major findings on how characteristics affect information utility.

7 The M&A advisor choice from a risk perspective

The theoretic foundations that have been developed in the previous chapters shall now be used to draw preliminary conclusions on the marketing of M&A advisory. The first part of this consists in dealing with the risk associated with choosing an M&A advisor.

7.1 Consequence associated with the M&A advisor choice

Making use of the risk component differentiation introduced in paragraph 4.1.2, this section is going to deal with the consequence component of risk. That is, the extent of differential impact that the choice of an investment bank advisor may have on the company's welfare, shall be assessed.

7.1.1 Influence of M&A risk on M&A advisor choice risk

Based on the findings of paragraph 4.1.4, it is proposed that the risk – more specifically, the consequence component of risk – associated with choosing an M&A advisor (primary transaction), strongly depends on the risk associated with the M&A project in question (underlying transaction), on the one hand, and the supposed importance of the bank's role in the M&A project, on the other (transfer lever). The reason for which a strong influence can be claimed, is that the sole purpose for hiring an investment bank is to get its advice on the M&A transaction in question. To use the terms illustrated in figure 4.3 on page 60, there are no other underlying transactions, and there is no stand-alone consequence associated with choosing an M&A advisor.

More specifically, the investment bank's role importance (transfer lever) and M&A risk (underlying risk) can be hypothesised to affect the consequence component of risk associated with the M&A advisor choice decision in a multiplicative way[1], while they can be expected to be independent of each other. Thus it is suggested that

R1. The multiplicative resultant of M&A risk and investment bank's supposed role importance increases the consequence component of risk associated with the M&A advisor choice decision[2].

More specifically, it is proposed that

R2. The risk associated with the M&A increases the consequence component of risk associated with the M&A advisor choice decision[2].

R3. The supposed importance of the investment bank's role in the M&A project increases the consequence component of risk associated with the M&A advisor choice[2].

R4. The supposed role of the investment bank in the project has no impact on the risk associated with the M&A project.

R5. The risk associated with the M&A project has no impact on the supposed importance of the investment bank's role in the project.

Since the consequence component of risk associated with the M&A advisor choice decision is thus expected to be strongly linked to the risk associated with making a transaction on the market for corporate control, some thoughts shall be devoted to the latter in the following.

7.1.2 Risk associated with an M&A transaction

As in the case of the primary transaction, the risk associated with making (or not making) a transaction on the market for corporate

1 See page 61.

2 The consequence component of risk is going to be operationalised as the importance of the M&A advisor choice, see paragraph 9.2.2 on page 178.

control shall be reviewed, from both an uncertainty and a consequence perspective. This approach is being chosen for the sake of theoretical soundness and consistency in the method of risk assessment.

Consequences

In order to assess the consequence component of risk associated with an M&A transaction, the extent to which the characteristics introduced in section 6.1 apply, shall be discussed. By virtue of the findings from section 6.2, such assessment will yield conclusions on the consequence component of risk associated with M&A transactions.

- **Production's degree of interaction.** The company[3] for purchase or sale constituting the subject of the transaction, the product for sale already exists at sale, which means that production's degree of interaction between potential buyer and seller is comparatively low[4]

- **Production's degree of non-automation.** The degree of non-automation can be considered high. People are the creators of companies, and a lot depends on their capabilities, as to whether companies are of "good or bad quality"

- **Product complexity.** No doubt about that, companies constitute complex "products"

- **Transaction's degree of self-containment.** The purchase or sale of a company does not constitute a fully self-contained transaction, since it impacts the respective company's future M&A options. Mergers and acquisitions thus somewhat limit (and shape) their counterparts' further development[5]. Transaction size and type are important determinants for the degree of such limitation

3 The term "company" is used as defined on page 32.

4 Price and specific contraction terms constituting part of the product, production's degree of interaction is not zero, though.

5 An acquisition may, for instance, constitute one step in a geographical expansion strategy, that may preclude other strategic postures. In particular, the merger with one specific company may preclude a merger with another one for cartel reasons.

- **Value of the product to the buyer.** From a product class perspective, the expected change in value of a company due to a company purchase or sale is high. Seen from the more granular transaction perspective, its expected value also strongly depends on (relative) size, in particular (relative) transaction volume

- **Organisational change when "using the product".** From a product class perspective, the purchase or sale of a company involves a high degree of organisational change. Again, it ought to be taken into account that such change may vary strongly by size and transaction type[6].

From paragraph 6.2.1, it follows that the consequence component of risk associated with a merger or acquisition, considered as a product class, is high. More specifically, size and type of the transaction are important determinants for the consequence componenet associated with a specific transaction. Figure 7.1 visualises this assessment.

Real-life observations support such theory-based discussion: the outcome and success of mergers and acquisitions varies a lot. While there are companies that have been able to make their merger or acquisition a success story, there are others whose value creation is likely to have been negative.

A high consequence component of risk means that it would be desirable for a company to be able to insure itself against adverse consequences[7]. But such insurances are not offered, due to the strong influence that exogenous factors have on transaction outcome and development, in combination with the lack of a control group[8]. This means that a company must be highly interested in decreasing the uncertainty of outcome associated with a specific M&A transaction.

6 In particular between acquisitions where the acquired company's management is not exchanged and just has to report to the acquiring company's management and board, in the one case, and acquisitions, where the acquired company is completely absorbed, in the other case. Frequent examples for the latter are acquisitions by direct competitors.

7 Cf. paragraph 4.2.4 (see for instance figure 4.6 on page 70).

8 Besides, the strong irreversibility would render such endeavour difficult.

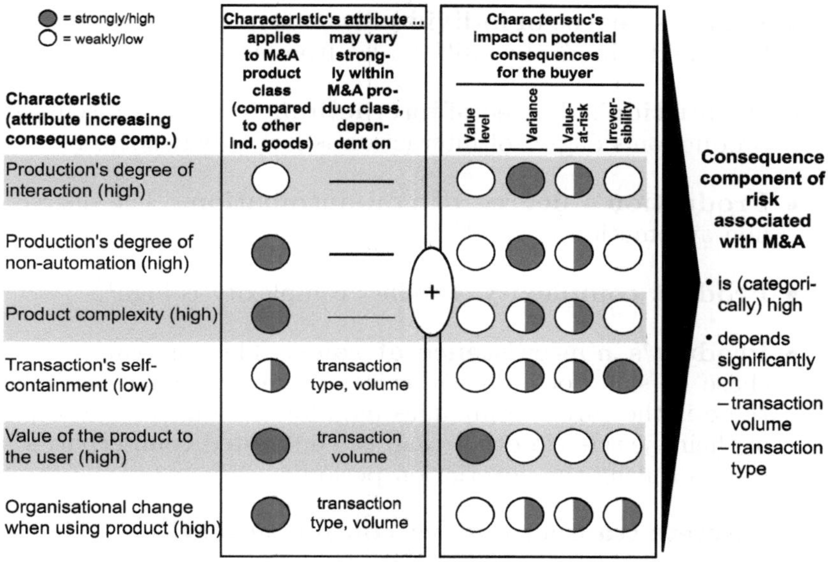

Figure 7.1: Consequence component of risk associated with M&A

Uncertainty and potential decrease by information search

Let us next take a closer look at the quality uncertainty associated with an M&A transaction. Similarly to the previous paragraph, M&A transactions' characteristics shall be linked to the utility of certain information types for quality uncertainty decrease. Thereby, the findings of section 6.3 shall be used.

- **Result's degree of immateriality.** The company[9], which constitutes the subject of a merger or acquisition, is dominated by intangible components, such as the skills of its employees, the quality of its production and management processes, etc. This observation must be put into the perspective that any company has tangible elements, such as for instance plants or buildings. The importance of the two may vary, dependent on the company type[10]

9 Again, the term "company" is being used as defined on page 32.

10 A producer of cloth, for instance, has a higher share of tangible elements (machinery and plant) than has a consulting company.

- **Result's degree of individualisation.** Companies are strongly individualised, they differ a lot from each other
- **Production's degree of interaction.** As already discussed[11], production's degree of interaction is low, albeit not zero
- **Production's degree of non-automation.** The degree of non-automation is high[11]
- **Product complexity.** Product complexity is high[11]
- **Product's non-existence at sales.** The company for purchase or sale does already exist at sales. Having said that, there is the threat companies may for instance try to dispose of their "jewels" in other than the interested counterpart's interests during the negotiation period[12]
- **Discrete transactions (vs. continuity services).** The purchase or sale of a company constitutes a discrete transaction
- **Transaction's self-containment.** Self-containment is moderate to high[13]
- **Purchase frequency.** In general, "buying cycles" can be considered long (at least for significant transactions). But, equally important, they do vary a lot from company to company
- **Newness of the problem definition to the buyer.** This is, in the field of mergers and acquisitions, buyer-specific, since the product class and its subclasses are not new
- **Intensity of the buyer-provider relationship.** Usually, companies buying or selling, respectively, parts of their business to each other, have not been in close contact for a long time before the transaction. But within the product class, intensity

11 See page 133.

12 The company for sale is subject to moral hazard and holdup. Besides, such strategies may constitute take-over-defense strategies, as for instance the "crown jewel strategy". An overview on such strategies can for instance be found in Jacob[124], pp. 54, 55, Gerpott[96], Achleitner[5], pp. 214–217, Klemm[146], pp. 4–6.

13 See page 133.

of relationship may vary. To give an example, such relationships can be expected to be more intense in the case of vertical integrations than in the case of horizontal integrations[14].

Many of the product characteristics being such that quality assessment by means of information collection is only of restricted utility, one can conclude that the quality of a specific company for purchase or sale, and its value to the seller or buyer, is difficult to determine. That is, the uncertainty component of risk associated with the purchase of a company is high. Figure 7.2 summarises this paragraph's findings.

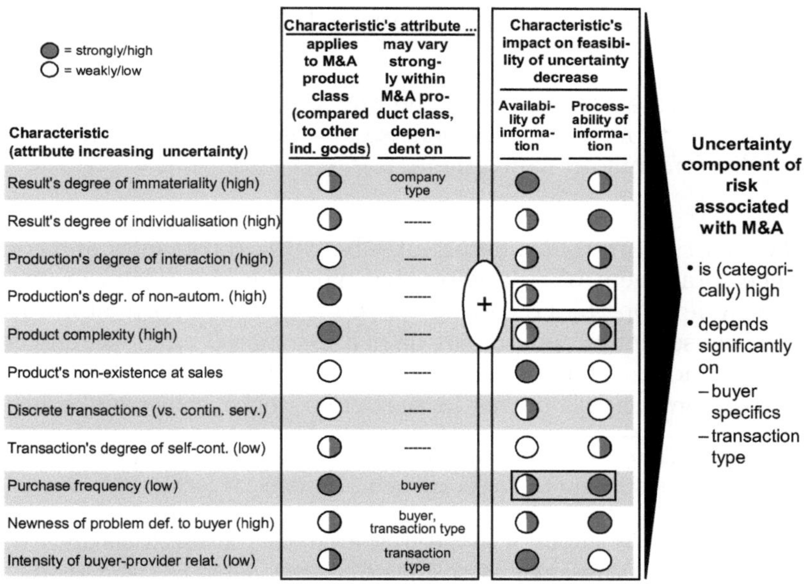

Figure 7.2: Uncertainty component of risk associated with M&A

14 In the case of vertical integration, the company buys a company which it has already had relationships with "at the edge of its own value chain" (for instance its component supplier, or its distributor). In the case of horizontal integration, a company may buy its competitor, which it has not had any relationships with.

Again, such theoretical arguments are strongly supported by empirical evidence: many of the M&A transactions fall short on value creation expectations[15], and the highly intensive information search that potential transaction counterparts perform on each other ahead of the closing of an M&A transaction[16] may be considered an indication for a high degree of uncertainty, and corresponding measures taken to relief it[17].

The formulation of the following hypotheses abstracts from the uncertainty and consequence component of risk associated with M&A transactions, but simply deals with risk as a "one-dimensional" concept[18].

R6. Relative transaction size increases the risk associated with the M&A.

R7. The risk associated with the M&A depends also on the transaction type: Take-over defense and mergers are chancier than divestments or acquisitions.

So far, a structure that differentiates between uncertainty and consequence component of risk associated with the M&A advisor choice, has been developed, and certain concepts' direct or indirect influence on the consequence component of risk associated with the choice of the M&A advisor has been proposed. A differentiation between the two risk components makes in particular sense, if certain concepts

15 See for instance Dibelius[73], pp. 42, 43. *Dibelius* adds that, in the longer run, the assessment of value creation is very difficult for the lack of a control group.

16 For instance by means of so-called "data rooms" in which potential transaction participants store information that their potential counterparts may use to assess their quality and value.

17 While information exchange can be considered a means to decrease the quality uncertainty, uncertainty of compliance in the underlying M&A transaction may be suspected to be pretty high, at least higher than in the primary transaction, cf. the discussion on page 106, where it was found that one reason for potential counterparts to employ an investment bank as their advisor is their superior ability to signal fairness.

18 This is done because the primary research focus is on the choice of the M&A advisor, and not on M&A transactions. To avoid excessive demand vis-a-vis survey invitees, M&A risk has been operationalised one-dimensionally.

influence only one of the two. Let us thus complement this section's hypotheses by the following:

R8. The risk associated with the M&A has no impact on the uncertainty component of risk associated with choosing an M&A advisor[19].

R9. The supposed role of the investment bank has no impact on the uncertainty component of risk associated with choosing an M&A advisor[19].

7.2 Uncertainty associated with the M&A advisor choice

Having dealt with consequence component of risk associated with choosing an M&A advisor, let us now deal with the uncertainty component of risk.

7.2.1 Drivers

The discussion of risk drivers on page 128 suggests that higher familiarity with the product renders the determination of the quality of the advice for sale easier. Thus

R10. The bigger a company's investment banking experience, the lower the uncertainty component of risk associated with the M&A advisor choice[19].

A company being more experienced, such company can be expected to be more effective and efficient in assessing a bank's capabilities,

19 The uncertainty component of risk is going to be operationalised as the perceived difficulty of assessing different banks' investment banking capabilities, cf. paragraph 9.2.2. Mostly, such difficulty *before* solicitation events is going to be used. If difficulty *after* solicitation is referred to, this shall be mentioned explicitly.

thus in decreasing the uncertainty component of risk associated with the M&A advisor choice. Conversely, there is no reason for which to believe that such company can limit the categorical consequences associated with its investment bank choice. Put differently, it is proposed that

R11. A company's investment banking experience has no impact on the consequence component of risk associated with the M&A advisor choice[20].

7.2.2 *Relievers*

The most common strategy of decreasing quality uncertainty is information search. In the case of M&A advisory, additional information may be requested and searched by employing a competitive solicitation procedure, where investment banks interested in acquiring the mandate give presentations[21]. These allow the company to gain a more specific understanding of suggested approaches, as well as the general background of the investment bank[22], that way providing it with additional information. Thus

R12. The higher the uncertainty component of risk associated with choosing an M&A advisor[19], the higher the buyer's willingness to employ a competitive selection process.

Since the utility of uncertainty decrease depends on the multiplicative resultant of consequence and uncertainty component of risk[23], hypothesis R12 yields the following corollaries:

20 In the area of consumer goods choices, researchers have repeatedly reported that higher newness of the problem definition yields higher involvement, and thus higher perceived risk, where the latter may arise from both risk components for psychological reasons. In the case of M&A advisory, one can expect such effects to be somewhat mediated by the rational-argument-based information exchange between decision makers.

21 Or, in a less formalised way, discuss the transaction in question with the company willing to make a merger or acquisition.

22 See paragraph 3.2.3, page 47.

23 Cf. paragraph 4.2.2, page 64.

R13. The higher the risk[24] associated with the M&A advisor choice, the higher the buyer's willingness to employ a competitive selection process.

R14. The higher the consequence component of risk associated with the choice decision, the higher the buyer's willingness to employ a competitive selection process.

Last but not least, reputation may constitute a device by which uncertainty may be decreased. It has been highlighted that, besides this purpose, a bank's reputation may serve its customer also in other ways, e. g., by rendering his signalling on the market for corporate control more effective. Thus, it is not without problems to look at reputation only from the risk reliever perspective.

Since reputation originates from a multitude of sources, such as for instance third party experience voiced through word-of-mouth, press summaries reflecting capital market experts' opinions on transactions, etc.[25], it represents a good "fall-back" guidance in cases where the buyer himself does not feel that capable of making up his mind about whom to choose. Thus

R15. The higher the uncertainty component of risk associated with the M&A advisor choice[26], the higher the importance of the bank's reputation as selection criterion.

24 Operationalised as the multiplicative resultant of uncertainty and consequence component.

25 Cf. paragraph 5.3.1, page 104.

26 Again, the uncertainty component of risk is going to be operationalised as the difficulty of assessing different banks' investment banking capabilities. This time, such difficulty *after* solicitation events seems a more appropriate measure for the following: supposing that difficulty of capability assessment before solicitation events is high, a company may employ competitive solicitation, in order to be able to collect more information on different banks' aptitude to advise on the transaction in question. If the information obtained is considered powerful for this purpose, then a company may not have to rely on other risk relievers. If the information obtained fails, though, to give further guidance as to which banks to choose, then the company may rely on reputation as the "fall-back" signal vehicle.

R16. The higher the risk[27] associated with the M&A advisor choice, the higher the importance of the bank's reputation as selection criterion.

R17. The higher the consequence component of risk associated with the M&A advisor choice[27], the higher the importance of the bank's reputation as selection criterion.

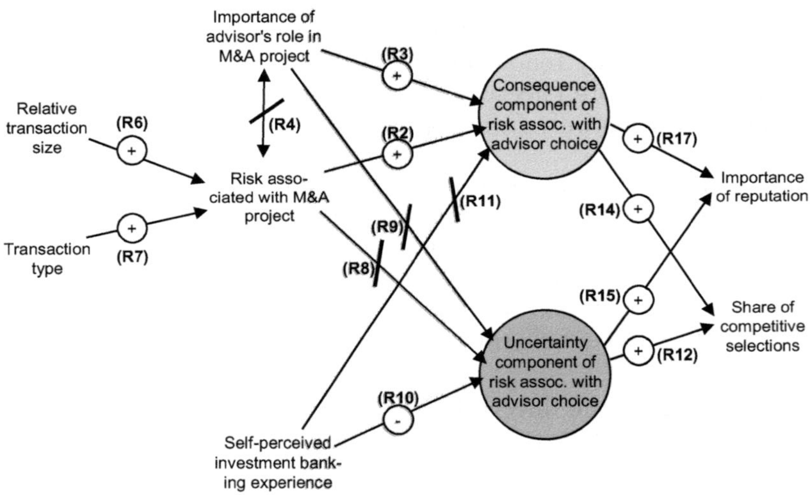

Figure 7.3: M&A advisor choice from a risk perspective

Thereby, hypotheses R16 and R17 follow as corollaries from hypothesis R15, by utility of risk decrease considerations from an uncertainty relief perspective[28]. But one also could have derived hypothesis R17 from a choice justification perspective. As discussed earlier[29], reputation may serve as a justification device, and justification sup-

27 Cf. footnote 24. Due to the arguments given in footnote 26, though, the multiplicative resultant of choice importance and perceived difficulty of capability assessment *after* solicitation events is being considered the most appropriate measure.

28 Cf. paragraph 4.2.2, page 64.

29 See page 107.

posedly plays a big role in corporate decision making[30]. Since the demand for justification can be assumed to increase with the importance of the decision to be made, hypothesis R17 follows.

Let us at this point provide a brief recap of the derived propositions on the marketing of M&A advisory from a risk perspective.

Figure 7.3 on page 142 gives an overview of the above propositions on risk antecedents and risk relievers, taking into account transaction and buyer specifics. Relationships hypothesised are signified by a "+" or "-", dependent on the proposed direction of influence. Crossed-out arrows between two concepts symbolise the expected absence of any directed influence of significance between the respective concepts. The number of the hypothesis that claims the illustrated relationship is enclosed in brackets.

To conclude this paragraph, let us take a step back and look at M&A advisory from a less granular, namely a product class perspective.

The consequence component of risk associated with an M&A advisor choice decision is proposed to be high, since the risk associated with an M&A transaction is high, and since this risk transfers directly due to the M&A advisor's significant role in the M&A project. Further, it is suggested that the uncertainty component of choice risk is high, since M&A advisors' capability assessment is difficult. The buyer will thus usually be motivated to decrease inherent risk to some tolerable level. As discussed in paragraph 4.2.2, this can be done through consequence or uncertainty relief.

As a complication, it has been found that consequence relievers for M&A advisory, resp. M&A transactions are not offered. The restricted solution of risk reduction lies thus in uncertainty relief. But among the uncertainty relievers, intrinsic cues are not available, due to the product's intangibility and its low degree of task programmability. This means the buyer is left with probabilistic risk relievers or self-selection mechanisms.

30 See page 29.

To summarise, the buyer knowing that his choice matters, he is left with reliever types that offer only low safety to him[31].

The availability and utility of these uncertainty relievers shall be further explored in the next chapter.

31 Namely the inner relievers of figure 4.6 on page 70.

8 The M&A advisor choice from an information perspective

The previous chapter having assessed risk and risk relievers from the angle of their mode of action, this chapter wants to concentrate on uncertainty relievers, more specifically, on information that may possibly be used to assess the quality of the M&A advice for sale. It has already been proposed in the previous paragraph that one such reliever might consist in inviting banks to give more information on the transaction in question and their capabilities. But, besides, other information vehicles might be in place, and this chapter wants to research the role they play for the buyer's investment bank choice decision.

The approach chosen here is different from approaches chosen so far[1] in that information shall not be categorised by personal vs. non-personal, and commercial vs. non-commercial sources, but by means of the characteristics introduced in section 5.2. Using the conclusions on availability and utility of these information types, this chapter is going to review the M&A advisory marketing situation from an information perspective, and to formulate according hypotheses[2].

8.1 Vehicles a company might base its choice on

To do this, the research at hand concentrates on the most commonly available signal vehicles in the case of M&A advisory. First, the information transmitted through these vehicles shall be systematised by means of the characteristics introduced in section 5.2. Making then use of the prerequisites for information characteristics to be-

1 Cf. Stock[226], Dawes[67], Brossard[43].

2 *Krishnan* has taken a somewhat related approach in researching memory associations for consumer goods along two dimensions, namely cognitive vehicle, and source (where sources have been differentiated as to whether they were commercial or non-commercial), see Krishan[150].

come reliable for product quality assessment[3], section 8.2 shall, in a second step, discuss the availability, reliability, and thus, supposed importance, of these vehicles for the marketing of M&A advisory.

8.1.1 Most important concepts

The vehicles to be dealt with, are, investment banking reputation, investment banking relationship, sales presentation, previous execution, and commercial banking relationship. They can be considered the most important vehicles through which the buyer can gain information on an investment bank's willingness and capabilities to advise on a deal[4]. Let us briefly clarify and review them.

- **Investment banking reputation.** Reputation originates from a multiplicity of sources, such as press' judgments of specific deals which the bank advised on, advertising conducted by the bank, word-of-mouth from peers, etc., and subsumes search as well as experience type information. As discussed in paragraph 5.3.1, a good or excellent reputation premises that an investment bank's qualities be consistently (highly) appreciated. Reputation can thus be thought of as the "aggregate opinion" market participants hold about an investment bank

3 An application on the M&A advisory marketing situation is provided in paragraph 8.1.3.

4 These vehicles are for instance discussed in Hunt[121], Jacob[124], Deiß[70], Jansen[127], Achleitner[5], Müller-Stewens[178], Morris[177]. In taking this perspective, this research is somewhat parsimonious by not dealing separately with advertising and external referrals, which supposedly play some, but not that important a role. The reasons for this scarceness, are, first, that a concentration is necessary for the sake of operational feasibility. Second, both advertising and referrals are reflected in reputation. As to advertising, much of the advertising commonly implemented in the M&A advisory business consists in displaying in some way or other what roles the advertising banks have played (this holds in particular for the most popular advertising type, so-called tombstone-advertising), and only minor parts of it consist in image-advertising. While, on the one hand, any type of advertising can be assumed to directly impact reputation, its more specific effects would be most appropriately assessed by means of stimulation-based research, a set-up that is not going to be chosen in this thesis. Similar thoughts hold for referrals, for which press articles and peers supposedly represent the most important sources.

- **Investment banking relationship.** This shall denote the interaction between the bank's individuals and the buyer's employees, whose motivation consists in a better mutual understanding of goals, capabilities, and weaknesses in the context of M&A and related investment banking businesses. As such, the investment banking relationship provides the means for an ongoing exchange of thoughts between the buyer and the bank. This dialogue may for instance comprise concerns and ideas as to how to further develop the buyer's business, or industry perspectives in general. Since a relationship is not transaction-focused, it is characteristic for relationships that they also do exist between transactions, resp. when no specific transaction is in sight[5]

- **Sales presentation or discussion.** Such solicitation events constitute meetings between the buyer and the bank, by means of which the bank wants to convince the buyer of its superior aptitude to advise the buyer on a specific deal. Solicitation events take place before the M&A advisor is being selected, and can be of more (presentation) or less (discussion) formal character. A company does not necessarily have to employ solicitation events. Rather, solicitation events can be considered an additional vehicle by means of which the buyer may gain some additional information about a certain bank's capabilities to advise him on a transaction[6]. As hypothesised in the previous section, theory suggests such events are likely to be more frequently employed if the buyer feels comparatively more uncertain about certain banks' capabilities

- **Previous execution.** This denotes the experience the buyer has possibly made with an investment bank during a previous M&A project, which it advised him on. Due to M&A advisory's high degree of intangibility and low degree of inspectability, this type of information – if available at all – can be supposed to play an important role in the selection of an M&A advisor, since it renders product experience more tangible, and since experience with the production process may provide an important surrogate for result type information,

5 See paragraph 5.3.3. Cf. also page 41 of paragraph 3.2.3 on strategic dialogue.

6 Cf. also paragraph 3.2.3, in particular page 46.

when the result is difficult to assess. Note that, in contrast to solicitation events, it lies outside the buyer's ad hoc power of whether he can access/generate this type of information for a specific bank or not

- **Commercial banking relationship.** This shall denote the interaction between the bank's individuals and the buyer's employees, whose motivation consists in obtaining the bank's commitment to provide ongoing credit and assistance. The bank, in contrast, is interested in having high assurance on the buyer's credit-worthiness by means of information sharing, in gaining a higher share of wallet, and thus in realising higher profits through economies of scope[7].

It should be noted that the individuals maintaining investment banking relationships differ from the ones maintaining commercial banking relationships, usually on both buyer and bank side[8].

8.1.2 Characterisation by means of natural characteristics

As to the information transmitted through these vehicles, it may be characterised as outlined in figure 8.1.

Let us briefly explain the main ideas. As to the cognitive vehicle, previous execution transmits experience type information, while sales presentation or discussion, respectively, transmit search type information. Through relationships, both search and experience type information may be transmitted, the latter in particular when a company has already made M&A projects with a company[9]. Reputation, finally, reflects both, search and experience type information. One may want to add that reputation – more than any other vehicle – may assess a bank's capabilities from a broader, longer-term perspective.

7 Cf. Moriarty[175], pp. 5–7. A review of the relationship concept from a broader perspective can be found in paragraph 5.3.3.

8 Cf. Hunt[121], page 107.

9 This represents an inevitable overlap with previous execution. Sticking to the relationship definition given earlier, though, such overlap should be limited.

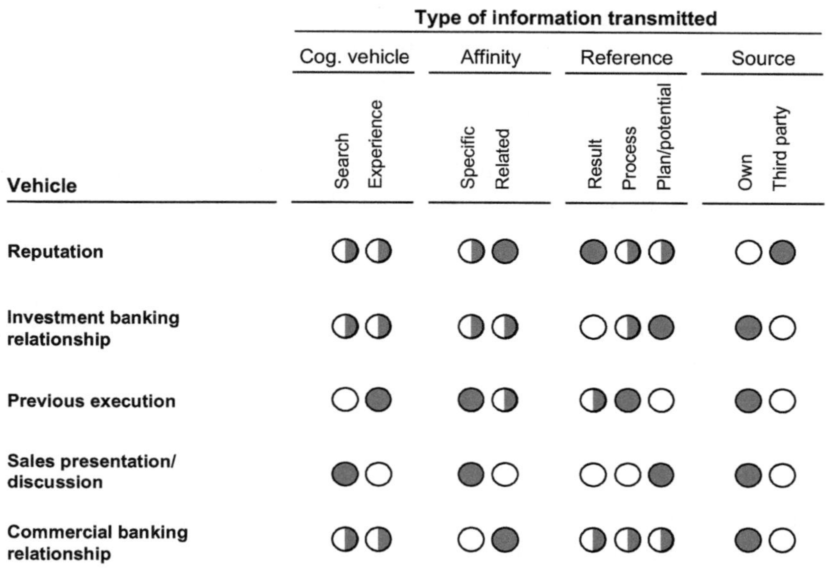

Figure 8.1: Information types transmitted through vehicles

As to affinity, the sales presentation or discussion, in containing suggestions as to how to approach the M&A transaction in question, how to organise the project, etc., is clearly the vehicle through which the most specific type of information is being transmitted. Commercial banking relationship, on the other hand, transmits information of hardly related type, and can thus be considered to be situated on the other extreme on this dimension. Previous execution of an M&A deal, again, can be considered close to specific, all the more, since the customer is the same (namely the buyer). One might want to add that the identity of the production-performing individual increases its affinity. Previous execution is pretty close to investment banking relationship on the affinity dimension. Finally, investment banking reputation is somewhat less specific in that it also subsumes third party information, which is less specific than own information, in particular due to the integration of external factors during production.

As to reference, the investment bank's goal of the solicitation event consists in demonstrating its superior potential to give the advice in question. On the other extreme, reputation more strongly reflects the results of investment bank advice. Due to the high degree of interaction during production, it is suggested that previous execution reflects, besides the result, also the process, while it is proposed that relationships significantly reflect potential type information[10].

As to source, all vehicles except for reputation reflect own type information. Since an individual's reputation assessment of a bank reflects what he thinks that others think about this bank, reputation is largely composed of third party information.

8.1.3 Assessment of information type prerequisites

Let us now check in how far these vehicles satisfy the utility prerequisites discussed in section 5.2.

Cognitive vehicle prerequisites

As to search type information, intrinsic cues do not exist in the case of M&A advisory. While surrogates may be observed, they do not have strong links to product quality.

Experience type information, on the other hand, is somewhat problematic in that it is even difficult to assess product quality from ex post, due to the immateriality of the product, a high degree of interaction during production, and the lack of a control group[11]. Non-automation of production and individualisation of the product, in combination with a low degree of task programmability, make it difficult to infer from experience type information on the quality of the product for sale. Section 5.2 has identified two means by which the processability of experience type information might be increased

10 The slight difference between investment banking relationship and corporate banking relationship in the information type assessment at hand can be attributed to the lower complexity and higher tangibility of commercial banking products (result), and the relatively lower importance of bank to company information flow in the case of commercial banking (potential).

11 Cf. section 6.3. Thus, experience type information can be expected to be highly process- and input-driven.

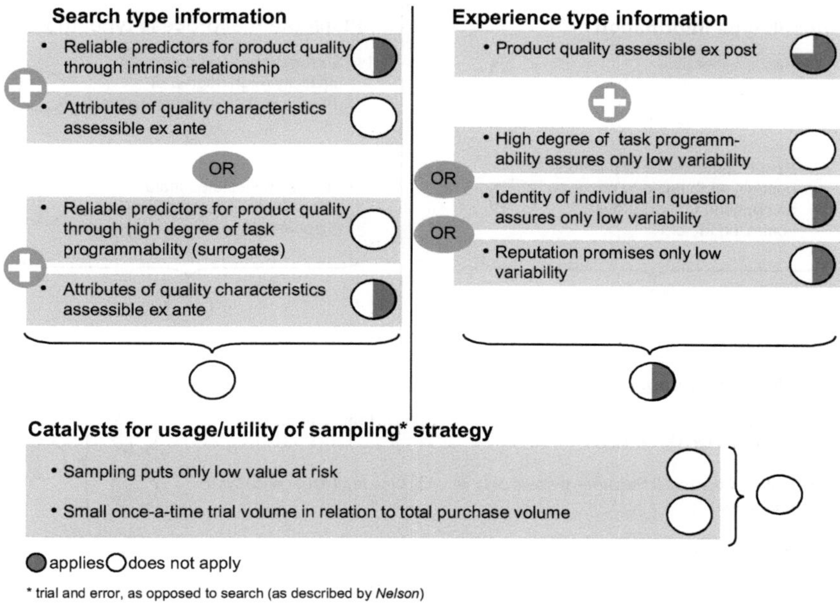

Figure 8.2: Cognitive vehicle perspective on M&A advisor choice

in such cases. First, if the banker in question is the same as the one with whom one has made experience, then IQV may be decreased. Second, this could also be achieved if the buyer has good reasons to believe that quality does not vary from individual to individual, that is, if the bank has a credibility for hiring and developing equally highly suited individuals. Such credibility for employing in equal measure excellent individuals is reflected in a bank's reputation. Figure 8.2 illustrates this paragraph's discussion.

Reference prerequisites

As to the reference of information, the product result, i. e., the advice given by the bank, is only assessible ex post, due to the product's non-existence at sales. An ex post assessment is somewhat difficult due to the immateriality of the product and the influence of external factors on it.

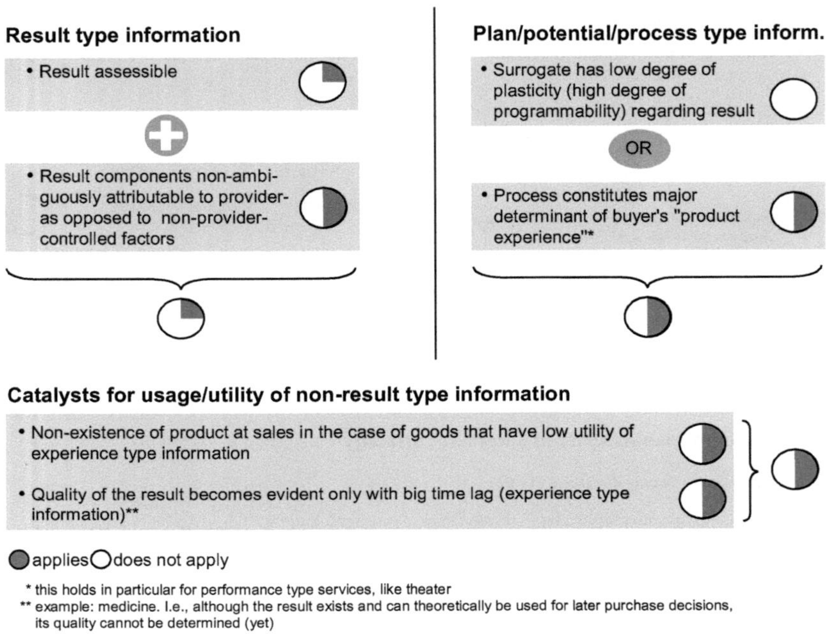

Figure 8.3: Reference perspective on M&A advisor choice

While being available ex ante, potential type information is difficult to evaluate due to high degrees of plasticity, and similar thoughts apply to an ex ante assessment of process/plan type information. As to the ex post assessment, process type information can be expected to play an important role, first, due to production's interaction, and second, for the rationale that process organisation and management represent important prerequisites for an M&A project's success. Figure 8.3 visualises these ideas.

Affinity prerequisites

The vehicles at hand may also be differentiated by the degree of affinity regarding the M&A advice in question. Most specific is the M&A project in question itself, next are a company's other M&A projects with the bank in question. Less specific information is provided by means of other investment banking projects with the bank in question, such as for example IPO business. Finally, information referring to the bank in question's commercial banking business can be considered least specific.

This ordering already reflects the degree of congruence in production factors, which has been found to constitute related information's most important utility driver for the quality assessment of products dominated by functional benefits: obviously, production factors for other M&A projects are most congruent compared to the ones of the project in question – again, one might want to add that the identity of the individual in question constitutes an additional utility driver. As to other investment banking services, most of them are also advice-dominated, which means knowledge and knowhow do constitute major production prerequisites (just as for M&A advisory). This should be put into the perspective that none of them is as purely knowledge- and knowhow-driven as M&A advisory; for instance does ownership or access to a retail distribution network constitute an additional major production prerequisite in the case of IPO business. Finally, commercial banking is least specific: major prerequisites for the provision of credit-lines to companies consist in a "big balance sheet", while advice may be considered only a supplement in the commercial banking business.

This means there is no intrinsic rationale for which banks that offer the best commercial banking products should be the ones offering the best investment banking advice. Accordingly, figure 8.4 visualises the utility assessment of related information in the case of M&A advisory.

Figure 8.4 complements the assessment of prerequisites by a review of in how far catalysts for the usage of the same provider in related product (class)es exist, and finds no major evidence for the advantageousness of "one-stop-shopping". Companies may merely find the re-engagement of an investment bank advantageous if they have already used it on an M&A project of highly related focus, for instance a project dealing with the same industry or geography.

The observation that there is neither an inherent rationale to use one bank for both commercial and investment banking, nor an obvious reason for which banks offering the best commercial banking products should also be the ones offering the best investment bank-

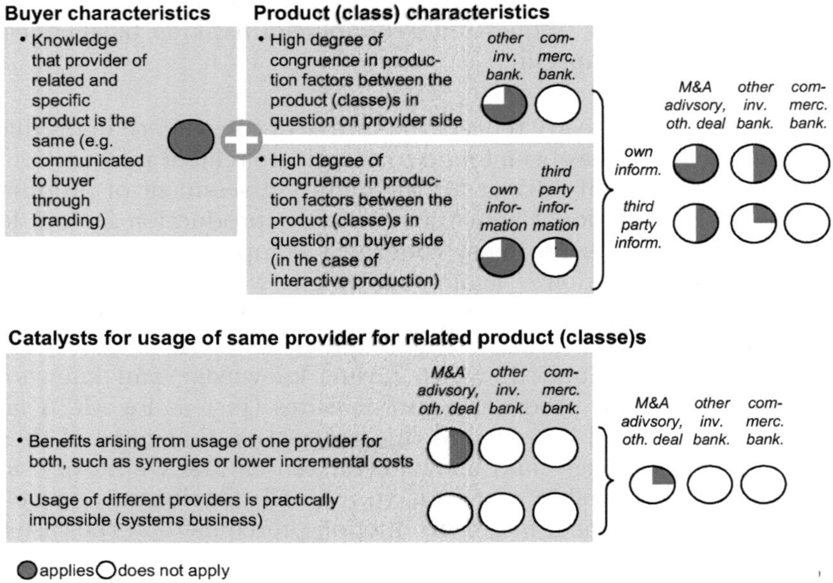

Figure 8.4: Affinity perspective on M&A advisor choice

ing services, constitutes a setback to the hopes expressed by many a universal bank to gain M&A advisory business via commercial business[12]. In the end, a strong commercial standing may only be "used" to subtly exert pressure on commercial banking clients not to be offered the most favourable commercial banking conditions if the universal bank is not, in turn, awarded M&A advisory business. The utility of such strategy can be doubted. First, pressuring clients to buy an additional product, for being offered a more favourable product in exchange, is a highly questionable practice, in particular from

12 Cf. for instance Currie[65], page 92, where a universal banker expressing his hopes that "if we help bail out a company now when they need us, and we can offer them a full range of investment-banking in the future, they'll come back" is being quoted. But, as *Currie* continues, "outside of high-grade debt, there are few deals where lending relationships have either directly or indirectly influenced the award of equity and M&A mandates", see page 94. – Rather, it is proposed that this may only happen – and then, it indeed may happen!–, if universal banks are able to offer M&A advice of equal quality.

a marketing perspective. – Commercial banking business should be attractive for both the customer and the bank on a stand-alone basis, and banks should convince by means of their potential, rather than by implicit threats. Second, since M&A transactions often constitute highly important an event in a company's history, one can question whether companies would even start thinking about such "horse-trading". To use colourful words, there are strong reasons to believe that "you don't choose your heart surgeon based on who owns the hospital"[13].

Source prerequisites

Availability and suitability of sources is difficult to assess for M&A advisory. This is due to the multiplicity of sources, as well as the varying ease of access that a buyer might possibly encounter to make use of them. While credibility should not constitute a major concern, accessibility may constitute a major restriction in making use of such sources, in particular peers. All the more, since advisors sometimes are not even being disclosed.

Another limitation to the utility of information gained from peers may arise from buyer-specifically different reference points[14]. Press, on the other hand, may take more of a bird's eye view, and thus not satisfactorily capture the M&A project as such, including process type information, but rather assess the result of it. In the case of M&A advisory, own experience can be expected to represent a more reliable information source than third party experience. But in lack of anything better, buyers may have to rely on third party opinions, and use third parties as justification device. Figure 8.5 illustrates these thoughts.

13 See Currie[65], page 94, where *Bob Greenhill*, a former Morgan Stanley banker running his own boutique, is being quoted.

14 That these have a significant impact on brand choice and satisfaction, has – in the context of consumer goods – repeatedly been shown, cf. for instance Hardie[106], Anderson[9].

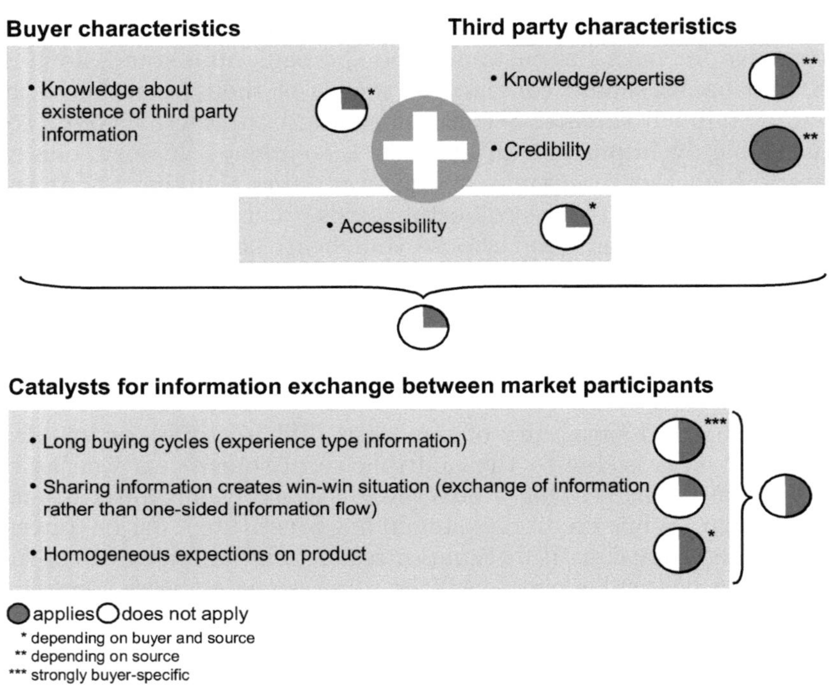

Figure 8.5: Source perspective on M&A advisor choice

8.2 Signal vehicles' role in the marketing of M&A advisory

Most of the hypotheses to be developed in the following are straightforward implications from the discussion in sections 5.2 and 8.1.

8.2.1 General importance of signal vehicles

Reputation has been found to potentially play a multifaceted role in the case of M&A advisory[15]. In particular, it was found that reputa-

15 Cf. paragraphs 5.3.1 and 5.3.2.

tion might serve four-fold, namely as probabilistic quality indicator, "hostage" in the buyer's hands, justification vehicle, and as a means by which the buyer himself may endeavour to economise signalling costs on the market for corporate control. By taking a closer look at reputation as a probabilistic quality indicator, it has been proposed that a company's reputation assessment can, in contrast to the other vehicles discussed, be expected to be highly fed by third-party-type information, which may provide important guidance for unexperienced users, all the more, since M&A advisory lacks intrinsic cues. Last but not least, while, for its generality, providing not that specific a guidance as information gained through previous experience, for instance, it is the signal vehicle most universally available. Therefore, reputation can be expected to play a dominant role in M&A advisor choice, at least as long as all types of buyers are being considered. Accordingly, it is hypothesised that[16]

I1. Reputation is the most important signal vehicle and choice criterion in the overall market.

While being the most specific signal vehicle, the sales presentation is problematic in that the link between performance potential – which constitutes its main content[17] – and actual product quality is only weak, since it lacks task programmability. The project schedule proposed in the sales presentation, for instance, might get changed by the bank for minor issues, and even academic and industry background of bankers in question to lead the deal, constitute no guarantee that these bankers are the ones suited best for the project in question[18]. Thus, sales presentation can be expected to only play a subordinate role in the selection of an M&A advisor; it may be considered a means to somewhat decrease the uncertainty associ-

16 Some of the hypotheses formulated in this and the following paragraph do not satisfy philosophy of sciences's requirements to the fullest extent, cf. Hildebrandt[117], page 41. Still, they may be considered viable from the perspective of utility prerequisites discussed in chapter 5, as well as from a practical implication perspective.

17 See paragraph 3.2.3.

18 If solicitation events are complemented by other signal vehicles (previous execution, relationship) by means of which the buyer may assess the banker in question's suitability, this situation might change.

ated with choosing an M&A advisor, but by far not as reliable as experience-based vehicles. Accordingly, it is proposed that

I2. Sales presentation or discussion, respectively, is less important as a signal vehicle than are reputation, investment banking relationship, and previous execution.

It has been suggested that sales presentation or discussion are mostly being employed when the buyer finds it difficult to assess different banks' capabilities[19]. One can expect that sales presentation, while, on the one hand, actually helping to decrease perceived uncertainty, offers, on the other hand, only comparatively limited help with respect to this purpose, due to its low task programmability. More specifically, it is proposed that

I3. The perceived uncertainty associated with choosing an M&A advisor shows a decrease after solicitation for companies employing competitive selection procedures.

I4. Perceived uncertainty associated with choosing an M&A advisor remains higher than the one perceived by companies that did not employ competitive procedures.

Commercial banking has been found to be hardly related to investment banking in terms of production factors. Thus, there exists no compelling reason for which to believe that being good in the one business (commercial banking) translates into being good in the other (investment banking)[20]. Furthermore, it was proposed that using one bank for both businesses brings no significant advantages to the buyer, such as for instance cost savings. Thus it is suggested that

I5. Commercial banking relationship is least important for M&A advisor selection.

19 See hypothesis R12.

20 Cf. paragraph 5.2.3, in particular page 99, and paragraph 8.1.3, in particular page 154.

8.2.2 Importance of signal vehicles for repeat buyers

The importance of signal vehicles can be expected to change, dependent on whether a bank is chosen for first or for repeat time as M&A advisor.

In contrast to switchers[21], repeat buyers have already made experience with the bank they are going to choose, during an earlier M&A project. Due to the comparatively high utility of own experience type information[22], and a high degree of interaction during production, previous execution can be expected to constitute highly important a signal vehicle – whose limitations mainly consist in availability issues[23]. This yields the propositions that[24]

I6. Repeat buyers consider previous execution among the most important signal vehicles.

I7. In particular, repeat buyers assign a significantly higher importance to previous execution as a choice criterion, than do switchers[23].

And since, for repeat buyers, investment banking relationship is supposedly more strongly based on experience and process/result type information, as opposed to search and potential type information, than for switchers, it also seems perspicuous that

21 The terms "switchers" and "repeat users" are clarified on page 31.

22 Cf. figure 8.2 of paragraph 8.1.3. Note that such reasoning is largely in line with Smith[217], Haugtvedt[109], Burnkrant[48], where – in the context of consumer goods – evidence has been found that direct experience with the brand generates stronger associations than indirect one.

23 While a company's bad previous execution experience with a bank can be expected to have a similarly strong impact on its choice decision (by resulting into the exclusion of this bank from selection), this effect can hardly be traced if previous execution's importance for the *lead selection* is being assessed, since bad previous execution would exclude only one (or two) banks from selection, rather than being decisive for lead selection.

24 Due to the multiplicity of roles that reputation plays, apart from serving as a probabilistic quality indicator, there is no reason for which the absolute importance of reputation should decrease, when own experience information is available, though.

I8. Repeat buyers consider investment banking relationship among the most important signal vehicles.

I9. In particular, repeat buyers assign a significantly higher importance to investment banking relationship as a choice criterion, than do switchers.

8.2.3 Signal vehicles' "natural owner"

Let us deal next with the individual-corporation antagonism, more specifically, with the question which of the signal vehicles are (relatively more) "owned" by banks, as opposed to bankers, and vice versa.

To start with reputation, this signal vehicle has been found to subsume a variety of information sources, references, and cognitive vehicles. Reputation covering such a broad range of information types, it is hypothesised that

I10. The perceived importance of reputation increases when the choice is based on the bank corporation rather than the individual banker.

Further, since different individuals agitate in the commercial and investment banking area of a bank, it is proposed that

I11. The perceived importance of the commercial banking relationship increases when the choice is based on the bank corporation rather than the banker.

Investment banking relationship, in contrast, constitutes more difficult of a matter, since it is clearly fostered by the bank corporation's individuals who might also do the project. This means that no clear picture as to whether investment banking relationships are "individual-" or "corporation-owned" can be expected. As outlined in paragraph 5.3.3, the quality of a relationship, while being motivated by two organisations' goals, depends a lot on the individuals maintaining it. In their empirical study on industrial relationships, *Diller* and *Kusterer* found that nearly half of their respondents spontaneously associated individuals with it, while an equally high share of respondents associated corporations with it, and roughly 10 percent both[25]. This issue shall be further explored by means of descriptive analyses in section 10.2[26].

As to experience type information, on the other hand, matters are less ambiguous. The low degree of task programmability and automation of M&A advisory have been found to put individuals into a decisive role with respect to product quality, which results in an only limited utility of experience type information when individuals change from transaction to transaction. This induces the propositions that

I12. The perceived importance of previous execution increases when the choice is based on the individual banker rather than the bank corporation.

I13. For highly renowned banks, this increase in perceived importance of previous execution is less strong than it is for others.

Vice versa, it is suggested that

I14. If previous execution is among the most important signal vehicles, the individual banker as opposed to the bank corporation plays a relatively more important role for the company's choice decision.

I15. If previous execution is among the most important signal vehicles, then the banker – as opposed to the bank – plays an incrementally more important role when a less renowned bank is selected, than when a highly renowned bank is selected.

25 See Diller[75], page 216. This is why in the empirical research at hand, respondents were asked for both, the perceived activity/intensity of their relationship with the investment bank, and the perceived activity/intensity of their relationship with the key banker, cf. chapter 9.

26 See page 211.

Thereby, hypotheses I13 and I15 are based on the following rationale. Besides identity of the individual in question, we have proposed that reputation might help increase the utility of experience type information for the quality of the M&A advice for sale. That way, reputation may substitute the missing intrinsic rationale of a high degree of homogeneity in production factors[27]. Vice versa, experience may not play that important a role to reassure the buyer about the mastery of the banker in question to lead the M&A project when this banker works for a highly renowned bank. This is the "reassurance benefit" of reputation[28].

Having in detail discussed the perceived importance of signal vehicles, which may be interpreted as their perceived utility, let us move on to the next step, which consists in determining how well they actually serve this purpose.

8.2.4 Signal vehicles' utility for uncertainty decrease

This shall be done by evaluating the companies' perceived ease of assessing the bank's capabilities, in dependence on the signal vehicles considered most important for the M&A advisor choice[29].

Since M&A advisory represents an example for a non-automated service, whose quality depends significantly on the individuals' capabilities, it is proposed that

I16. If the M&A advisor choice is based on the banker rather than the bank, the uncertainty associated with the advisor choice is perceived to be comparatively low.

Since relationship with the individual (per definition), and previous execution (if relationships claimed by hypotheses I12 and I14 hold) are signal vehicles "owned" by the individual, rather than the corporation, we formulate the following two corollaries to hypothesis I16:

27 This is the rationale for hypothesis I15.

28 Cf. paragraph 5.3.2, page 109. This is the rationale for hypothesis I13.

29 In the research at hand's operationalisation of uncertainty, difficulty *after* (possible) solicitation events is being employed.

I17. If investment banking relationship with the banker is among the most important choice criteria, the uncertainty associated with the advisor choice is perceived to be comparatively low.

I18. If previous execution is among the most important choice criteria, the uncertainty associated with the advisor choice is comparatively low.

As to reputation, investment banking relationship with the bank, sales presentation, and commercial banking relationship, one can expect them to be less powerful as quality assessment vehicles than the above mentioned ones, and thus to be dominated (overlaid in tests) by the presence or absence of the above vehicles[30].

8.2.5 Satisfaction with execution and re-engagement intention

Satisfactory product experience[31] has been shown to constitute one of the most important, if not *the* most important, antecedent of repurchase intention, and actual repurchase[32]. This induces the hypothesis that

I19. Higher satisfaction with a bank's execution yields higher re-engagement intention.

Since experience-based, own type information should be of comparatively high power for the prediction of the product for sale's quality, one can expect buyers to be more satisfied, and more willing to re-engage banks, if signal vehicles transmitting these types of information have played important roles in M&A advisor selection. Thus, the following can be considered corollaries to hypotheses I16 and I19.

30 Thus, while one can suppose them to be less powerful for uncertainty decrease, according hypotheses are not being formulated, since the test method employed is insufficient to verify or reject such claims.

31 A review of the satisfaction concept (contrasted with the quality concept), can for instance be found in Bolton[37], Oliver[182], Anderson[9].

32 Cf. footnote 33 on page 45. Herrmann[115] discusses why the strength of this relationship may vary between and within product classes.

I20. Investment bank choice decisions that are based on the banker, rather than the bank, yield a higher satisfaction with the execution.

I21. Investment bank choice decisions that are based on the banker, rather than the bank, yield a stronger re-engagement intention of the banker.

I22. Investment bank choice decisions that are based on the banker, rather than the bank, yield a stronger re-engagement intention of the bank.

I23. Investment bank choice decisions that are based on the banker, rather than the bank, are associated with a comparatively high banker, as opposed to bank, loyalty.

That way, it is proposed that banker choice has dichotomous consequences for the banker's bank: while on the one hand rendering the bank attractive as potential advisor for upcoming new business, it also increases the risk of loosing business in case the banker leaves the bank. The rationale for such argumentation is that personnel constitutes *the* production factor in highly non-automated services, like M&A advisory.

The following is a corollary to hypothesis I13, provided renowned banks keep their implicit promises, while hypothesis I49 represents a corollary to hypothesis I17:

I24. For highly renowned banks, this difference in satisfaction with banker- as opposed to bank-based mandates is less strong than it is for others.

I49. Satisfaction with projects where the relationship with the banker was among the most important signal vehicles is higher than for projects where other vehicles were considered most important.

Analogously, the following corollary to hypothesis I18 is proposed for projects where previous execution was among the most important M&A advisor choice determinants:

I50. Satisfaction with projects where previous execution was among the most important signal vehicles is higher than for projects where other vehicles were considered most important.

8.2.6 Importance of signal vehicles by type of selection procedure

In order to make their choice, companies may employ competitive or non-competitive selection procedures[33]. The employment of competitive procedures has already been proposed to constitute one means for a company to gain additional information on different banks' capabilities[34].

This paragraph is concerned with an assessment of which signal vehicles dominantly come into operation in either type of selection procedure. It is proposed that

I51. Sales presentation or discussion predominantly comes into force in competitive, as opposed to non-competitive, selection processes.

I52. Commercial banking relationship predominantly comes into operation in competitive, as opposed to non-competitive, selection processes.

The rationale for these propositions is the following. It has already been suggested that competitive selection is applied when it is difficult to assess different banks' capabilities[34]. This raises the presumption of relatively lower availability of the more reliable, that is, stronger experience-based, signal vehicles. This results in a relatively higher usage of potential and related type information.

Similar hypotheses for reputation ought not to be formulated, due to the multifaceted role it plays, which by far surmounts the single purpose of quality indication[35].

33 Cf. paragraph 3.2.3.

34 See hypothesis R12.

35 Cf. paragraphs 5.3.1 and 5.3.2. Still, one can expect that, compared to other signal vehicles, reputation plays a relatively more important role in compet-

Conversely, own specific and own experience type information can be expected to play a highly important role in non-competitive selection. Thus investment banking relationship is proposed to play a relatively more important role in non-competitive selection processes, more specifically

I53. Investment banking relationship with the bank predominantly comes into force in non-competitive, as opposed to competitive, selection processes.

I54. Investment banking relationship with the banker predominantly comes into operation in non-competitive, as opposed to competitive, selection processes.

And, similarly, it is suggested that

I55. Previous execution predominantly comes into force in non-competitive, as opposed to competitive, selection processes.

---

itive than in non-competitive selection procedures. This means, reputation can be expected to be most important in competitive selection processes, while it may get "flanked" by equally important signal vehicles in the case of non-competitive selection.

Part III

Research and discussion

9 Data collection and analytic methods

To validate hypotheses, field research has been conducted among companies that had used M&A advisors in their recent past. This chapter details the data collection procedure and analytic methods used for this purpose.

9.1 Data

Let us first revisit the the data collection process and its background.

9.1.1 Instrument

The instrument used was a written questionnaire, which was sent out to potential participants, with the accompanying letter asking them to complete the questionnaire[1] within the following four weeks. Two weeks after the proposed deadline, a reminder was sent to potential participants who had not answered yet[2]. Data collection was performed in two waves of comparable size. The first wave of questionnaires was sent out mid of December 2001, the second mid of February 2002.

M&A business constituting a highly delicate subject regarding confidentiality, participants were offered the opportunity to send back their completed questionnaires anonymously, and a copy of the questionnaire (which they could use alternatively) was presented on an internet page of Mainz university. Contacts were invited to pro-

1 This letter did not refer to a specific deal, but rather stated the company had been involved in an M&A transaction recently. Participants were asked to choose one specific M&A project in case their company had been involved in several projects, and complete the questionnaire by providing information on this specific project. Thus, if companies had been involved in several transactions, it was left in the participant's choice, which of them to assess.

2 Or for who this was not known (companies could respond anonymously).

vide a self-chosen username and password, by means of which they would later be able to view some of the key results[3] of the survey.

A copy of the complete questionnaire can be found in the appendix.

9.1.2 *Sample*

European companies that had been involved in an M&A transaction of significant size[4] in the time between October 2000 and mid of February 2002[5], constituted the universe for the empirical survey. Suitable candidates were identified by means of the *Mergermarket* database, which provided the information which companies had been involved into what kinds of M&A transactions[6] in the time horizon of interest. It also displayed information on what was known about companies' financial advisor employment for the projects. From all the companies displayed in this database, the ones that had been involved in transactions of significant size[4], and for which an advisor had been documented in the database, were selected, and their corresponding post addresses and contact persons were researched by means of firm directories or the internet sites of the companies. That way, nearly all companies of interest's contact details could be identified. Usually, the questionnaire was addressed to the Chief Financial Officer of the company, or the Head of M&A, if known. The accompanying letter invited them to fill out the questionnaire themselves, or to pass it on to people in the M&A department who had been involved in the M&A project and advisor selection.

3 To increase the utility of results for survey participants, data were evaluated from a company, rather than a bank perspective, the analyses dealing with issues such as "Which selection procedures offer highest satisfaction with selection?", "Which bank types offer highest satisfaction?", etc. The way of publishing via internet was chosen to offer survey participants the possibility to profit from such results, while remaining anonymous, if desired. This was the only incentive provided for participation. Roughly two thirds of respondents sent passwords with their responses.

4 Transaction volume in question surmounting Euro 100 million.

5 Announcement date.

6 Transaction volume, geographic reach, counterpart, company's geography, among others.

In addition to the companies for which it was known that they had used an advisor, some of the bigger companies satisfying transaction size and geography criteria, but for which the *Mergermarket* database lacked information on whether or not they had been using financial advice, were contacted.

Geography*

UK/Ireland	23	(31)
Germany	22	(11)
Switzerland	9	(4)
Austria	1	(1)
Scandinavia	18	(13)
Benelux	10	(10)
Italy	7	(8)
Iberia	5	(7)
France	1	(12)
Eastern Europe	2	(3)

Position

CEO	2
CFO/Financial Director	16
Board Member, M&A Director, Head of M&A, Vice President M&A, EVP Corporate Development	22
Member of the M&A Department	54
CFO support	2
Other: Project Leader Merger, Treasurer	4

* numbers in brackets indicate percentages of geographies in contact sample

Figure 9.1: Respondents' geography and company position
(Percent of core sample)

In total, 677 questionnaires were sent out, of which three quarters to companies for which it was known they had used financial advisors. 95 completed questionnaires were received in total, thus, response rate was 14 percent, which – in consideration of the confidentiality[7]

7 Indeed, some of the companies contacted indicated that they had not used an advisor, for which reason they could not participate in the survey, while

of the subject and the hierarchy of positions contacted – can be considered satisfactory[8]. Of the 95 questionnaires, one had been completed by a US American company[9], and another one by a private equity company. For homogeneity reasons, these two questionnaires were not used for analyses, and neither were two other questionnaires for quality reasons[10]. Two questionnaires assessed transactions of a volume of less than Euro 50 m and were excluded for this reason from M&A advisor choice, as well as satisfaction analyses[11]. Of the remaining 89 questionnaires, seven had been filled out by companies whose companies had not selected their financial advisor themselves, but had been assigned an investment bank by their parent companies. Thus, a core of 82 questionnaires usable for all kinds of analyses, and 89 questionnaires usable for analyses not directly concerned with M&A advisor choice, remained[12]. The sample of 82 questionnaires of respondents who chose the M&A advisor themselves, and where the transaction volume in question surmounted Euro 50 million, shall henceforth be called the *core sample*, the sample of 89 questionnaires including in addition companies that did not choose their M&A advisor themselves, shall be referred to by the term *main sample*, and the sample of 91 questionnaires that in addition contains the two companies that assessed small M&A projects, shall be called the *extended sample.*

As to response bias, the following observations may be recorded. With respect to the contact sample, German-speaking geographies were somewhat overrepresented among respondents, while French

others indicated they considered the topic too delicate of a matter and thus considered it more appropriate not to participate.

8 *Herrmann* and *Homburg* indicate response rates of 10 to 30 percent in written surveys are common, cf. Herrmann[114], page 27. Advantages and disadvantages of written surveys are discussed there, as well as in Scheffler[208], pp. 69, 70.

9 This constituted supposedly the new owner or parent company of one of the survey contacts, who apparently had passed on the questionnaire.

10 Due to double-checking of answers, strong inconsistencies, etc.

11 They were excluded, since the research goal consisted in an assessment of the "upper M&A advisory market", and since a difference in the importance of certain assets (for instance fees or reputation) between upper and lower market, the latter of which the bigger banks usually do not even compete for, could be expected.

12 Such as for instance analyses on satisfaction with execution, or reputation assessments.

companies were significantly underrepresented. The geography of companies contacted, and responding, as well as the position of respondents in their companies, are shown by figure 9.1 on page 171. As can be seen in the right part of the figure, all individual respondents' professional scope of duties included M&A business.

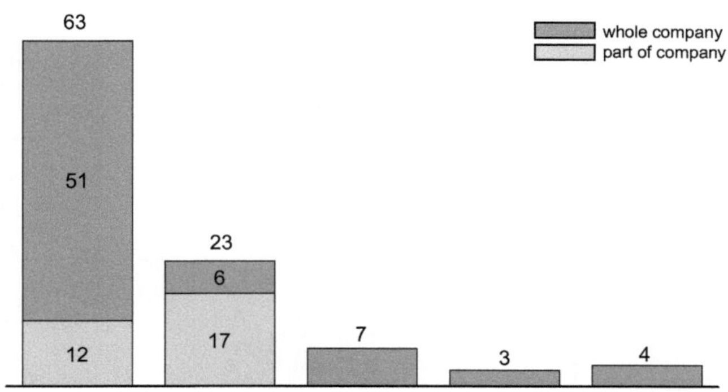

	Acquisition	Divestment	Merger	Take-over defense	Other*	TOTAL
Initiative						
- Company	47	19	3	-----	4	**73**
- Advising bank	4	-----	2	-----	-----	**6**
- Counterpart	12	4	2	3	-----	**21**

* demerger, take private

Figure 9.2: Companies' role in the M&A project assessed
(Percent of core sample)

While in the sample of contacts, targets had constituted a nearly equally high share as bidders, the response sample showed a strong bias towards bidders. Although such bias is deplorable, it is natural in the sense that the management of companies[13] that are being taken over is frequently exchanged by the company taking it over, which means targets may have lacked individuals who would have

13 Or parts of it.

been in the position to fill out the questionnaire. Indeed, some companies sent negative responses, explaining they could not participate for that reason[14]. Figure 9.2 shows the respondents' role in the transactions assessed.

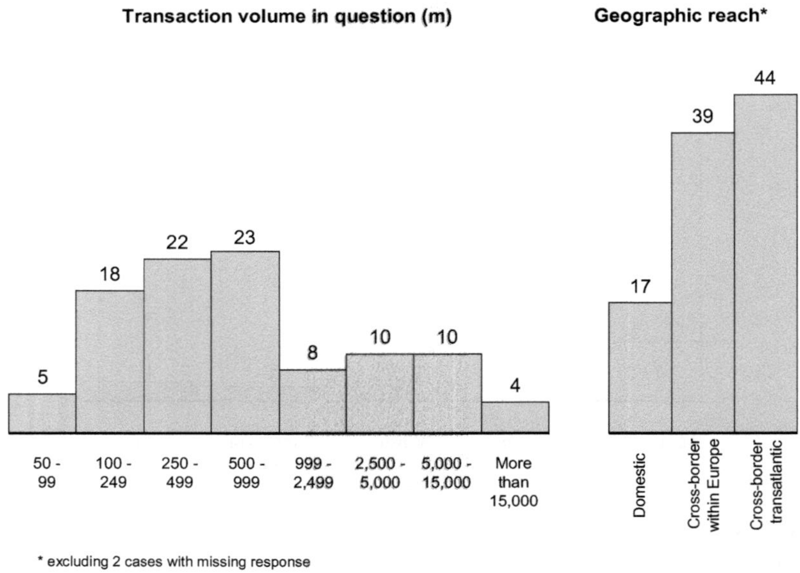

Figure 9.3: Size and geographic reach of M&A project
(Percent of core sample)

As to the transaction volume in question, the average size of deals assessed in the M&A advisory user survey was significant, and can be considered in excess of the average transaction size of contacts, which amounted to roughly Euro 290 million[15]. In spite of the lack of in-

14 Besides, the phenomenon that "survivors" of transactions are more willing to deal with this subject again than are those who "did not survive", can be attributed to the human character.

15 Due to the pooling of transaction sizes into size buckets, exact figures for the respondent sample cannot be calculated. But a proxy calculation based

formation on average revenues of companies contacted, there is some indication for a bias towards bigger size in the respondent sample as well – half of the survey respondents were companies that had annual revenues of Euro 5 billion or more[16]. The heuristic that bigger firms may employ more rigorous processes in M&A and M&A advisory business, and may also have dedicated resources, while for smaller companies, an M&A may rather constitute a singular event[17], may provide an explanation for this bias. Figure 9.3 depicts transaction volumes of deals assessed by respondents, and geographic reach of M&A projects.

	Survey (10/1999 - 02/2001)			Market (1999 - 2001)*		
M&A advisor	**Volume advised 1999-2001 (bn)**	**# resp. who chose as lead****	**Rank (# trans-actions)**	**Rank (volume advised)**	**Volume advised 1999-2001 (bn)**	**# trans-actions advised**
Morgan Stanley D.W.	17.1	9 (12)	1	2	1,130	406
Merrill Lynch	19.0	9 (7)	2	3	904	309
Goldman Sachs	40.3	9 (6)	3	1	1,367	366
Citibank	19.8	9 (2)	4	9	486	441
Cred. Suisse First Boston	43.1	7 (8)	5	6	640	583
J.P. Morgan Chase	11.4	7 (4)	6	4	749	504
UBS Warburg	41.3	7 (2)	7	5	685	401
Deutsche Bank	4.0	6 (15)	8	11	407	347
Lazard LLC	12.6	5 (8)	9	8	518	369
Dresdner Kleinw. Wass.	4.5	4 (3)	10	10	424	226
Lehman Brothers	0.4	1 (2)	13 ***	12	235	216
Rothschild	0	0 (1)	22 ****	7	566	449
Others	3.2	12 (15)				

* source: Thomson Financial Services. Aggregation for previous years to reflect current bank entities; double-counting for syndicates

** numbers in bracket indicate how frequently bank was financial advisor for project that directly preceded

*** behind ABN Amro and Enskilda (number of leads), resp. Enskilda and Lexicon (transaction volume)

**** behind ABN Amro, Enskilda (2 leads), and Bleichroeder, BNP, Handelsb., Lexicon, ING, KPMG, Lexicon, PWC (1 lead resp.)

Figure 9.4: Representation of lead advisors in survey sample *(Survey data based on core sample)*

on lower bounds of buckets, respectively bucket means (approximating the upper bucket by Euro 20 billion), hints at an average transaction size of 1.6 to 2.6 Euro billion in the core sample.

16 A bucket proxy calculation, in analogy to transaction volume, yields average company revenues of Euro 5.7 to 8.6 billion for respondents.

17 This would also decrease their interest in studies, as the one presented here.

Finally, the representativeness of lead banks chosen shall be examined. As depicts figure 9.4, the frequency (number of transactions) by which specific M&A advisors were assessed as lead advisors by respondents, corresponds well to the overall transaction volume advised in market[18].

In particular, the bulge bracket (Goldman Sachs, Morgan Stanley Dean Witter, and Merrill Lynch) were most frequently assessed by survey respondents, although they do not represent the banks that have advised on most transactions in the market. Rothschild is underrepresented, while Citibank is overrepresented with respect to market transaction volume advised, but not with respect to number of transactions advised in market.

The strong link between the number of survey lead assessments and market transaction volume is no surprising against the background of the survey's concentration on the upper M&A advisory market, and of overrepresentation of higher-volume transactions in our respondent sample[19].

To summarise, respondent data was found to be biassed towards bigger companies and transaction volumes, as well as towards companies taking rather than being taken over. For the research topics of interest in this thesis, this bias should not constitute a major setback. But one important implication of these observations is that the respondent sample's investment banking experience and uncertainty assessments can be expected to be biassed towards higher experience[20] and lower perceived risk[21]. Further, analyses taking into account specific transaction types may not show the implications that transaction types have on other concepts to an appropriate extent[22].

18 Rather than to the number of transactions advised in market.

19 Since market leaders in terms of fees earned, are not the ones advising on most transactions, but advising on the biggest transactions, cf. also paragraphs 2.1.1, 2.1.4.

20 Assuming bigger companies to be on average more experienced.

21 Assuming hypothesis R10 holds.

22 The reason being the small subsample size of divestments type transactions. In fact, for that reason, no further hypotheses dealing with transaction types have been formulated.

9.2 Methods

Let us now shortly revisit the methods that were employed to operationalise and evaluate the concepts of interest.

9.2.1 Measurement

Major parts of the questionnaire were designed to assess respondents' perceptions rather than objective facts, such as for instance the importance they attributed in their advisor choice to different signal vehicles, the satisfaction with the lead bank's execution, assessments of the intensity of the investment banking relationship maintained with different banks, or the assessment of specific banks' investment banking reputation.

Thereby, one aim consisted in complementing the perceived importance of selected items by an actual assessment of most prominent banks' positioning regarding these items – for instance, respondents were not only asked what important a role investment banking relationship played in their choice of the M&A advisor, but also asked to assess the quality of their company's relationship with the banks of relevance. The latter implied scarceness in concept operationalisation. In order to make questionnaire completion on the complex subject as easy a task as possible, respondents only had to check boxes, and a nine-point Likert scale was employed for all assessments to be made[23]. The reason for choosing an odd-numbered scale is that it was intended to give respondents the opportunity to express indifference where they felt this was appropriate[24]. The reason for which such a high number of grades was chosen, is that, by dealing with investment banks agitating in the upper market segment[25], respondents could be expected to view most of them well positioned, so that a lower point scale would have been too coarse to reflect the nu-

23 An exception provided investment banking experience, for which such detailed scale was considered pseudo-accurate, due to M&A advisory's long buying cycles.

24 Odd-numbered bipolar scales, in particular five- or seven-place, have been employed a lot in behavioural and marketing research, cf. Bearden[21].

25 That is, investment banks advising on the relatively small number of high volume deals which account for major market volume.

ances of importance. The market being highly concentrated around the top players that had to be assessed in the questionnaire, pseudo-accuracy could be ruled out as a potential problem of employing such a scale.

9.2.2 Operationalisation of specific concepts

Due to the multiplicity of the research task, one-dimensional measures were predominantly used.

An exception provided, first, the risk associated with choosing an M&A advisor, which was operationalised in accordance with major parts of theory[26], along the consequence and uncertainty dimension. This was done because risk was expected to be a major explanatory for selection behaviour and importance of signal vehicles. By employing such a split, a better understanding of the more specific ways which perceived risk is impacted by and does impact perceptions and behaviour[27], was aspired, on the one hand. On the other, the concept of "risk associated with choosing an M&A advisor" proved quite abstract to interviewees during the questionnaire pre-test phase, and became much more understandable by being split along these two dimensions.

Further, in order to use as simple a language as possible, the consequence component of risk associated with the M&A advisor choice was operationalised as the importance of this choice decision from a corporate perspective. Such operationalisation is largely in line with operationalisations of consequence component previously

26 Cf. paragraph 4.1.2. A description and discussion of selected risk operationalisation approaches can be found in Ross[200], pp. 2–4, Stem[224], pp. 314–315, Gemünden[95], pp. 82–85, Dowling[77], page 194. One of the earliest comparisons of different risk operationalisations has been performed by *Bettman*, who compares the power of his own operationalisation of uncertainty and consequences with the one suggested by *Cunningham*, see Bettman[30].

27 *Gemünden* for instance found evidence that a more-dimensional operationalisation of risk increases the explanatory power of risk for information search, as long as the number of risk components to be recalled does not surpass a critical threshold, see Gemünden[95], page 93.

employed by risk researchers[28]: the operationalisations by *Arndt*[29] or *Schiffman*[30], who were among the first to operationalise risk by importance and uncertainty, or by *Taylor*, who discusses adverse consequences as "importa[nce of] the possible loss"[31], as well as the operationalisation by *Bloch* and *Richins*, who employed the concept of "instrumental importance" for consequence component of risk[32], may serve as illustrative examples.

The uncertainty component of risk was operationalised as the perceived difficulty of assessing the banks in question's capabilities to advise on the deal. Such operationalisation also largely followed other research, cf. for instance the first item of the risk assessment instrument proposed by *Deering* and *Jacoby*[33], or the operationalisation suggested by *Schiffman*[30]. In order to be able to explain how uncertainty affects information search, two measures for uncertainty were employed: an interim measure of difficulty of capability assessment *before* possible solicitation events, and a final measure that assesses this difficulty *after* solicitation events.

Besides, a "two-dimensional" measure was also used for the assessment of investment banking relationships. Here, participants were asked to not only assess their company's relationship with the bank, but also with the banker. The rationale for this approach was provided by the highly important role that individuals play for the success of relationships[34], and by the observation that relationships may indeed vary with respect to individual as opposed to corporate importance.

Finally, the rationale for which perceived risk was *not* operationalised on a personal and corporate dimension, shall be given. As

28 Already *Cox* suggested consequence component of risk – in his terms, "amount at stake" – be a function of "the importance or magnitude of the goals to be obtained, the seriousness of the penalties that might be imposed for non-attainment, and the amount of means committed to achieving the goals", see Cox[60], page 38.

29 See Arndt[11], page 302.

30 See Schiffman[210], page 107.

31 See Taylor[228], page 57.

32 See Bloch[34], in particular figure 2 on page 78.

33 See Deering[69].

34 Cf. paragraph 5.3.3, and page 160 of paragraph 8.2.3.

depicted by paragraph 4.1.3, personal and corporate risk associated with the choice decision may strongly differ in their relative size, so that it may not be sufficient to assess only one of the two in the case of corporate decision-making. In the case of M&A and M&A advisory, the personal risk assessment was done without, the reasons for this being two-fold. First, since M&A and M&A advisory are dealt with on highest corporate hierarchy[35], it is proposed that personal risk is not in excess of corporate risk[36]. The second reason is a practical one. The choice decision being made by the buying centre, this would have meant to assess each of its members' personal risk associated with the decision in question, which would have been out of the feasibility and scope of the research at hand.

9.2.3 Dissonance reduction

By asking contacts to review their choice process from ex post, the empirical research conducted to substantiate theory-based propositions faced the problem that dissonance reduction processes[37] were likely to already have taken place, since respondents were asked for an ex post assessment of attitudes and behaviour. Dissonance reduction providing a threat to the explanatory power of the concepts researched[38], the structure of the questionnaire tried to preclude at least the more "superficial" of these processes. More specifically, it was avoided to let potentially explanatory concepts be directly assessed ahead of the concepts they potentially explain[39], and, similarly, it was avoided to let stated importance of a concept for choice decision be assessed directly ahead or directly after the assessment of perceived positioning of different banks with respect to this concept.

35 At least when they are of a significant size, which was the case in the research at hand, cf. figure 9.3.

36 See end of paragraph 4.1.3. Indeed, survey data show that only 9 percent of M&A advisor selections happened without the involvement of board members, and that the CEO or CFO were involved in 87 percent of the cases.

37 Cf. Festinger[89], page 131 and following pages.

38 Much of the empirical research on risk has faced this problem, see Ross[200], page 2.

39 The observation that perceived ease of capability assessment during selection process is, in the questionnaire data, not significantly linked to subsequent satisfaction with the chosen bank's execution in the M&A project, may be interpreted as a hint that such endeavours have been reasonably successful.

9.2.4 Philosophy of science background

Following the canon of critical rationalism[40], tests were conducted to possibly falsify the theory-based propositions. While such approach implies that empirical results can never serve the purpose of "verifying" a theory or parts of it, it enabled the critical re-assessment of theoretic considerations behind the hypotheses whose test results were not in line with expectations.

9.2.5 Data analysis technique

More specifically, non-parametric tests provided the basis for data analysis, since many of the variable distributions that were subject to research had been found to significantly deviate from normal distribution[41].

Let us in the following shortly revisit the two most important tests used for these purposes[42].

Location test for independent samples

To compare two independent samples with each other, the *Mann Whitney U test*[43] was used. This test goes back to *Mann* and *Whit-*

40 Cf. for instance Popper[189].

41 For instance, the importance of commercial banking relationship was frequently rated 1 on a 1–9 scale, and similarly, sales presentation and previous execution had "fat-tailed" distributions. Such approach was also justified from the more general perspective that Likert scale data, as being used in the survey, may be considered to only represent ordinal, but not interval-scaled data, see Gibbons[98], pp. 1, 2. Further, since for small sample sizes the deviation from normal distribution is most difficult to detect, while the effects from such deviation may be most devastating, non-parametric statistics proved the "safer" choice, cf. Bradley[40], pp. 23, 24. Eventually, relative efficiency of the tests discussed vis-à-vis their parametric counterparts is usually above asymptotic relative efficiency for small samples and very close to one in the case of normal distribution, see Bradley[40], page 18.

42 Besides non-parametric test statistics, regression and discriminant analysis were used to further depict the role of signal vehicles along the steps of the purchase funnel, and to compare stated with revealed importance of these vehicles, see chapter 11.

43 Also known as *Wilcoxon's rank sum test.*

ney, and constitutes the non-parametric alternative to the *Student's t-test*[44] that requires the assumption of a normal distribution with equal variances. Since an equivalent statistic was independently developed by *Wilcoxon*, *MWW* shall be used as an abbreviation for this test.

The MWW can be used to compare the location (median) of the random variables X and Y in two independent populations, provided their distributions can be assumed to have identical shapes[45]. Its main idea is to pool and jointly order the $N = n_1 + n_2$ observations into a single array, while keeping track of whether each of them is an X or a Y observation, where $x_1, \ldots, x_{n_1}$ and $y_1, \ldots, y_{n_2}$ denote the subsamples of order n_1 from X and n_2 from Y, respectively. By assigning each of the observations its rank in the joint array, the rank sum of X-observations,

$$T_X := \sum_X \text{ranks} = \text{rank}(x_1) + \ldots + \text{rank}(x_{n_1})$$ [46]

is calculated and used as the test statistic for the null hypothesis

$$\mathrm{H}_0 : M_X = M_Y,$$

where M_X and M_Y denote the medians of X and Y, respectively. Assuming X and Y are no different regarding their location, probabilities for the T_X values can be calculated, in dependence on n_1 and N[47]. Finally, dependent on whether the alternative[48] hypothesis H_1 is two- ($\mathrm{H}_1 : M_X \neq M_Y$) or one-sided ($\mathrm{H}_1 : M_X > M_Y$, or $\mathrm{H}_1 : M_X < M_Y$), the P-value for the observed test statistic can be

44 A brief recap of the *t-test* can for instance be found in Homburg[119], page 112.

45 This means that, under the null hypothesis, X and Y have identical distributions.

46 Equivalently, T_Y may be calculated and used as a test statistic, since $T_Y + T_X = 1 + \ldots + n = n \cdot \frac{n+1}{2}$.

47 Respectively $n_2 = N - n_1$ and N for T_Y.
The assumption of equal distribution shape means that, under the null hypothesis, X and Y have identical distributions. Thus, all single observations are equally likely to belong to X (probability: $\frac{n_1}{N}$) and to belong to Y (probability: $\frac{n_2}{N}$). This transfers to the probability of X rank combinations, which are thus all equally likely under the null hypothesis.

48 For a disambiguation of null and alternative hypothesis, see for instance Hildebrandt[117], page 45.

calculated. If P is sufficiently low, the assumption that M_X equals M_Y can be rejected[49].

It is important to note that, provided normal distribution, the MWW has the strong asymptotic relative efficiency[50] of .955 compared to the *Student's t-test.* This means that, by the possible employment of the MWW in cases where *Student's t-test* would be appropriate (namely in cases where the assumption of a normal distribution could be justified), only five percent of statistical power are being lost by employing the non-parametric alternative. If distributions are heavy-tailed, in contrast, relative efficiency increases to values larger than 1.00. The asymptotic relative efficiency of the test is 1.00 for continuous uniform distributions, and at least .864 for any continuous distribution[51].

Location test for paired samples

For the comparison of paired samples, the *Wilcoxon signed rank test* was employed, which shall be referred to by *WSR* in the following.

In addition to using signs[52], the WSR also takes into account the relative magnitudes of the differences $\delta_i := y_i - x_i$ between the paired observations. In order to calculate the test statistic

$$T_+ := \sum_+ \text{ranks} = \sum_{\delta_i > 0} \text{rank}(|\delta_i|),$$

49 Cf. Gibbons[98], pp. 30–35.

50 The term "asymptotic relative efficiency" is for instance discussed in Bradley[40], pp. 56–62. *Gibbons* loosely defines asymptotic relative efficiency by the following: "Suppose there are two tests, A and B, either of which can be used to carry out a test of a specific null hypothesis against a specific alternative hypothesis. The asymptotic relative efficiency of test A relative to test B is the ratio of the sample size required by test B relative to the sample size required by test A in order for both tests to achieve the same power at the same significance level under the same distribution assumptions with large sample sizes", see Gibbons[98], page 3.

51 See Gibbons[98], pp. 3, 39, 40.

52 As does the sign test, which has significantly lower statistical efficiency, see for instance Gibbons[98], page 25.

the absolute differences $|\delta_i|$ between the paired observations y_i and x_i are being calculated and ordered[53]. Thereby, track is being kept as to whether the difference δ_i was positive or negative, so that T_+ can be calculated. The probability under the null hypothesis

$$\mathrm{H}_0 : M = M_0,$$

where M denotes the median of $\delta = Y - X$ and M_0 is a fixed value[54], for the incidence of the observed T_+ or more extreme values[55] is then being calculated. If such probability is low, H_0 can be rejected. Again, dependent on the alternative hypothesis, one- or two-tailed probabilities are being employed.

By testing whether the magnitudes of those observations that exceed M_0 do approximately balance off the magnitudes of those smaller than M_0, the WSR is subject to the symmetry of the distribution of the difference δ in the population[56]. In the M&A advisory user research at hand, symmetry assumptions for the distributions of differences in question to be researched seemed reasonable[57], so that the application of the WSR seemed sensible.

By using the WSR instead of *Student's t-test* in the case of normal distribution, only little statistical power is being lost. The WSR's asymptotic relative efficiency to its parametric alternative, the *Student's t-test* for paired samples, is .955 for normal distributions, 1.00 for the continuous uniform distribution, at least .864 for any con-

---

53 Provided there are differences $\delta_i = 0$, these are excluded from the sample (if X and Y are continuous, no such differences should occur). Similarly, no differences of equal (absolute) value should occur. Alternative methods of dealing with 0-differences are for instance presented and discussed in Bradley[40], pp. 49–54. The most common approach (also used in this thesis) is to exclude the 0-differences from the sample and to assign midranks to tied observations. If midranks are to be used, the probability function of the test statistic changes, cf. for instance Gibbons[97], page 128.
Again, T_- may equivalently be used as a test statistic.

54 In the cases at hand, 0.

55 That is, the P-value for the observed T_+.

56 That way, any observation $|\delta_i|$ has a null probability of $\frac{1}{2}$ to have a positive, respectively negative, sign. This probability transfers to the rank order, cf. for instance Lehmann[156], page 125.

57 Plausibility checks were conducted by means of histogram representation.

tinuous symmetric distribution, and generally larger than 1.00 for longer-tailed distributions[58].

9.2.6 Statistical package

To conduct the tests and regression, respectively discriminant analyses, the program SPSS 10.0 was used.

As to location tests, SPSS usually provides the test statistics themselves, as well as asymptotic P-values by means of transforming the test statistic to a Z-value corresponding to the *Gauss distribution*, from which respective probabilities can be read. While in most cases[59] such approximation is sufficient, SPSS calculates in addition exact P-values for smaller-sized samples[60].

The research hypothesis being one-sided in most cases of the research conducted here, the two-sided P-value calculated by the SPSS package in respective cases could be divided by two, in order to derive the P-value by which the null hypothesis could possibly be rejected.

58 See Gibbons[98], page 25.

59 *Gibbons* suggests for instance for the WSR a total sample size of 16 or more, see Gibbons[98], page 17.

60 Since in such cases the Z-value provides only a coarse approximation, it is going to be parenthesised when test results for such cases are being displayed.

10 Review and discussion of results

This chapter contains the test results on the relationships hypothesised in chapters 7 and 8. Where test results conflict with the research hypothesis, potential reasons and implications shall be discussed. That way, test results are going to be reviewed on a very granular basis. Such review shall be complemented by a higher-level review of results and implications in chapter 12.

10.1 Risk associated with the advisor choice

Let us first review the hypotheses dealing with the risk associated with the M&A advisor choice, and the most basic risk relief strategies[1]. The following items are going to be used in this section.

- Company's risk associated with the M&A project (assessment on a 1–9 scale)
- Risk associated with the M&A advisor choice, operationalised by the multiplicative resultant of respective consequence and uncertainty, where
  - Consequence component of M&A advisor choice is operationalised as importance of the M&A advisor choice (assessment on a 1–9 scale)[2]
  - Uncertainty component of M&A advisor choice is operationalised as the difficulty to assess different banks' investment banking capabilities (assessment on a 1–9 scale)[2],

1 This corresponds to the hypotheses developed in section 7.1.

2 Cf. paragraph 9.2.2.

What about were your company's annual revenues **before** the M&A project? Please check.	O less than € 50m O € 50m - € 99m O € 100m - € 249m O € 250m - € 499m O € 500m - € 999m O € 1.0b - € 2.4b O € 2.5b - € 4.9b O € 5.0b - € 15.0b O More than 15.0b
...	...
What was your company's role in the M&A project? Please check.	O To acquire a company O To acquire some business of a company O To sell our company O To sell one of our bus. O To fend off take-over O To merge with a company O Other. Please specify: ____________
What about was the M&A transaction volume in question?	O less than € 50m O € 50m - € 99m O € 100m - € 249m O € 250m - € 499m O € 500m - € 999m O € 1.0b - € 2.4b O € 2.5b - € 4.9b O € 5.0b - € 15.0b O More than 15.0b
...	...
How would you rate your company's risk that was associated with the M&A project/ transaction itself?	Very low = 1 O, 2 O, 3 O, 4 O, 5 O, 6 O, 7 O, 8 O, 9 O = Very high
How would you rate the importance of your investment bank choice decision for your company's future welfare?	Very low = 1 O, 2 O, 3 O, 4 O, 5 O, 6 O, 7 O, 8 O, 9 O = Very high
...	...
How easy was it for you to make up your mind about the capabilities of different banks ... **before** the solicitation events ... **after** the soliciation events?	Very easy = 1, 2, 3, 4, 5, 6, 7, 8, 9 = Very diffic. (before: O O O O O O O O O; after: O O O O O O O O O)
How big was the role the lead bank was supposed to play in the course of the M&A project?	Not that important a role = 1 O, 2 O, 3 O, 4 O, 5 O, 6 O, 7 O, 8 O, 9 O = Highly important a role
What applied to the investment banking experience of your company, **prior** to the M&A project?	O First time we dealt with investment banking O Had some, but not much experience with investment banking O Had considerable experience with investment banking O Were already very experienced with investment banking

Which was the selection procedure your company applied to select the advising investment bank? Please check what applies.	O We invited several banks to make presentations, and selected thereafter
	O We discussed the transaction with several banks, and selected thereafter
	O We contacted only one bank for the transaction, and this was
	  O our existing investment banking relationship
	  O our existing commercial banking relationship
	  O some bank we did not have a relationship with
	  O the bank who brought us the idea
	  O the bank that has members on our board
	O We have a rotation scheme among a special set of investment banks, and assigned the mandate to the bank whose turn it was
	O We gave the mandate to the bank that was on retainer
	O Other. Please specify: ____________

...	...

Please rate the **importance** of the following factors for your final **selection of the lead bank.**

Please mark one check for each factor.

Factor	1 = Not at all important	2	3	4	5	6	7	8	9 = Extremely important
...				...					
Bank's reputation	O	O	O	O	O	O	O	O	O
Bank's investment banking relationship with us	O	O	O	O	O	O	O	O	O
Bank's commercial banking relationship with us	O	O	O	O	O	O	O	O	O
Key banker's relationship with our company	O	O	O	O	O	O	O	O	O
Bank had well executed one of our previous deal	O	O	O	O	O	O	O	O	O
Quality of sales presentation	O	O	O	O	O	O	O	O	O
...	O	O	O	O	O	O	O	O	O
Bank is on our company's board	O	O	O	O	O	O	O	O	O
Other. Please specify: ____________	O	O	O	O	O	O	O	O	O

Figure 10.1: Questionnaire excerpt I

where the content-wise more appropriate alternative of the following is chosen

* * Before solicitation
* * After solicitation[3]

- Transfer lever, operationalised as the importance of the role the bank was supposed to play in the M&A project (assessment on a 1–9 scale)
- Relative transaction size, operationalised as the ratio of bucket means of
  - M&A transaction volume in question (assessment in 9 size buckets)
  - Company revenues before the M&A transaction in question (assessment in 9 size buckets),
- Company's familiarity with the product, operationalised as company's investment banking experience (assessment on a 1–4 scale)
- Type of M&A project (merger, acquisition, divestment, etc.)
- Type of M&A advisor selection procedure employed, differentiated into
  - Competitive solicitation, comprising selections where a company contacted several banks, before awarding the mandate to one of them, in the form of beauty contests with sales presentation, or discussion
  - Non-competitive solicitation, comprising selections where the company contacted exclusively one bank, be it its main investment banking relationship, one of its relationships, or some other bank
- Importance of reputation, operationalised as importance that reputation had for the company's lead bank choice decision (assessment on a 1–9 scale).

3 Thus, difficulty of capability assessment before solicitation represents an "intermediary" measure of handled uncertainty. For M&A projects where no solicitation events have been employed, the two are equal to each other.

Figure 10.1 contains the respective excerpt of the questionnaire filled out by survey participants.

10.1.1 Consequence component

Hypotheses R1 to R9[4] are the ones concerned with the consequence component of risk associated with choosing an M&A advisor. Operationalising respective concepts in the way described in the previous paragraph, most of the hypothesised relationships were found to be supported by empirical evidence.

Table 10.1 on page 191 provides the more specific test results obtained by means of the SPSS package.

Before assessing the results, let us briefly look at the structure of the table. The third column contains the content of the research hypothesis by virtue of the operationalisation applied, while the fourth column describes the relationship of concepts claimed by the respective null hypothesis which is subject to the test – in this case, the MWW.

The second column indicates whether the test result was in the expected way. Thereby, "Y" means that the null hypothesis could be rejected in the way hypothesised, while "N" indicates this could not be done, but that this also was in accordance with the research hypothesis. Thus, "Y" or "N" indicate that test results were in the expected way. In contrast, "(Y)" or "(N)" indicate that results were not in the expected way. "(Y)" indicates that, although no significant deviation in the location of the groups tested against each other was expected, the test yielded that such difference was significant, while "(N)" denotes that, although a significant deviation of medians had been hypothesised, the test did not yield a P-value of small enough size. Thereby, 5% were chosen as significance level[5]. Most of the times, namely in all cases except for those where no deviation of significance of the group medians was expected[6], one-sided signif-

4 Formulated in section 7.1.

5 Problems associated with such approach, namely type 1 and type 2 errors, are for instance discussed in Hildebrandt[117], page 46.

6 That is, where research claimed a "o" relationship, and where the implication of the test outcome would be to reject or not to reject the null hypothesis.

1	2	3			4	5		6			7	8	9		10	11	12
Hypothesis	Null-hypothesis rejected?**	Research hypothesis			Null hyp.	Groups to be tested against each other		Group size			Asymp-totic, two-sided P-value	Asymp-totic, one-sided P-value	Mean rank		Z value	Mann Whitney U	Wilcoxon W
		Variable A	hypo-the-sised effect* →	Variable B		Group 1's variable A value range	Group 2's variable A value range	Total	Group 1	Group 2			Group 1	Group 2			
R1	Y	Multiplicative resultant of M&A risk and ib role	+	Importance of ib choice	o	<25	>=25	**79**	37	42	**(0.000)**	**0.000**	25.53	52.75	-5.330	241.5	944.5
R2	Y	Risk associated with M&A	+	Importance of ib choice	o	1-5	6-9	**81**	48	33	**(0.000)**	**0.000**	30.95	55.62	-4.695	309.5	1,485.5
R2	Y				o	1-6	7-9	**81**	59	22	**(0.000)**	**0.000**	35.21	56.52	-3.671	307.5	2,077.5
R3	Y	Importance of ib role	+	Importance of ib choice	o	1-5	6-9	**82**	33	49	**(0.001)**	**0.000**	31.32	48.36	-3.216	472.5	1,033.5
R3	Y				o	1-6	7-9	**80**	46	34	**(0.005)**	**0.003**	34.37	48.79	-2.780	500.0	1,581.0
R4	N	Importance of ib role	o	Risk associated with M&A	o	1-5	6-9	**79**	47	32	**0.178**	**(0.089)**	37.18	44.14	-1.346	619.5	1,747.5
R4	N				o	1-6	7-9	**79**	58	21	**0.443**	**(0.222)**	38.83	43.24	-0.768	541.0	2,252.0
R5	N	Risk associated with M&A	o	Importance of ib role	o	1-5	6-9	**80**	48	32	**0.176**	**(0.088)**	37.68	44.73	-1.354	632.5	1,808.5
R5	N				o	1-6	7-9	**80**	59	21	**0.436**	**(0.218)**	39.31	43.83	-0.779	549.5	2,319.5
R6	Y	Relative ta size (based on proxies)	+	Risk associated with M&A	o	<.4	>=.4	**81**	47	34	**(0.016)**	**0.008**	35.71	48.31	-2.400	550.5	1,678.5
R6	Y				o	<.7	>=.7	**81**	64	17	**(0.008)**	**0.004**	37.48	54.24	-2.634	319.0	2,399.0
R7	(N)	Merger or Take-over-defense	+	Risk associated with M&A	o	Other	Merger or take-over defense	**81**	7	74	**(0.225)**	**0.1125**	40.03	51.21	-1.213	187.5	2,962.5
R8	N	Risk associated with M&A	o	Difficulty of assessing ib capabilities bef. solicitat.	o	1-5	6-9	**81**	48	33	**0.128**	**(0.064)**	37.74	45.74	-1.522	635.5	1,811.5
R8	N				o	1-6	7-9	**81**	59	22	**0.436**	**(0.218)**	39.77	44.30	-0.779	576.5	2,349.5
R9	N	Importance of ib role	o	Difficulty of assessing ib capabilities bef. solicitat.	o	1-5	6-9	**82**	33	49	**0.456**	**(0.228)**	39.14	43.09	-0.746	730.5	1,291.5
R9	N				o	1-6	7-9	**80**	46	34	**0.672**	**(0.336)**	41.43	39.24	-0.423	739.0	1,334.0
R9	N				o	1-5	6-9	**79**	52	27	**0.163**	**(0.082)**	37.49	44.83	-1.395	571.5	1,949.5

*** + = increases, - = decreases, o = has not effect on**

**** Y = yes (in accordance with research hypothesis), (Y) = yes (not in accordance with research hypothesis), N = no (in accordance with research hypothesis), (N) = no (not in accordance with research hypothesis)**

Table 10.1: Consequences associated with the M&A advisor choice

icance was the measure of relevance[7], and to help the reader's easier orientation, the significance of non-relevance was parenthesised. P-values, for which 5% served as a hurdle rate (significance level), are displayed in columns 7 and 8.

Column 5 gives the respective ranges of variable A values, by means of which the groups tested against each other were defined[8]. For some of the hypotheses, two cuts were being applied, whose test results are then both displayed in the test result table. Column 6 depicts the group sizes obtained by means of the cut described in column 5.

Columns 9 to 12 display the more specific test items and results. Column 9 contains the mean ranks of the groups tested against each other, while columns 11 and 12 contain the test statistics. Column 10, eventually, contains the Z value by virtue of which an approximation for the test significance can be read from the *Gauss distribution*. Since Z is thus only of relevance in cases where an asymptotic significance was used, its value was parenthesised when such approximation, due to small sample size, was illegitimate and SPSS also provided the exact P-value.

As indicated by table 10.1, most of the relationships were in the hypothesised way. In the following, only the tests that yielded a result other than suggested by the respective research hypothesis – that is, the ones for which the second column of table 10.1 contains a bracketed entry –, shall be revisited.

- **Hypothesis R7.** Eventually, only hypothesis R7's test result is unsatisfactory, with a one-sided P-value of 11%, which is well above the significance level. Mergers or non-desired takeovers clearly being considered by respondents to represent the type of M&A transactions that most impact the corporate governance structure of a company[9], and relative transaction size being high, this may hint at additional risk drivers other than

7 Cf. paragraph 9.2.5, page 182.

8 These cuts were defined in such a way that the total sample was approximately balanced into two equally big groups, respectively in such a way that the "high-risk" group was slightly lower-sized than the group whose variable A values hinted at lower risk.

9 The one-sided P-value here is .000.

the ones identified for overall M&A risk, which may constitute an interesting field for further research[10].

10.1.2 Uncertainty component

Next, let us revisit the hypotheses dealing primarily with the uncertainty component of risk associated with the M&A advisor choice, that is, with hypotheses R10 to R17[11].

Table 10.2 on page 194 shows the test results of the MWW, which was applied in order to possibly reject the null hypotheses. Again, only those hypotheses for which test results conflicted with the research hypothesis, shall be revisited – with the exception of hypothesis R17. The latter is going to be reviewed, since the reader's suspicion that the explanation given for the test results of hypothesis R13 conflicts with the rationale of hypothesis R17, ought to be precluded.

- **Hypotheses R13, R14.** While the test results suggest that the difficulty of capability assessment may indeed motivate a company to search further information by means of employing a competitive selection process[12], the test results of hypothesis R14 suggest that such endeavour may not be affected by the consequence component of risk. And, as a consequence, also hypothesis R13's test result shows a P-value missing the significance level.

  An explanation for the insignificance of our test results may be provided by the proposition that companies may employ other strategies than information search to cope with risk, dependent on the amount at stake. For instance may companies be more willing to re-engage one of their "in-suppliers" with whom they have already made satisfactory usage experience, than taking

10 The research data set, in contrast, is clearly too small to deal with this topic in a more differentiated way, e. g., by differentiating merger from take-over-defense projects. As already mentioned on page 176 of paragraph 9.1.2, our sample is biassed regarding transaction types, and may not constitute the most appropriate basis for their evaluation.

11 These have been derived in section 7.2.

12 See hypothesis R12.

1 Hypothesis	2 Null-hypothesis rejected?**	3 Research hypothesis: Variable A	hypothesised effect*	Variable B	4 Null hyp.	5 Groups to be tested against each other: Group 1's variable A value range	Group 2's variable A value range	6 Group size: Total	Group 1	Group 2	7 Asymptotic, two-sided P-value	8 Asymptotic, one-sided P-value	9 Mean rank: Group 1	Group 2	10 Z value	11 Mann Whitney U	12 Wilcoxon W
R10	Y	Investment banking experience	-	Difficulty of assessing ib capabilities bef. solicitat.	o	1-3	4	**81**	43	38	**(0.053)**	**0.0265**	45.70	35.68	-1.934	615.0	1,356.0
R11	N	Investment banking experience	o	Importance of ib choice	o	1-3	4	**82**	44	38	**0.457**	**(0.229)**	43.30	39.42	-0.744	757.0	1,498.0
R12	Y	Difficulty of assessing ib capabilities bef. solicit.	+	Employment of competitive solicitation process	o	1-4	5-9	**82**	42	40	**(0.007)**	**.004**	35.57	47.72	-2.696	591.0	1,494.0
	(N)	Multiplicative resultant of choice importance and difficulty of capability assessment before solicit.	+	Employment of competitive solicitation process	o	<=16	>16	**82**	50	32	**(0.227)**	**0.114**	39.32	44.91	-1.209	691.0	1,966.0
R13	(N)				o	<=20	>20	**82**	57	25	**(0.198)**	**0.099**	39.58	45.88	-1.287	603.0	2,256.0
	(N)	Importance of ib choice	+	Employment of competitive solicitation process	o	1-4	5-9	**82**	47	35	**(0.634)**	**0.317**	42.43	40.26	-0.476	779.0	1,409.0
R14	(N)				o	1-5	6-9	**82**	59	23	**(0.928)**	**0.464**	41.63	41.17	-0.090	671.0	947.0
R15	(N)	Difficulty of assessing ib capabilities after solicit.	+	Importance of bank's reputation	o	1-4	5-9	**74**	49	25	**(0.132)**	**0.066**	34.90	42.60	-1.507	485.0	1,710.0
	Y	Multiplicative resultant of choice importance and difficulty of capability assessment after solicit.	+	Importance of bank's reputation	o	<=16	>16	**79**	54	25	**(0.069)**	**0.035**	36.91	46.48	-1.820	508.0	1,993.0
R16	Y				o	<=20	>20	**70**	60	10	**(0.012)**	**0.006**	36.82	47.29	-2.509	358.5	2,188.5
	Y	Importance of ib choice	+	Importance of bank's reputation	o	1-4	5-9	**79**	46	33	**(0.002)**	**0.001**	33.59	48.94	-3.032	464.0	1,545.0
R17	Y				o	1-5	6-9	**79**	57	22	**(0.090)**	**0.045**	37.37	46.82	-1.696	477.0	2,130.0

*** + = increases, - = decreases, o = has not effect on**

**** Y = yes (in accordance with research hypothesis), (Y) = yes (not in accordance with research hypothesis), N = no (in accordance with research hypothesis), (N) = no (not in accordance with research hypothesis)**

Table 10.2: Uncertainty associated with the M&A advisor choice and most basic relievers

the risk of selecting a bank that gave a a good sales presentation and has an excellent reputation, but which they have never used before[13].

Alternatively, the non-significance of the relationship claimed by hypothesis R14 may hint a consequence component of risk that categorically surmounts the threshold that makes risk reduction through search a desirable strategy. In such case, uncertainty component of risk would constitute the sole determinant of whether or not to employ competitive selection processes. Put differently, if the potential differential consequences arising from the choice of the M&A advisor are always so big that it always pays to better assess a bank's capabilities, then choice importance, i. e., the consequences arising from choosing the advising bank, is not a differentiating but a categorical driver for the utility of comparison, i. e., uncertainty decrease. Then, the decision as to whether or not not employ competitive solicitation – which offers the opportunity of further information collection –, solely depends on the question whether the buyer thinks he can assess different banks' capabilities to a satisfactory extent, and, provided he thinks that not, whether competitive solicitation constitutes an appropriate mean to increase his knowledge about different banks' capabilities

- **Hypothesis R17.** But such categorically high consequence component of risk raises the question why reputation does then show significantly different levels of importance, dependent on the perceived importance of M&A advisor choice, as proposed by hypothesis R17[14]. One explanation for the differing importance of reputation may lie in its nature: if consequences are perceived to be of significant size, then companies may tend to more strongly rely on the opinion that third parties, in particular more experienced peers, or opinion leaders, have on M&A advisors, and which are subsumed in a respondent's reputation

13 That is, priority may be given to banks for which comparatively useful information types are available, even if there may be better choices.

14 That is, in the following, one has to give arguments that would not categorically be applicable to other uncertainty relievers, as for instance information search, but arguments that have to reflect reputation specifics.

assessment[15]. In addition to that, and as already mentioned, one would take by far too restricted a perspective by looking at the importance of reputation only from the uncertainty decrease perspective. In particular, reputation may provide a justification device, and as discussed on page 143 following hypothesis R17, this rationale by oneself may be sufficient to derive the relationship claimed by hypothesis R17

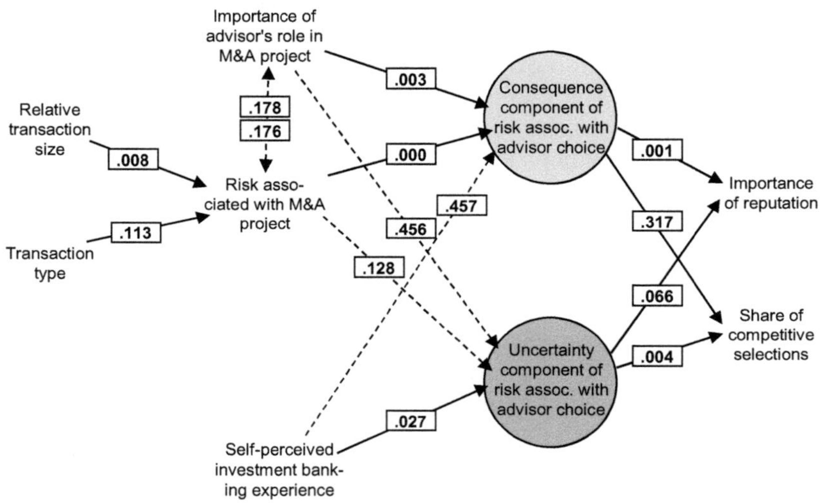

Figure 10.2: Test results on M&A advisor choice risk
(Relationships assessed are in positive direction, except for the effects of self-perceived investment banking experience)

- **Hypothesis R15.** As to hypothesis R15, test levels are close to being significant, so that there is no major need to discuss relationships other than the one proposed by the hypothesis. Rather, the MWW analysis of hypothesis R15 may be complemented by an additional MWW analysis. As to the influence

15 Further, reputation constituting a hostage in the buyer's hands, its importance may be particularly crucial for the buyer if choice importance is high, cf. paragraphs 4.2.3 and 5.3.1, 5.3.2.

that difficulty of investment banking capability assessment *before* solicitation has on the perceived importance of the bank's reputation, it is found that the significance of this relationship is lower[16]. This hints at reputation as a "fall back" option from an uncertainty relief perspective. That is, buyers who have not been able to gain a satisfactory insight into a bank's capabilities in other, more direct ways may, "willy-nilly", have to rely on reputation.

Figure 10.2 visualises the test results revisited in this section. Dashed arrows indicate that no significant relationships had been expected, while drawn-through lines visualise relationships that had been hypothesised to be of significance. The P-values for the respective relationships are provided in the boxes.

10.2 Information used to determine the advisor choice

Let us now revisit the hypotheses dealing with the signal vehicles which a buyer might base his choice on[17].

The items that are going to be used in this section, besides some of the ones mentioned in the previous section, are the following.

- Importance of the investment banking reputation for the choice of the lead bank (assessment on a 1–9 scale)
- Importance of the investment banking relationship with the company for the choice of the lead bank, operationalised as
  - Importance of the company's investment banking relationship with the investment bank (assessment on a 1–9 scale)

16 Dependent on cuts ((1-4) vs. (5-9), or (1-5) vs. (6-9), respectively), one-sided P-value is .244 or .082.

17 Thus, the hypotheses developed in chapter 8 shall be revisited.

  - Importance of the company's investment banking relationship with the key banker[18] for the choice of the lead bank (assessment on a 1–9 scale)

- Importance of the bank's previous execution of one of the past M&A transactions for the company for the choice of the lead bank (assessment on a 1–9 scale)

- Importance of the sales presentation/discussion for the choice of the lead bank (assessment on a 1–9 scale)

- Importance of the commercial banking relationship for the choice of the lead bank (assessment on a 1–9 scale)

- Importance of individual banker as opposed to bank corporation for choice of M&A advisor (assessment on a 1–9 bipolar scale)

- Satisfaction with the bank's execution (assessment on a 1–9 scale)

- Company's re-engagement intention, operationalised as its

  - Re-engagement intention of the bank (assessment on a 1–9 scale)

  - Re-engagement intention of the banker (assessment on a 1–9 scale)

- Company's banker as opposed to bank loyalty, operationalised by the presence or absence of its willingness to follow the banker to another bank in case he would leave (digital variable)

- Investment banking reputation of any of Goldman Sachs, Morgan Stanley Dean Witter, Merrill Lynch, J.P. Morgan Chase, UBS Warburg, Credit Suisse First Boston, Rothschild, Lazard LLC, Citibank, Deutsche Bank, Dresdner Kleinwort Wasserstein, and Lehman Brothers (assessment on a 1–9 scale)[19]

---

18 The "key banker" being defined as "banker who leads the bank's team during solicitation resp. execution. The key banker is the main contact between the bank and the advised company's senior management" (this clarification was appended to the questionnaire).

19 Respondents were asked to complement these assessments by respective assessments for other banks of relevance in their choice.

Please give us your opinion about the following investment banks' public reputation.

Please mark one check for each bank.

	Poor reputation = 1	2	3	4	5	6	7	8	Excellent reputation = 9	Have no opinion about their reputation
ABN Amro	O	O	O	O	O	O	O	O	O	O
Credit Suisse First Boston	O	O	O	O	O	O	O	O	O	O
Deutsche Bank	O	O	O	O	O	O	O	O	O	O
Dresdner Kleinwort Wasserst.	O	O	O	O	O	O	O	O	O	O
Goldman Sachs	O	O	O	O	O	O	O	O	O	O
J.P. Morgan Chase	O	O	O	O	O	O	O	O	O	O
Lazard LLC	O	O	O	O	O	O	O	O	O	O
Lehman Brothers	O	O	O	O	O	O	O	O	O	O
Merrill Lynch	O	O	O	O	O	O	O	O	O	O
Morgan Stanley D.W.	O	O	O	O	O	O	O	O	O	O
Rothschild	O	O	O	O	O	O	O	O	O	O
Salomon Smith Barney	O	O	O	O	O	O	O	O	O	O
UBS Warburg	O	O	O	O	O	O	O	O	O	O
Other:_______________	O	O	O	O	O	O	O	O	O	O
Other:_______________	O	O	O	O	O	O	O	O	O	O

Which of these **investment banks** did your company have an investment banking <u>relationship</u> (i.e., an ex-change of ideas on an ongo-ing basis) with, **ahead of the M&A project?**

Please indicate the type of relationship, if any, your company had with the following investment banks, and indicate the duration of this relationship.

	Had no relationship with this bank	Only for banks you had a relationship with — Character of relationship: loose/inactive 1	2	3	4	5	6	7	8	intense/active 9
ABN Amro	O	O	O	O	O	O	O	O	O	O
Credit Suisse First Boston	O	O	O	O	O	O	O	O	O	O
Deutsche Bank	O	O	O	O	O	O	O	O	O	O
Dresdner Kleinwort Wass.	O	O	O	O	O	O	O	O	O	O
Goldman Sachs	O	O	O	O	O	O	O	O	O	O
J.P. Morgan Chase	O	O	O	O	O	O	O	O	O	O
Lazard LLC	O	O	O	O	O	O	O	O	O	O
Lehman Brothers	O	O	O	O	O	O	O	O	O	O
Merrill Lynch	O	O	O	O	O	O	O	O	O	O
Morgan Stanley D.W.	O	O	O	O	O	O	O	O	O	O
Rothschild	O	O	O	O	O	O	O	O	O	O
Salomon Smith Barney	O	O	O	O	O	O	O	O	O	O
UBS Warburg	O	O	O	O	O	O	O	O	O	O
Other: _______________	O	O	O	O	O	O	O	O	O	O

How about these banks' <u>**key bankers?**</u> You might have had a relationship with certain key bankers* **ahead of the M&A project.**

Please indicate the type of relationship, if any, your company had with the key bankers, and indicate the duration of this relationship.

	Had no relationship with him/her	Only for key bankers you had a relationship with — Character of relationship: loose/inactive 1	2	3	4	5	6	7	8	intense/active 9
ABN Amro	O	O	O	O	O	O	O	O	O	O
Credit Suisse First Boston	O	O	O	O	O	O	O	O	O	O
Deutsche Bank	O	O	O	O	O	O	O	O	O	O
Dresdner Kleinwort Wass.	O	O	O	O	O	O	O	O	O	O
Goldman Sachs	O	O	O	O	O	O	O	O	O	O
J.P. Morgan Chase	O	O	O	O	O	O	O	O	O	O
Lazard LLC	O	O	O	O	O	O	O	O	O	O
Lehman Brothers	O	O	O	O	O	O	O	O	O	O
Merrill Lynch	O	O	O	O	O	O	O	O	O	O
Morgan Stanley D.W.	O	O	O	O	O	O	O	O	O	O
Rothschild	O	O	O	O	O	O	O	O	O	O
Salomon Smith Barney	O	O	O	O	O	O	O	O	O	O
UBS Warburg	O	O	O	O	O	O	O	O	O	O
Other: _______________	O	O	O	O	O	O	O	O	O	O

... ...

What applies to the **lead bank** to which you finally awarded the mandate? Please check **all that apply.**

- O Bank did previous M&A project with us
- O Was the first time we used this bank for M&A
- O We had used another bank for previous M&A
- O Bank had already done IPO for us
- O Bank had already led equity offerings or debt offerings for us
- O Bank we always use for investment banking
- O Had an investment banking relationship with bank prior to selection
- O Had a commercial relationship with them
- O Bank we had never used for anything before
- O Bank has members on our board

... ...

Considering the **lead bank** that won your mandate. Was it more the **bank corporation** which made you choose this bank, or was it more due to the **key banker** that you awarded them

The key banker was by far most important = 1 O — 2 O — 3 O — 4 O — 5 O (Key banker and bank were equally important) — 6 O — 7 O — 8 O — 9 O = The bank was by far most important

... ...

How satisfied were you with...

	Completely unsatisfied = 1	2	3	4	5	6	7	8	Extremely satisfied = 9
... the M&A project **overall?**	O	O	O	O	O	O	O	O	O
... the **outcome** of the project?	O	O	O	O	O	O	O	O	O
... the smoothness and clarity of its **process?**	O	O	O	O	O	O	O	O	O
... the **lead bank's overall** contribution/execution?	O	O	O	O	O	O	O	O	O

... ...

Thinking about some future transaction to come, what applies to the **bank to which you awarded the lead mandate?** Pls. check **all that apply.**

- O Would avoid using them again
- O May possibly invite them to pitch
- O Would definitely invite them to pitch
- O Have <u>shortlisted</u> them for the next transaction
- O Would probably award them the mandate
- O Would most likely award them the mandate, without seriously considering other banks
- O Would recommend them to others

How likely would you re-engage this bank?

Definitely **not** re-engage = 1 O — 2 O — 3 O — 4 O — 5 O — 6 O — 7 O — 8 O — 9 O = Definitely re-engage

Thinking about a future transaction, what applies to the **key banker** to which you awarded the mandate? Please check **all that apply.**

- O Would avoid using this key banker
- O Would like to engage her/him also in future
- O Would like to engage only her/him in future
- O Would like to engage only her/him, independent of the bank she/he may be with then
- O Would recommend her/him to others

How likely would you re-engage this banker?

Definitely **not** re-engage = 1 O — 2 O — 3 O — 4 O — 5 O — 6 O — 7 O — 8 O — 9 O = Definitely re-engage

* such relationship may have been built at times when this banker was with another bank

Figure 10.3: Questionnaire excerpt II

- Intensity/activity of investment banking relationship maintained with any of Goldman Sachs, Morgan Stanley Dean Witter, Merrill Lynch, J.P. Morgan Chase, UBS Warburg, Credit Suisse First Boston, Rothschild, Lazard LLC, Citibank, Dresdner Kleinwort Wasserstein, Deutsche Bank, and Lehman Brothers ahead of the M&A project in question (assessment on a 1–9 scale)[19]

- First time M&A advisory buyer vs. switcher vs. repeat buyer self-assessment[20], derived from whether a respondent's company used a bank for first or repeat time for M&A advisory, and whether the M&A transaction was the company's first M&A transaction

- Bulge as opposed to major bracket customer, where bulge bracket customers comprised companies that chose any of Goldman Sachs, Morgan Stanley Dean Witter, and Merrill Lynch as their lead advisor, and major bracket customers comprised companies that chose any of J.P. Morgan Chase, UBS Warburg, Credit Suisse First Boston, Rothschild, Lazard LLC, Citibank, Dresdner Kleinwort Wasserstein, Deutsche Bank, and Lehman Brothers as their lead advisor.

Figure 10.3 contains the respective excerpt of the questionnaire filled out by survey participants.

10.2.1 Importance of signal vehicles in general

Hypotheses I1 to I5[21] are the ones concerned with the general importance of different signal vehicles. The operationalisation of respective concepts in the way described in the previous paragraph yields that most of the hypothesised relationships are being supported by empirical evidence.

Table 10.3 gives an overview of the test results. As can be seen, besides the MWW, the WSR served as a tool to assess in how far empirical data matched expectations.

20 Defined as on page 31.

21 Formulated in paragraph 8.2.1.

Location test for paired samples

1	2	3			4	5	6			7	8	9		10
Hypothesis number	Null-hypothesis rejected?**	Research hypothesis: Var. A	hypothesised relationship*	Var. B	Null hypoth.	Postitive ranks defined by	Group size***: Total	Negative ranks	Positive ranks	Asymptotic, two-sided P-value	Asymptotic, one-sided P-value	Mean rank of... neg. ranks	... positive ranks	Z value****
I1a	Y	Importance of reputation	>	Importance of investment banking relationship bank	=	Other variable > importance of reputation	78	33	22	(0.006)	0.003	33.24	20.14	-2.771
I1b	Y			Importance of investment banking relationship banker	=		79	40	19	(0.003)	0.002	31.98	25.84	-2.996
I1c	Y			Importance of previous execution	=		78	44	15	(0.000)	0.000	33.28	20.37	-4.393
I1d	Y			Importance of sales presentation/ discussion	=		78	53	11	(0.000)	0.000	35.79	16.64	-5.750
I1e	Y			Importance of commercial banking relationship	=		78	64	8	(0.000)	0.000	39.30	14.06	-6.763
I2a	Y	Importance of sales presentation/ discussion	<	Importance of reputation	=	Importance of sales presentation > other variable	78	53	11	(0.000)	0.000	35.79	16.64	-5.750
I2b	Y			Importance of investment banking relationship bank	=		79	48	24	(0.000)	0.000	40.83	27.83	-3.638
I2c	Y			Importance of investment banking relationship banker	=		78	47	22	(0.001)	0.000	37.06	30.59	-3.207
I2d	(N)			Importance of previous execution	=		78	38	26	(0.183)	0.091	32.59	32.37	-1.332
I5a	Y	Importance of commercial banking relationship	<	Importance of reputation	=	Importance of commercial banking relationship > other variable	78	64	8	(0.000)	0.000	39.30	14.06	-6.763
I5b	Y			Importance of investment banking relationship bank	=		77	53	4	(0.000)	0.000	30.42	10.25	-6.261
I5c	Y			Importance of investment banking relationship banker	=		78	51	10	(0.000)	0.000	34.90	11.10	-6.001
I5d	Y			Importance of previous execution	=		78	41	20	(0.000)	0.000	35.06	22.67	-3.545
I5e	Y			Importance of sales presentation/ discussion	=		77	40	19	(0.002)	0.001	32.58	24.58	-3.173
I3	Y	Difficulty of making up mind about investment banking capalitites after solicit. events	<	Difficulty of making up mind about investment banking capalitites before solicit. events	=	Difficulty of making up mind after solicitation > Diff. before solicitation	44	20	6	(0.006)	0.003	14.07	11.58	-2.749

* > = higher than, < = lower than

** Y = yes (in accordance with research hypothesis), (Y) = yes (not in accordance with research hypothesis), N = no (in accordance with research hypothesis), (N) = no (not in accordance with research hypothesis)

*** ties can be calculated by subtracting postive and negative ranks from group size

**** based on positive ranks

Location test for independent samples

Hypothesis	Null-hypothesis rejected?**	Research hypothesis: Variable A	hypothesised effect* →	Variable B	Null hypoth.	Groups to be tested against each other: Group 1's variable A value range	Group 2's variable A value range	Group size: Total	Group 1	Group 2	Asymptotic, two-sided P-value	Asymptotic, one-sided P-value	Mean rank: Group 1	Group 2	Z value	Mann Whitney U	Wilcoxon W
I4	Y	Employment of competitive solicitation process	+	Difficulty of making up mind about investment banks' capabilities (after solicit. events)	o	Companies employing non-com. selection	Companies employing competitve selection	77	33	44	(0.036)	0.018	32.92	43.56	-2.101	525.5	1,086.5

* + = increases, - = decreases, o = has not effect on

** Y = yes (in accordance with research hypothesis), (Y) = yes (not in accordance with research hypothesis), N = no (in accordance with research hypothesis), (N) = no (not in accordance with research hypothesis)

Table 10.3: General importance of signal vehicles

Let us first take a closer look at the structure of the WSR part of the table. As for the MWW, the third column contains the research hypothesis, the fourth indicates the relationship claimed by the null hypothesis, the second column indicates whether the test result was in the expected way, and P-values are displayed in columns 7 and 8.

Column 5 contains the definition of positive ranks, and column 6 displays sample size, number of positive, and number of negative ranks[22].

Columns 9 and 10 display the more specific test items and results. Column 9 contains the mean rank of positive ranks, and the mean rank of negative ranks[23]. Column 10 contains the Z value, by virtue of which an approximation for the P-value could be read from the *Gauss distribution.*

As indicated by table 10.3, most of the relationships were in the hypothesised way. Figure 10.4 illustrates the perceived overall importance of different signal vehicles for the choice of the M&A advisor.

As shows table 10.3, some of the hypotheses had to be split into subhypotheses. As proposed, reputation was found to play the most important role for selection in the overall market[24], while commercial banking relationship was found to be least important[25].

- **Hypothesis I2.** As to sales presentation/discussion, its importance was found to clearly fall behind the ones of reputation and investment banking relationship, but not to be significantly lower than the one of previous execution. As sales presentation/discussion itself, previous execution is not always applicable in selection processes. But, in contrast to sales presentation, the previous execution's applicability does not lie in the "ad hoc" control of the buyer[26]. Thus, it is proposed that levels of difference in importance should significantly increase, as

22 From these three figures, the number of ties can be calculated. For analysis purposes, ties were excluded from the sample.

23 Thus the information which the WSR uses in addition to the number of positive and negative ranks, which is also used by the sign test.

24 Hypothesis I1.

25 Hypothesis I5.

26 You either have made experience during a past project, or you have not. A sales presentation, in contrast, can always be requested by the buyer.

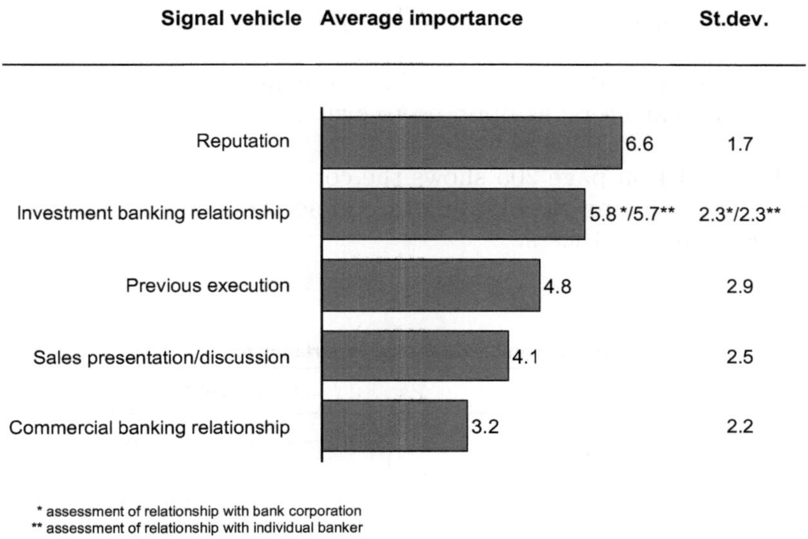

Figure 10.4: Signal vehicles' general importance
(Average on a 1–9 scale; core sample)

soon as previous execution as a signal vehicle is available, that is, in the case of repeat purchase[27]. Consequently, the proposition that previous execution offers the buyer more safety in his quality assessment is being maintained, while the restriction to such utility, which lies in the non-availability of previous execution type information, may be higher than suspected.

As to the issue in how far solicitation events help decrease the uncertainty component of risk associated with the M&A advisor choice, test results of hypotheses I3 and I4 do suggest that uncertainty can indeed be decreased[28], but that sales presentation, by being largely focused on potential type information, constitutes only a weak backup for other signal vehicles.

27 This is what was proposed by hypotheses I6 and I7.

28 A high share of ties (18/44), which were excluded from the sample, relativises the highly significant P-value.

10.2.2 Importance of signal vehicles for repeat buyers

Hypotheses I6 to I9[29] deal with the importance that signal vehicles have for repeat users, as opposed to switchers.

Table 10.4 on page 205 shows the corresponding test results. As can be seen, all empirical findings are in accordance with the respective research hypotheses.

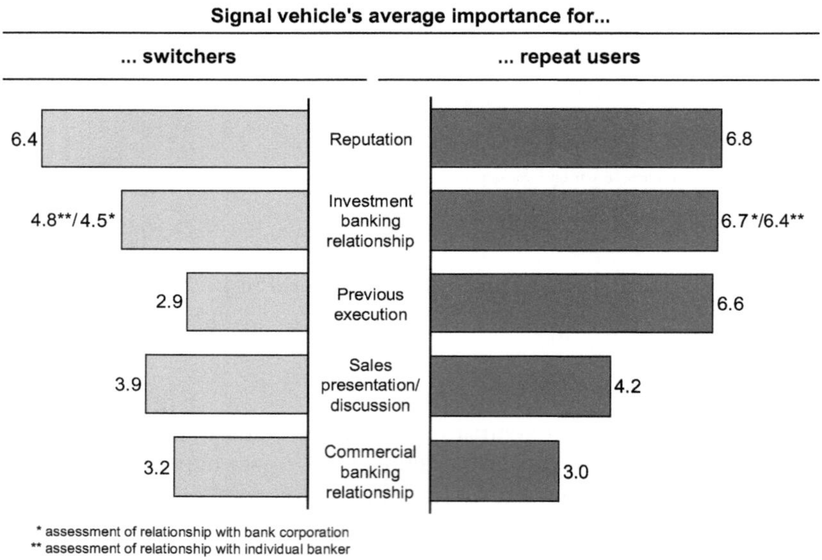

Figure 10.5: Signal vehicles' importance for repeat buyers
(Average on a 1–9 scale; core sample)

As shows figure 10.5, previous execution and investment banking relationship were found to play indeed a relatively more important role when a bank is chosen for repeat time. It is interesting to note that, in the case of repeat purchase, sales presentation/discussion plays

29 Proposed in paragraph 8.2.2.

Location test for paired samples

Hypothesis number	Null-hypothesis rejected?**	Var. A	hypothesised relationship*	Var. B	Null hypoth.	Postitive ranks defined by		Group size*** Total	Negative ranks	Positive ranks	Asymptotic, two-sided P-value	Asymptotic, one-sided P-value	Mean rank of... neg. ranks	... positive ranks	Z value****
16a	N	Importance of previous execution	=	Importance of reputation	=	Repeat buyers	Importance of previous execution > Importance of other	41	14	12	0.699	(.350)	13.61	13.38	-0.387
16b	N		=	Importance of investment banking relationship bank	=			41	13	15	0.825	(0.413)	14.88	14.17	-0.221
16c	N		=	Importance of investment banking relationship banker	=			41	10	13	0.278	(0.139)	10.30	13.31	-1.085
16d	Y		>	Importance of sales presentation/ discussion	=		Importance of previous execution < Importance of other	42	29	7	(0.000)	0.000	19.60	13.93	-3.714
16e	Y		>	Importance of commercial banking relationship	=			41	33	4	(0.000)	0.000	20.03	10.50	-4.681
18a	N	Importance of investment banking relationship bank	=	Importance of reputation	=	Repeat buyers	Importance of ib relationship > Importance of other	41	13	13	0.539	(0.270)	15.31	11.69	-0.614
18b	N		=	Importance of investment banking relationship banker	=		Importance of ib relationship < Importance of other	41	15	10	0.203	(0.102)	13.91	11.60	-1.274
18c	N		=	Importance of previous execution	=			41	13	15	0.825	(0.413)	14.88	14.17	-0.221
18d	Y		>	Importance of sales presentation/ discussion	=			43	29	10	(0.000)	0.000	22.47	12.85	-3.662
18e	Y		>	Importance of commercial banking relationship	=			40	34	1	(0.000)	0.000	18.44	3.00	-5.122

* > = higher than, < = lower than

** Y = yes (in accordance with research hypothesis), (Y) = yes (not in accordance with research hypothesis), N = no (in accordance with research hypothesis), (N) = no (not in accordance with research hypothesis)

*** ties can be calculated by subtracting postive and negative ranks from group size

**** based on positive ranks

Location test for independent samples

Hypothesis	Null-hypothesis rejected?**	Variable A	hypothesised effect* →	Variable B	Null hypoth.	Groups to be tested against each other: Group 1's variable A value range	Group 2's variable A value range	Group size: Total	Group 1	Group 2	Asymptotic, two-sided P-value	Asymptotic, one-sided P-value	Mean rank: Group 1	Group 2	Z value	Mann Whitney U	Wilcoxon W
17a	Y	Repeat buyer as opposed to non-repeat user	+	Importance of previous execution as signal vehicle	o	Repeat buyer	Switcher or first time buyer	79	42	37	(0.000)	0.000	53.79	24.35	-5.788	198.0	901.0
17b	Y	Repeat buyer as opposed to switcher	+	Importance of previous execution as signal vehicle	o	Repeat buyer	Switcher	70	42	28	(0.000)	0.000	45.65	20.27	-5.180	161.5	567.5
19a	Y	Repeat buyer as opposed to non-repeat user	+	Importance of investment banking relationship as signal vehicle	o	Repeat buyer	Switcher or first time buyer	80	43	37	(0.000)	0.000	48.79	30.86	-3.428	439.0	1,142.0
19b	Y	Repeat buyer as opposed to switcher	+	Importance of investment banking relationship as signal vehicle	o	Repeat buyer	Switcher	71	43	28	(0.000)	0.000	42.97	25.30	-3.570	302.5	708.5

* + = increases, - = decreases, o = has not effect on

** Y = yes (in accordance with research hypothesis), (Y) = yes (not in accordance with research hypothesis), N = no (in accordance with research hypothesis), (N) = no (not in accordance with research hypothesis)

Table 10.4: Importance of signal vehicles for repeat buyers

only a less important role in relative terms to other signal vehicles, but not in absolute terms. One interpretation of this observation is that the sales presentation/discussion might represent a "hygiene factor", that is a signal vehicle that mainly holds downside potential for the bank, in the sense that disappointing potential buyers with it yields loss of mandate, while giving a convincing sales presentation is by far no sufficient to obtain the mandate.

Vice versa, sales presentation/discussion is no more important for switchers than for repeat users. This can be seen to substantiate the low reliability that sales presentation offers for the assessment of the quality of the M&A advice for sale, by being focused on transmitting potential and process type information, and due to its low task programmability.

10.2.3 Signal vehicles' "natural owner"

Hypotheses I10 to I15[30] address the individual-corporation antagonism, in that they make propositions which of the signal vehicles are banker- rather than bank-owned. Their verification shall be accomplished by pinpointing in how far the importance between signal vehicles shifts, dependent on whether the banker or the bank is being considered more important for the M&A advisor choice.

As table 10.5 indicates, all test results but two support the theory-based propositions. Let us briefly revisit these findings.

- **Hypothesis I10.** As to the proposition that importance of reputation increases when the choice is based on the bank rather than the banker, the significance of the test result is only moderate[31]. This is not so surprising when one takes into

30 Proposed in paragraph 8.2.3.

31 The inversion of the relationship claimed by hypothesis I10 holds as well, but is of lower significance. I. e., if reputation is among the most important signal vehicles, then bank as opposed to banker importance increases (an explanation for the comparatively high P-value may lie in the rationale that when renowned banks do keep their implicit promise to deliver better products – which, due to product class characteristics, means they must have the better-suited people –, then the effect of the relationship claimed by the hypothesis is partially set off). Hypothesis I14 already represents the inversion

Hypothesis	Null-hypothesis rejected?**	Research hypothesis: Variable A	hypothesised effect* →	Variable B	Null hypoth.	Groups to be tested against each other: Group 1's variable A value range	Group 2's variable A value range	Group size: Total	Group 1	Group 2	Asymptotic, two-sided P-value	Asymptotic, one-sided P-value	Mean rank: Group 1	Group 2	Z value	Mann Whitney U	Wilcoxon W
I10	(N)	Choice based on bank rather than banker	+	Importance of reputation as signal vehicle	o	Companies for which banker was more important than bank for choice (1-4)	Companies for which banker was less important than bank for choice (6-9)	**57**	25	32	**(0.169)**	**0.085**	25.72	31.56	-1.376	318.0	643.0
I11	Y	Choice based on bank rather than banker	+	Importance of commercial banking relationship as signal vehicle	o			**57**	25	32	**(0.029)**	**0.015**	23.70	33.14	-2.180	267.5	592.5
I12	Y	Choice based on banker rather than bank	+	Importance of previous execution as signal vehicle	o			**57**	25	32	**(0.047)**	**0.024**	33.88	25.19	-1.989	278.0	806.0
I13	Y	Major bracket customers: Choice based on banker rather than bank	++ ↑	Importance of previous execution as signal vehicle	o			**31**	16	15	**(0.066***)**	**0.033*** **	18.94	12.87	(-1.885)	73.0	193.0
	N	Bulge bracket customers: Choice based on banker rather than bank	lower than	Importance of previous execution as signal vehicle	o			**18**	7	11	**(0.479***)**	**0.240*** **	10.64	8.77	(-0.735)	30.5	96.5
I14	(N)	Previous execution among most important signal vehicles	+	Importance of banker as opposed to bank	o	Previous execution not considered most important	Previous execution among most important signal vehicles	**74**	52	22	**(0.140)**	**0.070**	41.58	33.64	-1.475	516.0	841.0
I15	Y	Major bracket customers: Previous execution among most important signal vehicles	++ ↑	Importance of banker as opposed to bank	o			**40**	26	14	**(0.076)**	**0.038**	13.78	12.88	(-1.788)	119.5	224.5
	N	Bulge bracket customers: Previous execution among most important signal vehicles	lower than	Importance of banker as opposed to bank	o			**26**	18	8	**(0.807***)**	**0.404*** **	13.78	12.88	(-0.283)	67.0	103.0

*** + = increases, - = decreases, o = has not effect on**

**** Y = yes (in accordance with research hypothesis), (Y) = yes (not in accordance with research hypothesis), N = no (in accordance with research hypothesis), (N) = no (not in accordance with research hypothesis)**

***** Exact P-value (2-sided: 2 x (1-sided P-value); 1-sided: 1 x (1-sided P-value))**

Table 10.5: Importance of signal vehicles by banker as opposed to bank choice

account that uncertainty decrease considerations may only constitute one of several perspectives to sufficiently assess the roles that reputation might play

- **Hypothesis I11.** As proposed, commercial banking relationship has more to do with the bank than with individual bankers

- **Hypothesis I12.** If choice is based on the banker, rather than the bank, then previous execution is of incrementally higher importance. An interpretation of this relationship is that good experience with bankers during previous deals renders their capabilities to advise on the project in question more credible. Thus, previous experience offers reassurance on a specific banker's capabilities

- **Hypothesis I13.** Test results on hypothesis I13 show that, when the M&A advisor choice is based on the banker rather than the bank, then the increase in perceived importance of previous execution is higher when a major bracket bank is being chosen, than when the most renowned banks are being chosen. In fact, in the latter case, the increase in importance of previous execution is insignificant. An interpretation of this finding is that reputation offers reassurance, that is, bankers working for the most renowned banks do not have to give proof of their capabilities as much as those working for less renowned banks

- **Hypothesis I14.** Test results of hypothesis I14 indicate that the relative importance of the banker, as opposed to the bank, increases when previous execution is considered among the most important signal vehicles. The P-value of the test results falls somewhat above the 5% significance level for the overall market. An interpretation of the relationship proposed by the hypothesis is that utility of experience type information increases when it refers to a specific individual, rather than the bank corporation – which is plausible due to M&A advisory's low task programmability and high degree of non-automation

of hypothesis I12. Only commercial banking relationship as most important signal vehicle has no impact on increase in bank as opposed to banker importance, but this can be explained by the small number base (only 8 companies considered commercial bank relationship among their top choice criteria).

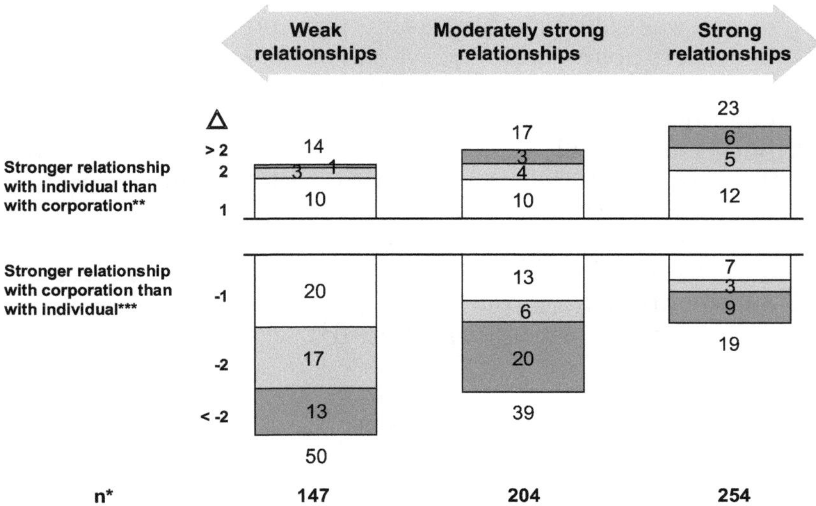

* weak: relationships where the maximum of banker and bank relationship activity/intensity was perceived to be between 1 and 3 on a 1-9 scale. Moderate: relationships where the maximum of banker and bank relationship activity/intensity was perceived to be between 4 and 6 on a 1-9 scale. Strong: relationships where the maximum of banker and bank relationship activity/intensity was perceived to be between 7 and 9 on a 1-9 scale

** difference between banker and bank relationship strength (assessed on 1-9 scale) positive, i.e. 1, 2, or >2

*** difference between banker and bank relationship strength (assessed on 1-9 scale) negative, i.e. -1, -2, or <-2

Figure 10.6: Role of individuals in relationships
(Percent of relationship bucket; extended sample)

- **Hypothesis I15.** Significance targets are met when the relationship proposed by hypothesis I14 is tested for major bracket customers only. Here, the importance of the banker as opposed to the bank increases significantly, when choice is based on previous execution. Similarly to hypothesis I12, the relationship suggested by hypothesis I14 is insignificant for bulge bracket customers. An interpretation of these findings is that experience type's utility increases when IQV is decreased. This can, on the one hand, be achieved by re-engaging the same banker, since intra-person quality variability is lower than inter-person quality variability, and people constitute the most important production factor in M&A advisory[32]; in section 5.2.1, such

32 This relationship is represented by the major bracket customer sub-sample.

device was called an "intrinsic utility increaser"[33]. But if the buyer sees no reason to believe that different individuals within a bank corporation are differently apt to perform the service in question, then such device is redundant. The banks for which buyers may hold such belief are the most renowned banks. That is, reputation may substitute the missing a priori rationale of a high degree of homogeneity in production factors, and thus render experience type information equally helpful for uncertainty decrease, independent of whether the individual in question to perform the service differs from the one which experience type information refers to[34].

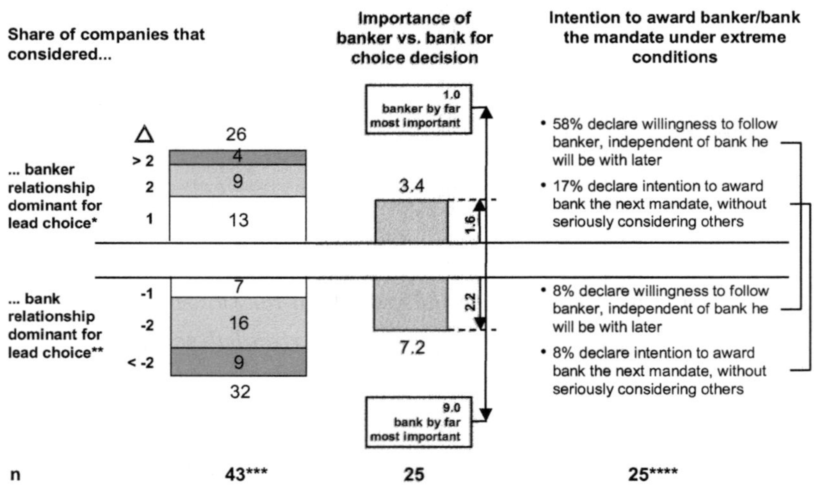

* difference between perceived importance of banker and bank relationship (on 1-9 scale) is positive, i.e. 1, 2, or >2
** difference between perceived importance of banker and bank relationship (on 1-9 scale) is negative, i.e. -1, -2, or <-2
*** of which 18 state equal importance
**** small number basis. Difference regarding willingness to follow banker is significant (P = .015), difference regarding straight re-engagement intention of bank is not

Figure 10.7: Role of individuals and implied loyalty transfer *(Respondents that considered investment banking relationship among most important choice criteria; core sample)*

33 See page 92.
34 This relationship is represented by the bulge bracket customer sub-sample.

Analogous hypotheses have not been formulated for the investment banking relationship, since this represents more difficult of a matter in the following sense. Investment banking relationships are clearly fostered by the bank corporation's individuals, who might also be the ones in question to advise on the project. If companies feel attached to an individual banker, this may transfer into an attachment to the bank corporation[35]. Vice versa, maintaining an active relationship with a specific investment bank means maintaining an active relationship with one or several of its banker individuals.

As illustrates figure 10.6 on page 209, looking at investment banking relationships from a "life cycle" perspective, one finds that the relative importance of the role of the individuals, as opposed to the corporation, increases with the intensity of the relationship. That is, investment banking relationships "need some face" to become active and intense.

Finally, if the banker relationship is perceived to be more important as a choice criterion than the bank relationship, the share of companies that would follow the banker no matter what, increases significantly. But on the other hand, active individual relationships do also foster a company's willingness to re-engage the bank. These findings are illustrated by figure 10.7 on page 210, and are consistent with with relationships claimed by hypotheses I21 to I23, which paragraph 10.2.5 shall deal with.

10.2.4 Signal vehicles' utility for uncertainty decrease

Next, let us revisit hypotheses I16 to I18[36], which make propositions on different signal vehicles' effectiveness regarding uncertainty decrease.

Table 10.6 on page 212 contains the results of the MWW. As can be seen, all relationships are in the hypothesised directions. To summarise, if M&A advisor choice is based on the banker rather than the bank, then the uncertainty component of the risk associated with

35 This is why respondents were asked to give an assessment of both, the investment relationship with the bank, as well as the relationship with the key banker.

36 Derived in paragraph 8.2.4.

Hypothesis	Null-hypothesis rejected?**	Research hypothesis			Null hypoth.	Groups to be tested against each other		Group size			Asymp-totic, two-sided P-value	Asymp-totic, one-sided P-value	Mean rank		Z value	Mann Whitney U	Wilcoxon W
		Variable A	hypothe-sised effect* →	Variable B		Group 1's variable A value range	Group 2's variable A value range	Total	Group 1	Group 2			Group 1	Group 2			
I16	Y	Choice based on banker rather than bank	-	Difficulty of assessing investment banking capabilitites (after solicitation events)	o	Companies for which banker was more important than bank for choice (1-4)	Companies for which banker was less important than bank for choice (6-9)	**58**	25	33	**(0.000)**	**0.000**	18.96	35.00	-3.762	155.0	455.0
I17	Y	Investment banking relationship with banker among most important signal vehicles	-	Difficulty of assessing investment banking capabilitites (after solicitation events)	o	Investment banking relationship with banker not considered most important	Investment banking relationship with banker considered most important	**77**	50	27	**(0.020)**	**0.010**	43.27	31.09	-2.320	461.5	839.5
I18	Y	Previous execution among most important signal vehicles	-	Difficulty of assessing investment banking capabilitites (after solicitation events)	o	Previous execution not considered most important	Previous execution considered most important	**77**	51	26	**(0.063)**	**0.032**	42.32	32.48	-1.858	493.5	844.5

*** + = increases, - = decreases, o = has not effect on**

**** Y = yes (in accordance with research hypothesis), (Y) = yes (not in accordance with research hypothesis), N = no (in accordance with research hypothesis), (N) = no (not in accordance with research hypothesis)**

Table 10.6: Signal vehicles' effectiveness for uncertainty decrease

the advisor choice decreases. Similarly, if investment banking relationship with the banker or previous execution are considered among the most important signal vehicles, uncertainty decreases.

Other signal vehicles (reputation, investment banking relationship with the bank, sales presentation, commercial banking relationship) offering less reliable links to product quality compared to these signal vehicles (previous execution, investment banking relationship with the banker), the former's inferior aptitude to decrease uncertainty may get overlaid by the latter's superior aptitude, in case they are simultaneously considered most important[37]. Indeed, complementary test findings substantiate this suspicion.

An exception provides reputation, which is tested to have a positive relationship with the difficulty of capability assessment[38]. Contrary to "superior" signal vehicles' importance, the importance of "inferior" signal vehicles might constitute an effect, rather than, or in addition to, a cause for increased uncertainty. If increased importance of reputation is an effect, rather than a cause for uncertainty, this means reputation represents a "fall-back" rather than an "actively preferred" signal vehicle. Such proposition is consistent with the findings of paragraph 10.1.2[39].

10.2.5 Satisfaction with execution and re-engagement intention

Next, hypotheses I19 to I50[40] shall be revisited, which propose relationships between the importance of the vehicles for the advisor choice and subsequent satisfaction with the bank's execution.

37 That is, the test method employed is not suitable to assess signal vehicles' inferior aptitude to decrease uncertainty. For that reason, no according hypotheses for reputation, investment banking relationship with the bank, sales presentation, and commercial banking relationship have been formulated.

38 The one-sided P-value for difficulty of capability assessment after solicitation is .015. That is, if reputation is considered among the most important signal vehicles, then uncertainty decrease is comparatively low.

39 In particular hypothesis R15. An incrementally stronger significance of the relationship between importance of reputation and difficulty of capability assessment *after* solicitation (P-value is .015), as opposed to *before* solicitation (P-value is .050), supports such argumentation.

40 Derived in paragraph 8.2.5.

Table 10.7 on page 215 displays the MWW test results for the hypotheses.

- **Hypothesis I19.** As proposed, increased satisfaction with execution yielded significantly higher re-engagement intention
- **Hypotheses I20 to I23.** If the M&A advisor choice had been based on the individual rather than on the corporation, subsequent satisfaction with the advice delivered was significantly higher. As a secondary implication, re-engagement intention of bank and banker were also significantly higher in these cases. A drawback, from a bank's perspective, provides the finding that in these cases, banker as opposed to bank loyalty did also sharply increase

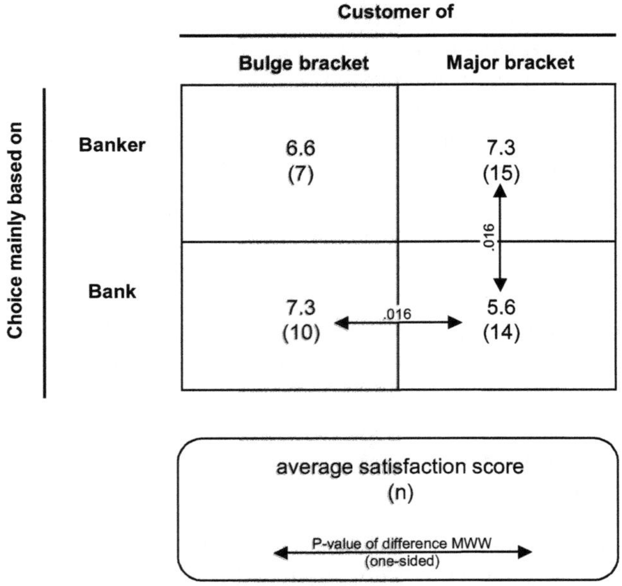

Figure 10.8: Customer satisfaction by choice and bank type
(Average satisfaction score of group; core sample)

Hypothesis	Null-hypoth. rejected?**	Research hypothesis: Variable A	hypothesised effect*	Variable B	Null hypoth.	Groups to be tested against each other: Group 1's variable A value range	Group 2's variable A value range	Group size: Total	Group 1	Group 2	Asymptotic, two-sided P-value	Asymptotic, one-sided P-value	Mean rank: Group 1	Group 2	Z value	Mann Whitney U	Wilcoxon W
I19	Y	Satisfaction with bank's execution	+	Re-engagement intention of bank	o	Rather low satisfaction (1-6)	High satisfaction (7-9)	**80**	28	52	**(0.000)**	**0.000**	22.05	50.43	-5.305	211.5	617.5
	Y				o	Low or moderate satisfaction (1-7)	Extreme satisfaction (8,9)	**80**	52	28	**(0.000)**	**0.000**	32.87	54.68	-4.078	331.0	1,709.0
I20	Y	Choice based on banker rather than bank	+	Satisfaction with execution	o			**58**	25	33	**(0.096)**	**0.048**	33.62	26.38	-1.667	309.5	870.5
I21	Y	Choice based on banker rather than bank	+	Re-engagement intention banker	o	Companies for which banker was more important than bank for choice (1-4)	Companies for which banker was less important than bank for choice (6-9)	**55**	23	32	**(0.001)**	**0.000**	36.13	22.16	-3.245	181.0	709.0
I22	Y	Choice based on banker rather than bank	+	Re-engagement intention bank	o			**58**	25	33	**(0.019)**	**0.010**	34.72	24.53	-2.342	257.0	785.0
I23	Y	Choice based on banker rather than bank	+	Willingness to follow the banker to a new bank if he leaves the bank he currently works for	o			**57**	25	32	**(0.000)**	**0.000**	35.54	23.89	-3.723	236.5	764.5
I24	Y	Major bracket customers: Banker as opposed to bank choice	++	Satisfaction with execution	o	Major bracket customers for who banker was more important than bank (1-4)	Major bracket customers for who banker was less important than bank (1-4)	**32**	16	16	**(0.015***)**	**0.008*** **	20.47	12.53	(-2.456)	64.5	200.5
	(N)	Major bracket customers: Banker as opposed to bank choice	↑ lower than	Satisfaction with execution	o	Bulge bracket customers for who banker was more important than bank (1-4)	Bulge bracket customers for who banker was less important than bank (1-4)	**18**	7	11	**(0.246****)**	**0.123******	7.64	10.68	(-1.238)	25.5	53.5
I25	Y	Investment banking relationship with banker among most important signal vehicles	+	Satisfaction with execution	o	Investment banking relationship with banker not considered most important	Investment banking relationship with banker considered most important	**81**	51	30	**(0.100)**	**0.050**	37.80	46.43	-1.643	602.0	1,928.0
I26	Y	Previous execution among most important signal vehicles	+	Satisfaction with execution	o	Previous execution not considered most important	Previous execution considered most important	**81**	54	27	**(0.030)**	**0.015**	37.12	48.76	-2.164	519.5	2,004.5

* + = increases, - = decreases, o = has not effect on

** Y = yes (in accordance with research hypothesis), (Y) = yes (not in accordance with research hypothesis), N = no (in accordance with research hypothesis), (N) = no (not in accordance with research hypothesis)

*** Exact P-value (2-sided: 2 x (1-sided P-value); 1-sided: 1 x (1-sided P-value))

**** Exact P-value (2-sided: 2 x (1-sided P-value); 1-sided: 1 x (1-sided P-value)). Mean ranks show even order inverse to hypothesis' claim

Table 10.7: Satisfaction with the bank by signal vehicle importance

- **Hypothesis I24.** Interestingly, the increase for satisfaction with the execution when the choice is based on the banker rather than the bank is significantly higher for major than for bulge bracket banks[41]. More specifically, and as illustrated by figure 10.8, difference in satisfaction with banker mandates' execution is non-significant between bulge and major bracket[42], while bulge bracket banks score significantly better in bank mandates (7.3 vs. 5.6; P-value: .008). These results may be interpreted in the way that highly renowned banks keep their implicit promise[43] to deliver superior quality, while for less renowned bank, "cherry picking" individual bankers seems to pay off. Further, figure 10.9 shows that, while universal banks had the "institutional power" to attract customers, they were not viewed to deliver as good a service quality as bulge bracket banks. Conversely, many of the remaining major bracket banks seem to have lacked the power to attract by corporate means; respondents frequently felt relatively more attracted by the individual as opposed to the bank corporation. On the other hand, these banks were viewed to deliver a high service quality

- **Hypotheses I49, I50.** Test results here were analogous to the ones of hypothesis I20. That is, when the incrementally more "individual-owned" signal vehicles had been among the most important selection criteria, this yielded higher subsequent satisfaction rates[44].

One could now feel tempted to argue that all these findings are no surprising from a dissonance reduction perspective. That is, companies sanction or dissociate themselves from their choice by indicating they felt it was easy or difficult to assess different banks' capabilities. But perceived ease of capability assessment after solicitation showed, on an aggregate level, no significant directed relationship with subsequent satisfaction with the bank's execution[45]. This finding can

41 In fact, for bulge bracket banks, satisfaction with execution is somewhat lower when the bank was based on the banker, rather than the bank.

42 6.6 vs. 7.3 on average.

43 Provided by their reputation.

44 A further investigation shows that the importance of investment banking relationship with the banker and previous execution are somewhat, though not strongly positively correlated.

45 Based on a (1–4) vs. (5–9) cut of difficulty of capability assessment, the increase of satisfaction with subsequent execution is strongly insignificant.

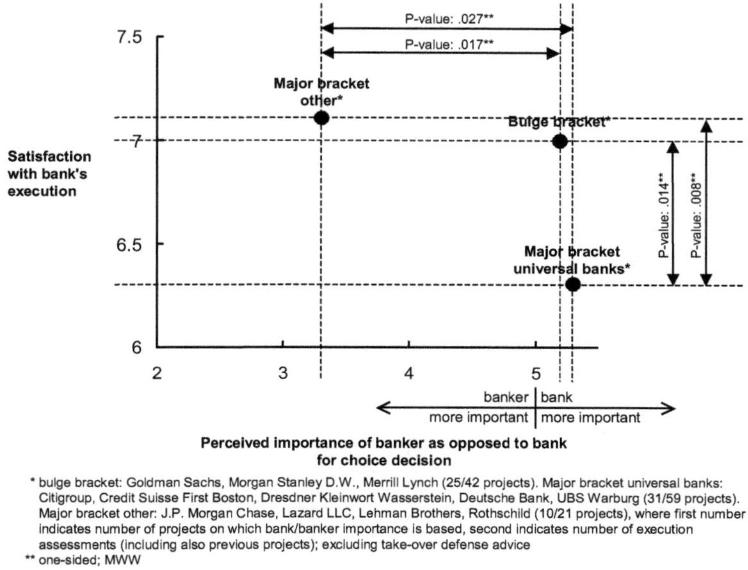

Figure 10.9: Customer satisfaction by choice and bank subtype
(Average satisfaction score of subgroup; core sample)

be seen to give indication that dissonance reduction processes played only a minor role in responses[46].

The group of companies who felt that the difficulty of capability assessment was low (1–4) had a mean satisfaction rank of 40.04 in the MWW, while the group of companies that found it difficult to assess the banks' capabilities (5–9) had a mean satisfaction rank of 43.14 (thus subsequent satisfaction scores were even in reverse order).

46 Again, reputation, investment banking relationship (bank), sales presentation/discussion, and commercial bank relationship cannot be expected to have any impact of significant difference on satisfaction, the rationale being that these vehicles might be dominated by other vehicles considered equally important. Indeed, the differences in satisfaction are not significant for reputation, investment banking relationship (bank), and sales presentation. In cases where commercial banking relationship was considered the most important signal vehicle, a negative impact on subsequent satisfaction with the execution was found (with a one-sided P-value of .028).

Hypothesis	Null-hypothesis rejected?**	Research hypothesis			Null hypoth.	Groups to be tested against each other		Group size			Asymp-totic, two-sided P-value	Asymp-totic, one-sided P-value	Mean rank		Z value	Mann Whitney U	Wilcoxon W
		Variable A	hypothe-sised effect* →	Variable B		Group 1's variable A value range	Group 2's variable A value range	Total	Group 1	Group 2			Group 1	Group 2			
I27	Y	Employment of competitive solicitation process	+	Importance of sales presentation	o	companies employing non-compet. selection	companies employing competitve selection	79	32	47	(0.000)	0.000	28.43	50.57	-4.272	365.0	995.0
I28	Y		+	Importance of commercial banking relationship	o			80	33	47	(0.004)	0.002	30.58	45.38	-2.891	452.0	948.0
I29	Y		-	Importance of investment banking relationship with bank	o			79	32	47	(0.073)	0.037	46.00	36.64	-1.796	594.0	1,722.0
I30	(N)		-	Importance of investment banking relationship with banker	o			81	35	46	(0.121)	0.060	44.80	36.73	-1.551	598.5	1,726.5
I31	(N)		-	Importance of previous execution	o			78	31	47	(0.293)	0.147	43.23	37.80	-1.052	648.5	1,776.5

* + = increases, - = decreases, o = has not effect on

** Y = yes (in accordance with research hypothesis), (Y) = yes (not in accordance with research hypothesis), N = no (in accordance with research hypothesis), (N) = no (not in accordance with research hypothesis)

Table 10.8: Signal vehicles' importance by selection type

10.2.6 Importance of signal vehicles by type of selection procedure

A company might use competitive or non-competitive selection procedures when choosing its M&A advisor. Hypotheses I51 to I55[47] make propositions what signal vehicles come into force in competitive as opposed to non-competitive selection processes.

Table 10.8 on page 218 shows the MWW test results. Most of the hypotheses are supported.

- **Hypothesis I54.** As to the proposition that investment banking relationship with the banker plays a significantly more important role in non-competitive, as opposed to competitive selection processes, significance levels of the test are close to being satisfactory. The dichotomous role that individuals play in business relationships might provide an explanation for these somewhat ambiguous test results[48]
- **Hypothesis I55.** As to the propositions that previous execution plays a significantly more important role in non-competitive, as opposed to competitive selection processes, the *P*-value is insufficient to reject the null hypothesis. This means that, albeit applying competitive selection procedures, companies might, eventually, strongly rely on the experience they have made with specific banks during previous projects when making their M&A advisor choice. Previous execution's importance is thus more strongly determined by the question whether a lead advisor is chosen for first or repeat time, than by the criterion whether the selection process applied is competitive or not[49].

---

47 Proposed in paragraph 8.2.6.

48 Cf. paragraph 10.2.3 on page 211.

49 In fact, the "competitive vs. non-competitive selection dimension" is pretty independent from the "repeat user vs. switcher dimension", i. e., you cannot say that M&A advisors are predominantly chosen through competitive selection processes for first time, or that non-competitive processes are predominantly applied in the case of repeat buy. In the research sample, 57% of first time buyers, 61% of switchers, and 53% of repeat buyers applied competitive selection processes.

11 Complementary and deepening analyses

By containing descriptive analyses, this chapter is meant to provide an embedment for the hypothesis-based research of the previous sections. The results given in it may not be fully representative for the market, due to relatively small sample size and partial bias[1]. Still, they may help a better understanding of the concepts discussed, by showing what average perception, common practice, and actual behaviour are like in the M&A advisory market, and by putting hypothesis-driven results into a practical perspective.

11.1 Convictions and perceptions

From a practical standpoint, it is no sufficient to know that certain concepts impact risk perception, but it is also important to know in how far risk, choice importance, etc., are actually perceived to be high. The analyses included in this section shall provide evidence that the concepts that have been discussed in previous parts of the thesis are of a broad practical relevance.

11.1.1 Investment banking experience

As depicted by figure 11.1, the self-perceived investment banking experience of the core sample is rather high: only one fifth of respondents considered themselves rather unexperienced[2].

Against the background of the argument that a huge number of first time users is entering the M&A market in any new M&A wave, this finding is somewhat surprising. But the respondent sam-

1 See paragraph 9.1.2.

2 Of the seven companies in the sample for who the M&A project assessed constituted their first M&A project, some had apparently already dealt with other investment banking businesses, such as IPO.

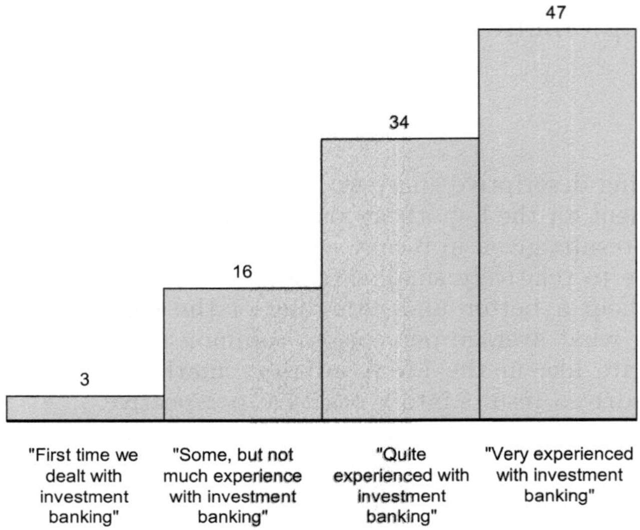

Figure 11.1: Self-perceived investment banking experience
(On a 1–4 scale; percent of core sample)

ple being biassed towards bigger companies and bidders, it may be reconciled with the argumentation on page 23.

11.1.2 Importance of investment bank's role in M&A

Next, let us take a closer look at the perceived importance of the investment bank's role in the M&A project.

Figure 11.2 shows that three quarters of respondents considered the importance of the investment bank's role significant. This can be considered indicative for the proposition that the consequence component of risk associated with choosing an M&A advisor is largely linked to the risk associated with the underlying M&A transaction[3].

3 Cf. paragraph 4.1.4, and hypotheses R1 to R5.

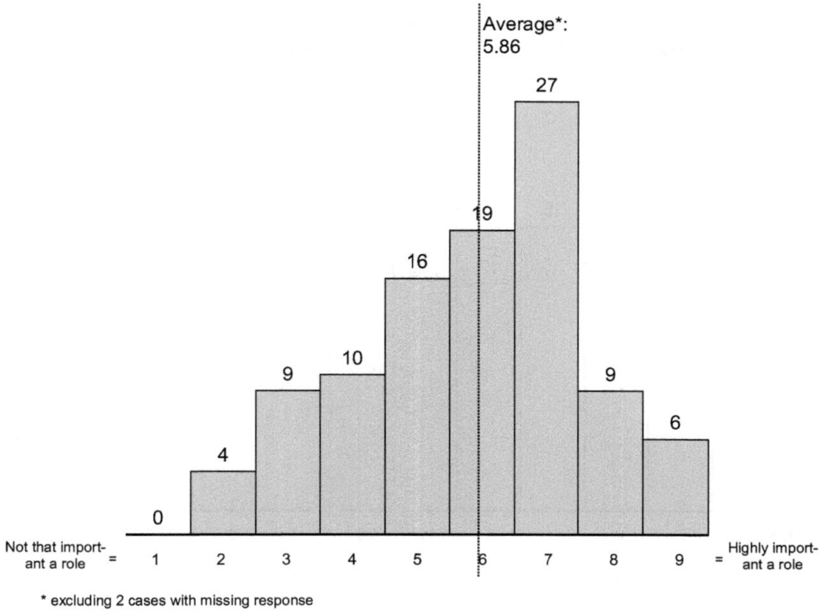

Figure 11.2: Perceived importance of lead bank's role
(On a 1–9 scale; percent of core sample)

11.1.3 Risk associated with the M&A project

The research conducted restricts itself to the upper M&A market in terms of transaction volumes in question. Therefore, perceived risk associated with such M&A transactions should be significant.

As illustrated by figure 11.3 on page 224, three fifths of respondents did indeed find that their company's risk associated with the M&A project in question was high[4].

4 5 or higher on a 1–9 scale.

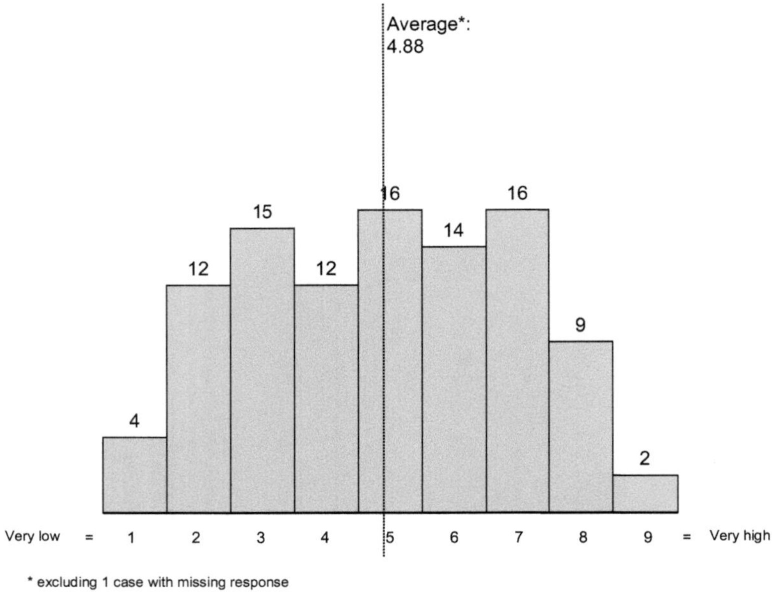

Figure 11.3: Perceived risk associated with the M&A project
(On a 1–9 scale; percent of core sample)

11.1.4 Consequence component of risk associated with the bank selection

As shows figure 11.4, consequence component of risk associated with choosing an M&A advisor, operationalised as the importance of M&A advisor choice for the company's future welfare[5], was perceived to be somewhat lower. While the underlying M&A transaction represents the sole purpose of engaging an M&A advisor, its success also depends significantly on the company itself, as well as its potential transaction counterpart(s). Thus, a somewhat lower level of choice importance, as opposed to risk associated with the M&A transaction, is plausible.

5 Cf. paragraph 9.2.2.

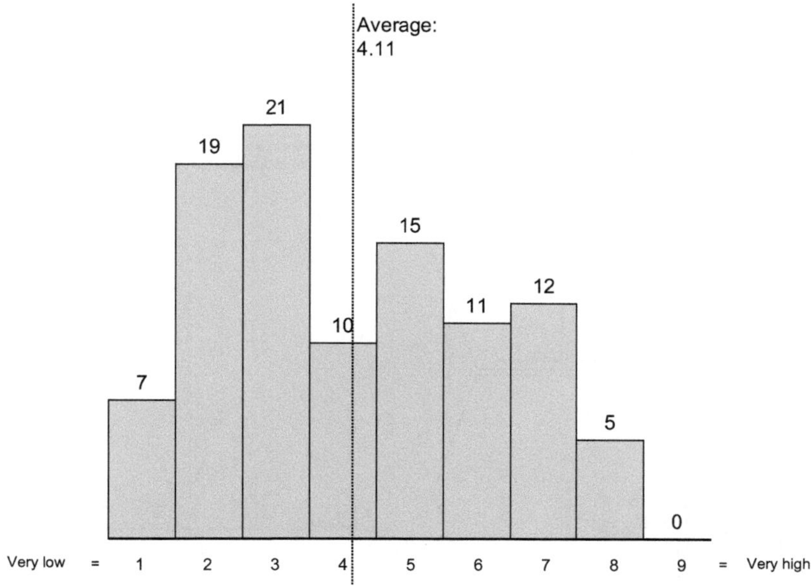

Figure 11.4: Perceived importance of M&A advisor choice
(On a 1–9 scale; percent of core sample)

Two fifths of respondents perceived M&A advisor choice to have high impact on their company's future welfare[6]. Since, from a company perspective, there is no higher level of concern than the company's future welfare, perceived consequence component of risk associated with choosing an M&A advisor can be considered high.

11.1.5 Uncertainty component of risk associated with the bank selection

Uncertainty component of risk has been operationalised as the perceived difficulty to assess different banks' M&A advice capabilities[7].

6 5 or higher on a 1–9 scale.

7 Cf. paragraph 9.2.2.

Thus, the employed operationalisation reflects handled, rather than inherent risk[8].

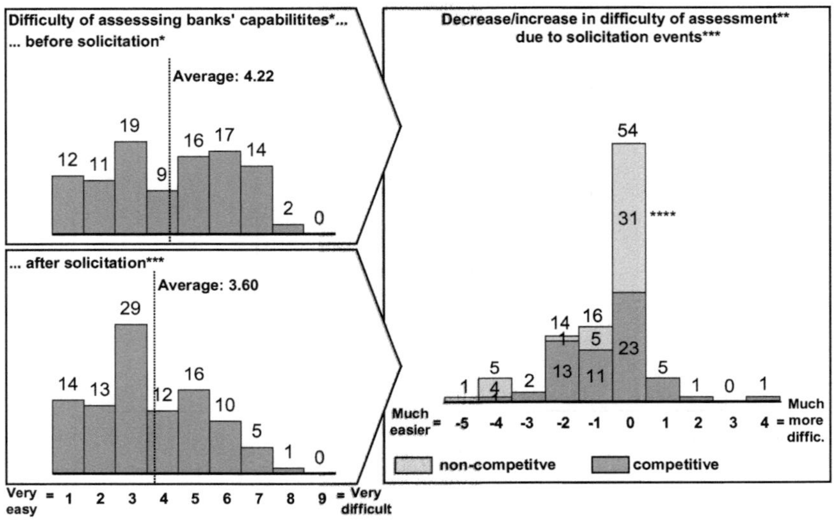

* includes all companies (i.e., also companies that did not employ solicitation events)
** zero for 24 of the 33 companies that did not employ competitive solicitation (corresponding to 31 % of total)
*** excluding 5 cases with missing response
**** of which 22 without sales presentation

Figure 11.5: Perceived difficulty of capability assessment
(On a 1–9 scale; percent of core sample)

Thereby, the difficulty of assessing the banks' capabilities before solicitation has been differentiated from the one after solicitation[9]. This was done in order to be able to evaluate solicitation events' power to decrease uncertainty[10]. As shows figure 11.5, the majority of respondents found it rather easy to assess different banks' capa-

8 Cf. paragraph 4.2.4.

9 For companies that did not employ competitive solicitation, the difficulty of capability assessment after solicitation has been set equal to the one before solicitation.

10 Cf. hypotheses R12, I3, and I4.

bilities, at least after solicitation[11]. But it should also be noted that, on the other hand, one third of respondents still found this task difficult, even after solicitation[12].

Taking into account that the respondent sample is biassed towards bigger, more experienced companies, and that it was found that experience is likely to impact handled uncertainty[13], the market's share of companies that find it difficult to assess different banks' capabilities can be expected to be even higher.

The results depicted in this and the previous paragraphs of this section give indication that perceived risk associated with choosing an M&A advisor is high, compared to a company's other purchase and decision tasks.

11.1.6 Banker-bank importance

Last but not least, let us deal with the banker-bank antagonism. The individual-corporation antagonism has been discussed a lot in service literature[14]. In particular, the issue has recently been raised in the context of M&A advisory[15], and the observation that many a universal bank has tried to obtain investment banking business by hiring the most renowned individuals and teams from renowned players, only highlights the importance that also practitioners attribute to the issue[16]. Paragraphs 10.2.3 to 10.2.5[17] have already dealt with this antagonism, and have found evidence that banker as opposed to bank choice may, from a customer's perspective, constitute a viable risk decrease strategy, at least, and most prominently, for major bracket banks.

The insights developed in paragraphs 10.2.3 to 10.2.5 may be complemented by the depiction of whether banker selection – as op-

11 Scores of 1 to 3 on a 1–9 scale.

12 Scores of 5 or more on a 1–9 scale.

13 Cf. hypothesis R11.

14 See for instance Lovelock[160], page 70.

15 See Brown[44].

16 *Lechler* emphasises the importance of individual performance for any type of business project, see Lechler[153].

17 Cf. in particular hypotheses I16 and I20.

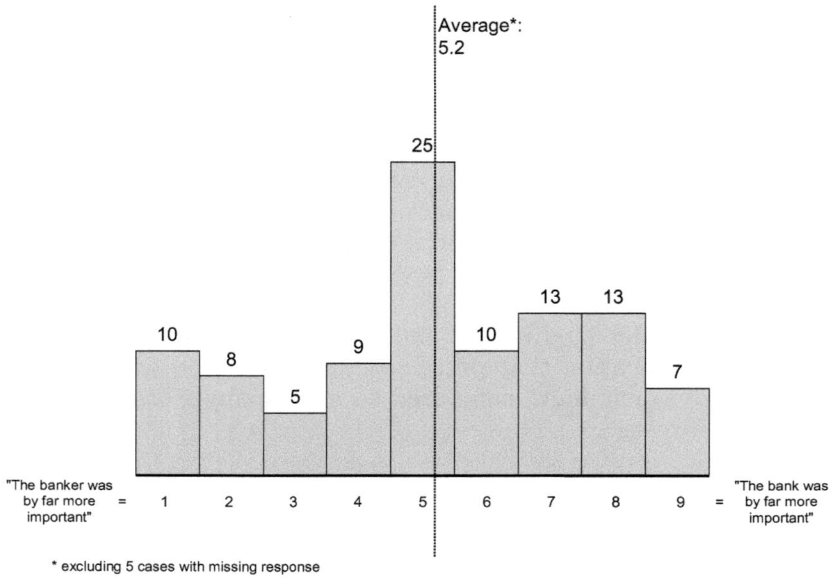

Figure 11.6: Perceived importance of banker vs. bank
(On a 1–9 scale; percent of core sample)

posed to bank selection – was more of a common, or more of a rare strategy taken by survey participants.

With this respect, figure 11.6 shows a pretty balanced picture of implemented choice strategies. While one fourth of respondents considered corporation and individual of similar importance for their choice decision, somewhat more than half of the remainder felt their decision was determined by the bank rather than the banker, whereas the remaining third of respondents felt the opposite way.

11.1.7 Summary

To summarise this section's findings, it was found that perceived risk and advisor choice are matters that customers care about in the context of M&A. Thus, a risk-information perspective to analyse the marketing of M&A advisory is justified.

The individual-corporation antagonism is an issue of further interest in the research of M&A advisory marketing. One third of buyers basing their bank choice on individuals rather than corporations, banks should consciously think about how to cope with this issue[18].

11.2 Actual behaviour and implementation

This section aims at depicting the market's application of certain selection types, and the quantity structures behind them. Again, this section's goal is to complement causative insights, given in the previous chapter, by evidence on actual incidence, in order to substantiate the practical implications of the concepts discussed.

11.2.1 Incidence of selection types in market

Let us first take a closer look at the frequency by which certain selection types are being employed in the market.

As shows figure 11.7, about 60 percent of respondents employed competitive solicitation procedures. One in two of these companies employed formal beauty contests, while the other half settled for discussion with banks it considered apt to advise on the transaction in question. Among the non-competitive selection procedures, the exclusive contacting of one of the relationship banks proved most popular, confirming the importance of relationships in non-competitive selection[19]. Only five percent of the M&A projects assessed were initiated by the advising banks[20].

18 Paragraph 12.2.5 shall expand on this topic.

19 Cf. hypotheses I53 and I54.

20 Comparing this result with literature, cf. figure 3.2 on page 40, this is surprisingly low. Apart from sample bias, this difference could be attributed to an interim market development. This is to say that most (Anglo-American) investment banks nowadays may have a well-developed European relationship

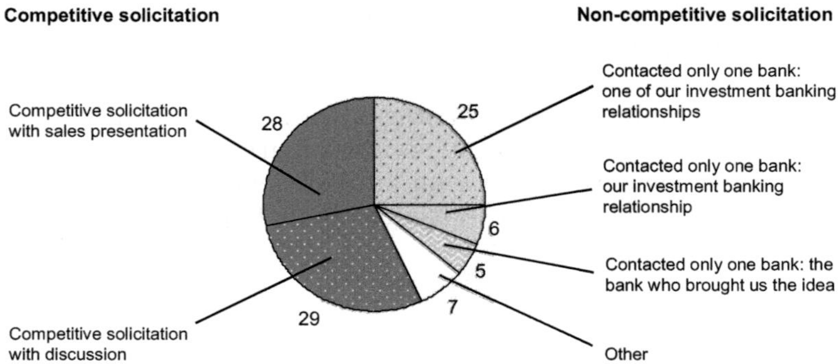

Figure 11.7: Incidence of selection procedures
(Percent of core sample)

Competitive and non-competitive selection processes having similar incidence in the market, this means the passing of either type of selection procedure constitutes an important prerequisite for a bank's overall market success. Average transaction volume, based on a size bucket proxy calculation, amounted to Euro 1.87 bn for competitive, and Euro 3.38 bn for non-competitive selection procedures[21].

11.2.2 Quantity structure of the purchase funnel

Dependent on whether a company is going to employ competitive or a non-competitive selection, what is the quantity structure along the purchase funnel[22]? – The answer to this question is useful for an

base, and that this increased local presence may have fostered a predominance of the reactive solicitation type.

21 That is, major parts of the transaction volume were awarded directly to banks, without competitive solicitation. Our data indicate that the vast majority companies that were involved in high volume transactions and whose M&A advisory mandates were not solicited competitively, chose banks they had already used before. This substantiates the importance that experience type information (previous execution) plays in M&A advisor selection, provided it is available.

22 Cf. paragraph 3.2.3, in particular figure 3.4 on page 44.

M&A advisor's cost-benefit considerations, such as whether to invest forces into sales presentations, or relationship enhancement[23].

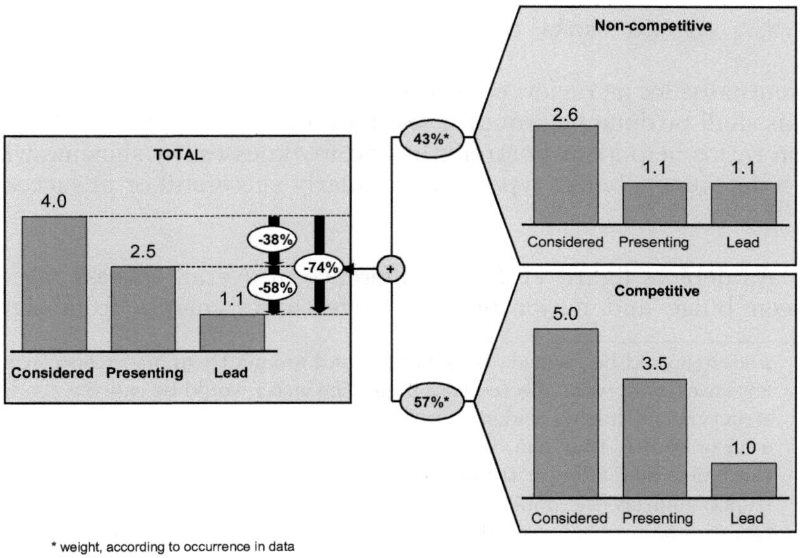

Figure 11.8: Quantity structure of purchase funnel
(Average number of banks per mandate; core sample)

Figure 11.8 shows that, in the respondent sample, on average four banks were considered potential candidates. Of these, two to three were most commonly invited to present their ideas[24]. The quantity

23 Paragraph 10.2.6 found that sales presentation comes into force in competitive solicitation, while relationship comes mainly into force in non-competitive and repeat business.

24 This includes also the non-competitive cases, where only one bank, namely the bank chosen lead, was left at this stage. About half of the respondents employing non-competitive selection procedures asked the bank chosen lead to actually give a presentation, while the other half did not. In the analysis depicted in figure 11.8, also banks directly chosen that were not asked to

structure was calculated by combining non-competitive and competitive quantity structures, using the core sample incidence of competitive and non-competitive selection procedures as a weight[25].

11.2.3 Specific banks' conversion rates

Eventually, let us review conversion ratios along the purchase funnel. This shall be done by grouping similar banks into buckets[26]. Conversion ratios help identify strengths and weaknesses, by showing which specific steps a bank (type) is particularly successful or unsuccessful at[27].

As depicts figure 11.9, the difference in overall success rate between bulge and major bracket[28] effectuates mainly from signifi-

---

present would be termed "presenting", and among them one, respectively in few cases, two, were selected lead bank (the latter would be called a "co-lead" structure). While co-lead structures somewhat diversify risk associated with advisor choice, they can, but need not, prove impractical in practice, when the banks co-leading a transaction find it difficult to cooperate, and when responsibilities are ambiguous.

25 Questionnaires that partially lacked assessments, as for instance indication of how many banks were considered, were excluded from the respective sub-analyses (in this example, consideration to presentation ratio calculation), but included into the remainder of analyses (presentation to lead ratio calculation).

26 Banks are grouped due to small sample sizes.

27 The analysis is somewhat inexact in that no adjustments were made for incomplete purchase funnel assessments (e. g., if it was only known who was invited and selected, the invited banks were simply taken as considered, and all the rest as non-considered). Seven of the 35 core sample companies that had employed non-competitive selection procedures, had not indicated in their questionnaires which other banks they had considered. Six of the 47 core sample companies that had employed competitive selection procedures had not indicated who they had considered, and another three had given neither indication on banks considered, nor on banks invited. Companies with incomplete assessments of the purchase funnel were not excluded from these analyses, for the sake of a broader data base.

28 The latter was composed of the banks occupying ranks 4 to 12 in the advised volume 1999–2001 ranking (cf. figure 9.4 on page 175), namely J.P. Morgan Chase, UBS Warburg, Credit Suisse First Boston, Rothschild, Lazard LLC, Citibank, Dresdner Kleinwort Wasserstein, Deutsche Bank, and Lehman Brothers. As to universal banks, this group included banks that also had a

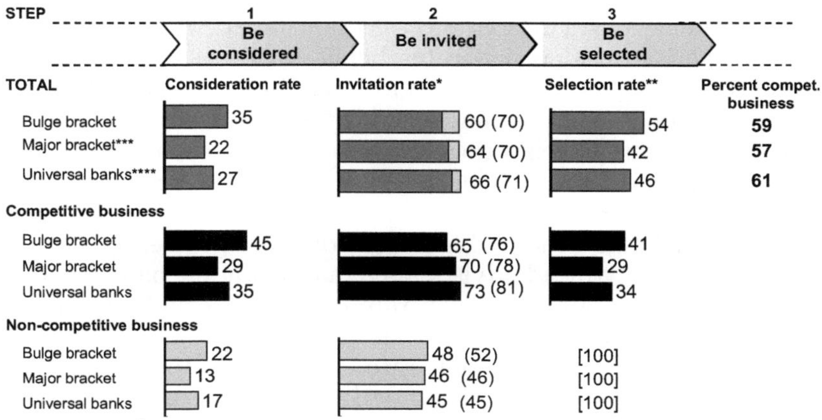

* from being considered to being invited. In brackets: from being considered to being invited or hindered.
Hinderance rates as percentage of considered: bulge bracket: 11 %, major bracket: 8%, universal banks: 7%
** from presenting to being selected lead. Only cases included where bank was not hindered
*** Citibank, Credit Suisse First Boston, Deutsche Bank, Dresdner Kleinwort Wasserstein, J.P. Morgan Chase, Lazard LLC, Lehman Brothers, Rothschild, UBS Warburg
**** Citibank, Credit Suisse First Boston, Deutsche Bank, Dresdner Kleinwort Wasserstein, UBS Warburg

Figure 11.9: Conversion rates by bank group
(Percent; core sample)

significant retail and commercial banking business. While Citibank, as US American bank, was included in this group, J.P. Morgan Chase was not included, the reason being two-fold. First, the combined J.P. Morgan Chase is made up of two widely autonomous parts, namely J.P. Morgan, which comprises investment banking, research, private equity, investment management, private banking, treasury and securities services, and middle market, while Chase offers consumer banking, small business services, auto finance, education finance, credit cards, home finance, investments, and insurance. Thus, J.P. Morgan's focus was on corporate investment banking, whereas Chase's banking area was the retail market, which meant J.P. Morgan represented a classical investment bank, and corporate commercial banking (in particular, credit business, as extensively covered by Citibank, Credit Suisse, Deutsche Bank, Dresdner Bank, and UBS) did not constitute a core business area of the combined bank. – Note also that, in contrast to other banks, J.P. Morgan Chase did not employ umbrella branding, but used separate names for its commercial and investment banking entities. The second and more important reason was that the closing of the J.P. Morgan-Chase merger was only in December 2000, thus in the time covered by this thesis' research. A fourth subgroup may thus be composed of J.P. Morgan Chase, Lazard LLC, and Lehman Brothers, which would represent major bracket "pure" investment banks.

cantly different consideration and selection rates. More specifically, bulge bracket's consideration rates being 1.6 times as high as major bracket's consideration rates, and bulge bracket's selection rates being 1.3 times as high as major bracket's selection rates, the step to consideration represents the purchase funnel step in which bulge bracket banks most strongly outperform major bracket banks[29].

Overall, a bulge bracket bank was, on average, nearly twice as frequently appointed lead advisor, as a major bracket bank. The differences in this overall conversion rate can, in theory, be attributed to bank-group-specific differences in competitive, as well as non-competitive business' conversion rates, as well as to differences in franchise composition (share of competitive vs. non-competitive business). Bulge bracket outperforms major bracket in both franchises by a factor of approximately two[30], and no major differences in franchise composition between bulge and major bracket banks can be observed.

11.2.4 Summary

To summarise, field research indicates that competitive and non-competitive selection procedures are about equally common in the upper M&A advisory market. Non-competitive selection means in most cases that one of the relationship banks is being chosen, underlining the importance of active relationships for mandate acquisition.

The comparison of quantity structures of competitive and non-competitive solicitation showed that the number of banks considered in non-competitive selection amounts to only half the number of banks considered in competitive selection (put differently, considered banks have double the chances to be awarded the mandate), and that in competitive selection, on average 5 banks are being considered, of which 3.5 are going to be invited. Sales presentation/discussion may then tip the scales for banks that have made it to that stage.

29 Similar, although relatively weaker, observations hold for the comparison of bulge bracket with universal banks (the consideration multiple is 1.3, the selection multiple is 1.2).

30 2.0 for competitive, 1.8 for non-competitive business.

As to a comparison of major and bulge bracket banks, the latter were found to achieve significantly higher consideration rates, and also widely better selection rates in case of competitive selection. Similar observations were made for the comparison between major bracket universal banks and bulge bracket banks, although differences were somewhat smaller.

The quantity structures researched provide an interesting perspective for the analyses that shall be reviewed in the next section[31].

11.3 Revealed importance of signal vehicles

So far, factors that influence the perceived importance of signal vehicles have been examined. This has the advantage that, even when banks are perceived to be equally strong or weak positioned with respect to several of these signal vehicles, the respondent could voice what actually made him choose or not choose his bank. On the other hand, putting these findings into the perspective of which banks actually *did* make it to the next step of the purchase funnel[32], dependent on their perceived positioning regarding these signal vehicles, may be highly interesting. Corresponding analyses shall be provided in this section.

11.3.1 Data and method

The research of the steps of the purchase funnel by means of discriminant and regression analyses, respectively, was based on the respondents' assessments for each of the banks considered, or not considered, regarding the following[33]:

31 The last paragraph of the following section provides one synthesis of this and the next section's findings.

32 As introduced on page 43 and following pages.

33 The questionnaire contained a fixed list of the most popular M&A advisors, namely Goldman Sachs, Morgan Stanley Dean Witter, Merrill Lynch, J.P. Morgan Chase, UBS Warburg, Credit Suisse First Boston, Rothschild, Lazard LLC, Citibank, Dresdner Kleinwort Wasserstein, Deutsche Bank, and Lehman Brothers. Survey participants were asked to assess each of these

- Public investment banking reputation (on a 1–9 scale, where 1 = "poor", 9 = "excellent", and alternative response was "don't have an opinion about that bank's reputation"[34])

- Activity/intensity of the company's relationship with the investment bank (on a 1–9 scale, where 1 = "loose/inactive", 9 = "intense/active", and non-existence of relationship was given a 0 on this scale)

- If applicable, quality of sales presentation/discussion (on a 1–9 scale, where 1 = "poor", 9 = "excellent", and alternative response was "no sales presentation/discussion")

- Satisfaction with the bank's execution (on a 1–9 scale, where 1 = "completely unsatisfied", 9 = "extremely satisfied").

Further, respondents were also asked to give an according assessment of their previous M&A project regarding their satisfaction with the lead bank's execution. This means, for some, but by far not all banks, the following data were also available:

- Satisfaction with the execution of the advisor most recently employed in an M&A project (on a 1–9 scale, where 1 = "completely unsatisfied", 9 = "extremely satisfied").

These data were fed into a discriminant or regression model, respectively, that pictured the steps in the purchase funnel, namely

- To being considered (discriminating banks that were considered from banks that were not considered)

- From consideration to invitation (discriminating considered, invited banks from considered, non-invited banks)

banks, and to complement these assessments by the assessment of other banks that had played a role in their advisor selection.

34 This variable was split into two, one that indicated reputation assessment, where a bank's missing reputation assessment was replaced by the respective company's average reputation assessment, and a binomial one that indicated whether the respondent had an opinion about a bank's investment banking reputation or not.

- From presentation to being selected lead (discriminating banks that were presenting and not chosen lead, from banks that were presenting and chosen lead[35])

- From selection to being awarded repeat business (regressing re-engagement intention on reputation, investment banking relationship, and satisfaction with execution).

11.3.2 Vehicles' influence along the purchase funnel

Figure 11.10 gives an overview of the results on aggregate level, i. e., for all solicitation types in combination, and shows which method has been applied to what number base. Note that many a signal vehicle was only applied to some of the steps within the funnel, for instance was "opinion about reputation" only applied in the first step, while sales presentation/discussion, for obvious reasons, could only be employed to analyse the third step in the funnel[36].

While significance of difference in means of discriminated groups has been high in the first and third[37] step of the funnel, it has been unsatisfactory in the second. This is no surprising, since it was already suspected that tactical considerations and situational effects might play an important role in this step[38]. As to the test statistics, the eigen value and canonical correlation[39] can be considered satisfactory in the first and third step. Shares of correctly assigned

35 Again, this did not have to mean that banks actually gave a presentation or discussion in non-competitive selection, cf. footnote 24 on page 232.

36 Thus restricting base cases to cases where a presentation/discussion was given at all.

37 At least if one restricts oneself to solicitations where sales presentation or discussion was applied.

38 Cf. page 45.

39 The eigen value captures the ratio of variance *between* to variance *within* the discriminated groups, and thus should be as high as possible. Canonical correlation measures the correlation between actual and calculated group affiliation (the latter is given by virtue of the discriminant function), and thus should also be high, cf. Brosius[42], pp. 771–814, Bühl[47], pp. 427–445, Decker[68], pp. 305–313. Thus, in the case of two discriminated groups, the square of the canonical correlation corresponds with regression analysis' R^2, cf. Backhaus[18], page 172.

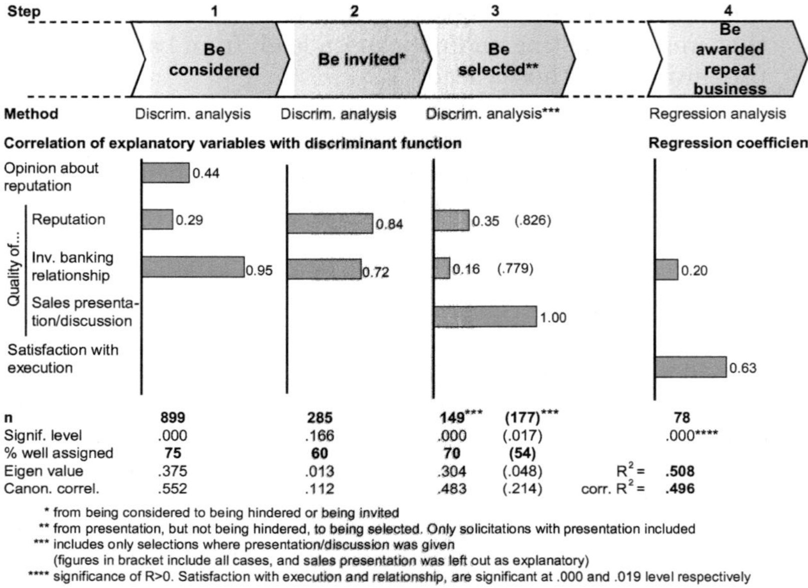

Figure 11.10: Vehicles' explanatory power along funnel
(Core sample)

values substantially surmount shares of correctly assigned values being achieved by means of default assignment[40], which substantiates the discriminant function's explanatory power.

As to content-wise results, relationship was found to play a dominant role in the first step of the purchase funnel. Thus, the presumption that the "evoked set" be mainly composed of relationship banks[41] is substantiated from this perspective. But such finding should be put into the perspective that 25 percent of discriminant assignments were faulty, which means that, in a significant share of

40 75% in the first step vs. 69% (meaning that 69% of banks are not being considered), and 70% vs. 63% in the third. Such approach to assess the goodness of discrimination is for instance suggested in Backhaus[18], pp. 170, 171.

41 Cf. page 75 of paragraph 4.2.4, and page 111 of paragraph 5.3.3.

cases, relationship may not have been the most influential factor for consideration. Second, reputation and relationship assessment may strongly converge in intense relationships[42], which means that in another part of cases, reputation may provide similarly explanatory power for consideration.

In fact, the latter is supported by the survey data, as shows figure 11.11 on page 240[43].

As to the fourth step of the funnel, a step-wise regression analysis on re-engagement intention was conducted[44], and satisfaction with the bank's execution was found to be the best explanatory for re-engagement intention. This fits with theory, and in particular with hypothesis I19.

The test statistics show that results are significant[45], and that half of the variance in repurchase intention is explained by variances in satisfaction and investment banking relationship. Thus, R^2 can

42 There is good reason to believe that intense relationships are being maintained with banks that are considered renowned, and where own experience does not negatively infer with such positive reputation assessment.

43 It is interesting to note that many a bank's reputation assessment, dependent on relationship quality, is v-shaped, rather than a slope (Goldman Sachs and Lazard provide the only exceptions). Thus, companies may maintain (weak to moderate) relationships with banks they perceive – compared with companies that *do not* maintain relationships with these banks – to be weakly positioned on reputation. Against the background that companies may strengthen relationships with banks they have made very positive acquaintance with, one may thus suspect that a significant share of low to moderate quality relationships are relationships that mainly emanate from banks, rather than the companies, or relationships that were initiated at times companies held a better opinion about a bank's reputation, and that relationship intensity decreased, as reputation assessment worsened, possibly in interference with own experience.

44 Reputation, the company's investment banking relationship with the bank, and satisfaction with the bank's execution were admitted as independent variables.

45 The F-statistic hints at a significance level of .000. Further, the t-statistic for coefficients yields significance levels of .000 for the satisfaction measure, and of .019 for the relationship measure (the constant of 1.913 is also significant at the .001-level). Background on the F- and t-statistics is for instance given in Backhaus[18], pp. 26–31, or Skiera[216], pp. 211, 212.

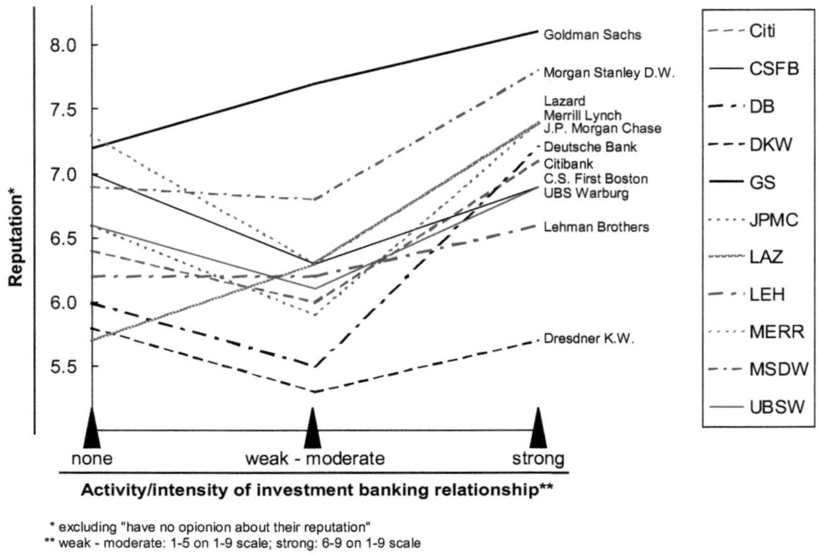

Figure 11.11: Reputation assessment by relationship bucket *(Extended sample)*

be considered satisfactory[46]. Further, a *Durbin-Watson* statistic of 1.959[47] shows autocorrelation is non-substantial, and a respective *VIF value* of 1.098 and *tolerance value* of .911 for both satisfaction and relationship assessment show that multicollinearity does not constitute a problem[48]. Finally, figure 11.12 illustrates that heteroscedasticity is not given[49], since the size of standardised residuals does not depend on the size of the standardised dependent variable. Autocorrelation, multicollinearity, and heteroscedasticity represent-

46 (Corrected) R^2 captures the ratio of explained to non-explained variance, and should thus be as high as possible, cf. for instance Backhaus[18], pp. 20–25, Skiera[216], pp. 209, 210.

47 Values close to 2 show autocorrelation is non-substantial, cf. for instance Brosius[42], pp. 471–504, Bühl[47], pp. 333–348, Skiera[216], pp. 225, 226.

48 Cf. for instance Backhaus[18], pp. 41–43, Skiera[216], page 222.

49 Cf. for instance Skiera[216], pp. 229, 230.

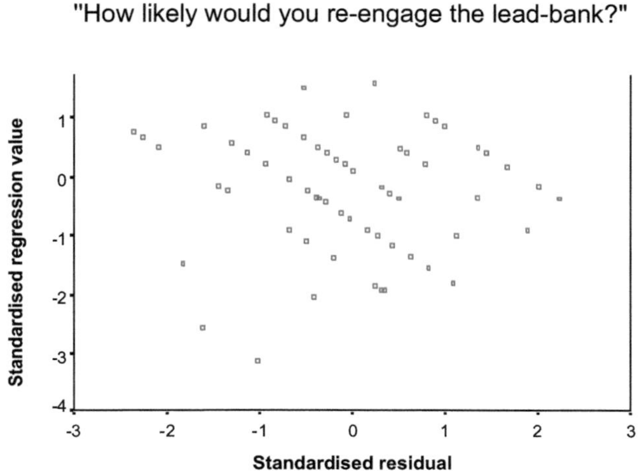

Figure 11.12: Heteroscedasticity assessment for fourth funnel step *(Main sample)*

ing the major reasons for which estimators may not be optimal, the identified estimators can be assumed to be both "unbiassed" and "best"[50].

11.3.3 Vehicles' influence by selection and buyer type

As to the second and third step, a further differentiation within the core sample seemed desirable, due to the inhomogeneity of choice situations. Accordingly, a differentiation was made between competitive and non-competitive selection procedures[51], on the one hand, and repeat buyers and non-repeat buyers[52], on the other.

---

50 Cf. Skiera[216], page 221.

51 Since in non-competitive processes, presenting constitutes already the selection step, which means steps 2 and 3 are combined.

52 Since, after consideration, one can expect switchers' and first time buyers' reliance on certain signal vehicles to be different from repeat buyers' one.

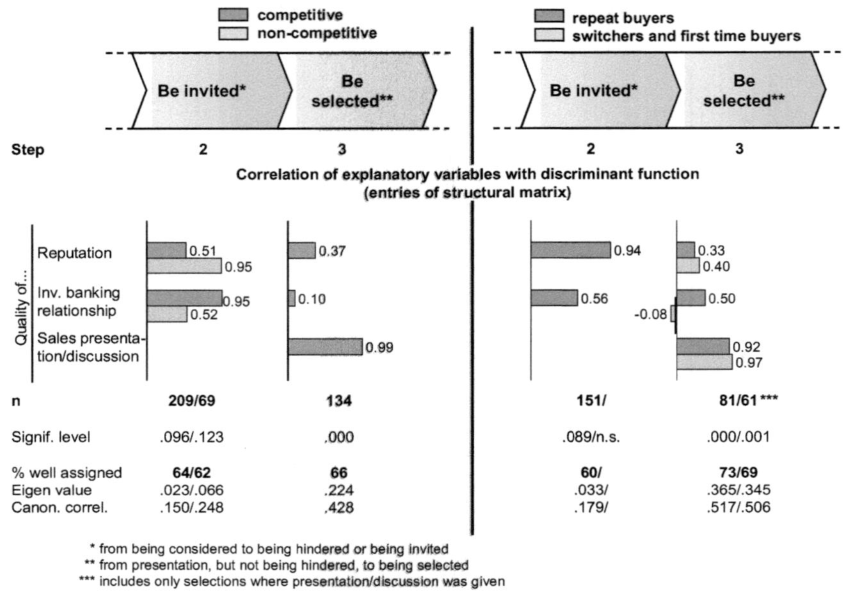

Figure 11.13: Vehicles' explanatory power by selection/buyer type
(Second and third step of funnel; core sample)

Basic results of discriminant analyses for the second and third step, in dependence on selection process and customer type, respectively, are shown in figure 11.13.

As to non-competitive selection, the explanatory power of the considered variables for invitation (that is, selection), is unsatisfactory. If analyses are restricted to the sample of companies that used non-competitive selection procedures, and the bank universe to banks for which the previous execution was assessed, the significance level can somewhat be improved, and results hint that previous execution may in particular play an important role in the second step of the funnel[53].

53 Unfortunately, the sample size of 34 on which such analysis is based for the second step for non-competitive selection is small. As to correlations of

As to competitive selection, sales presentation is found to play a dominant role in the third step, while relationship proves a bad explanatory. Results of the second step are insignificant, supporting the presumption that tactical considerations and situational specifics might play an important role.

A closer look at the second and third step of the purchase funnel from the repeat buyer vs. non-repeat buyer perspective reveals that explanatory power of the examined variables for the second step of the purchase funnel is poor. As to the third step, if analyses are restricted to choice procedures in which sales presentation or discussion was employed[54], sales presentation is repeatedly found to constitute the best explanatory for selection. The discriminant function for non-repeat buyers has no relation to investment banking relationship, and reputation plays a more important role. Repeat buyers, in contrast, seem to rely more on relationship[55], apart from sales presentation, which also constitutes the best explanatory variable for this kind of buyers.

Admittedly, danger of choice dissonance reduction is very high for sales presentation assessment. This is why the step three discriminant analysis was also conducted for repeat buyers and non-repeat buyers without admitting quality of sales presentation/discussion as an explanatory. Test statistics being significantly weaker than for the analyses where quality of sales presentation was included as explanatory[56], results support that for repeat purchase, investment

---

explanatory variables with the discriminant function, it yields .843 for own reputation assessment, .523 for investment banking relationship, and .639 for previous execution, at a significance level of .085, and 65 percent of the cases are being assigned correctly. Eigen value is .242, and canonical correlation is .442.

54 Including non-competitive solicitations with presentation/discussion.

55 For repeat buyers, modelling the third step by restricting the sample to banks whose previous execution had been assessed by the company, showed that previous execution as an explanatory was correlated with the discriminant function by .482, but results were not significant (.120), and only weakly supported by eigen value (.100) and canonical correlation (.301).

56 For repeat buyers, significance is .011, eigen value is .101, and canonical correlation is .303, and only 59 percent of cases are well-assigned by virtue of the discriminant function. For first time buyers and switchers, significance is .061, eigen value is .083, and canonical correlation is .277, and 59 percent of cases are well-assigned by virtue of the discriminant function.

banking relationship plays a dominant role, while first time buyers and switcher predominantly rely on reputation[57].

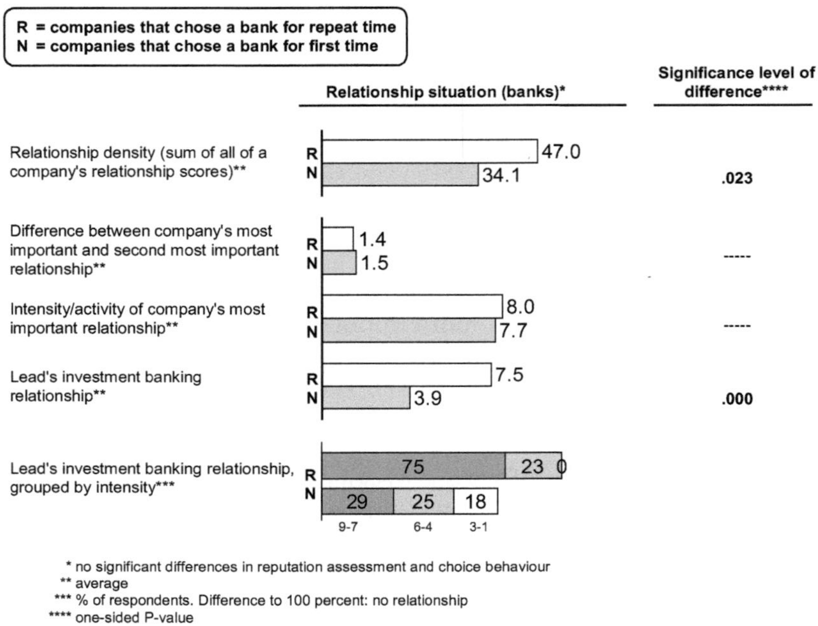

Figure 11.14: Switchers' vs. repeat buyers' relationship situation *(Core sample)*

Eventually, these findings are substantiated by the profiling of repeat buyers and switchers regarding their relationship situation. As shows figure 11.14, relationship does not play that prominent a role when an investment bank is chosen for the first time: switchers chose banks whose relationship intensity amounted only to an average of 3.9 on a 1–9 scale, although such behaviour could *not* be explained

57 Correlations with discriminant function amount to .403 (reputation) and .995 (relationship) for repeat buyers, and .996 (reputation) and .330 (relationship) for first time buyers and switchers.

by the general absence of strong relationships, as shows the third row in figure 11.14[58].

11.3.4 Summary

To summarise the findings of this paragraph, discriminant and regression analyses along the steps of the purchase funnel yield the following results: investment banking relationships play a highly important role in the M&A advisory market. In particular, the "evoked set" of banks considered potential advisor candidates, is largely composed of relationship banks. Further, intense relationships are commonly associated with relatively higher reputation scores for the banks with whom these relationships are maintained.

As to the second step of the purchase funnel, decision as to which banks to invite for presentation/discussion (respectively choose in the case of non-competitive solicitation), seems strongly influenced by situational factors and tactical considerations; the concepts researched do not provide satisfactory explanation. Besides, the quality of previous execution may, in particular, play an important role in the second step for non-competitive selection procedures.

As to the step from presentation/discussion to selection, it seems strongly influenced by the quality of presentation/discussion. Results also indicate that in case of repeat purchase, investment banking relationship might play an important role, while in the case of non-repeat purchase, reputation may constitute an important choice determinant[59].

Re-engagement intention, eventually, has been found to strongly depend on satisfaction with the bank's execution.

As to reputation, this paragraph shows that it plays highly important a role as door opener for new business. Taking into account

58 From the perspective of observations documented in figure 11.11, it is no surprising that no significant deviation in the lead's reputation assessment by switchers vs. repeat buyers was found.

59 All of these results should be put into the perspective that the survey data basis was insufficient to adequately picture the role of previous execution in these analyses.

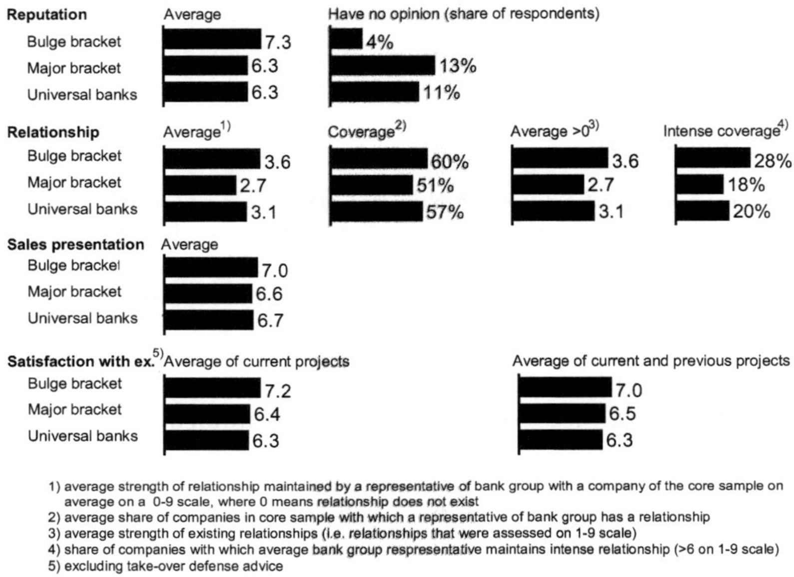

Figure 11.15: Market positioning by bank group
(On a 1–9 scale; core sample)

that initial business, then, offers a bank the opportunity to build and maintain a relationship with the respective company, and that intense relationships usually enhance reputation, this paragraph's findings support the importance of reputation in selection decisions, as perceived by survey participants, from an "as is" perspective.

Figure 11.9 of the previous section shows that major bracket banks have lower conversion rates in the first, as well as the third and fourth step of the purchase funnel. The findings of this section suggest that major bracket banks thus fall behind bulge bracket regarding quality of relationship (consideration rate), sales presentation/discussion, reputation (selection rate, in particular first time purchase), and execution (re-engagement intention).

Indeed, as illustrated by figure 11.15, bulge bracket banks score better on all vehicles. While such findings do not help much to

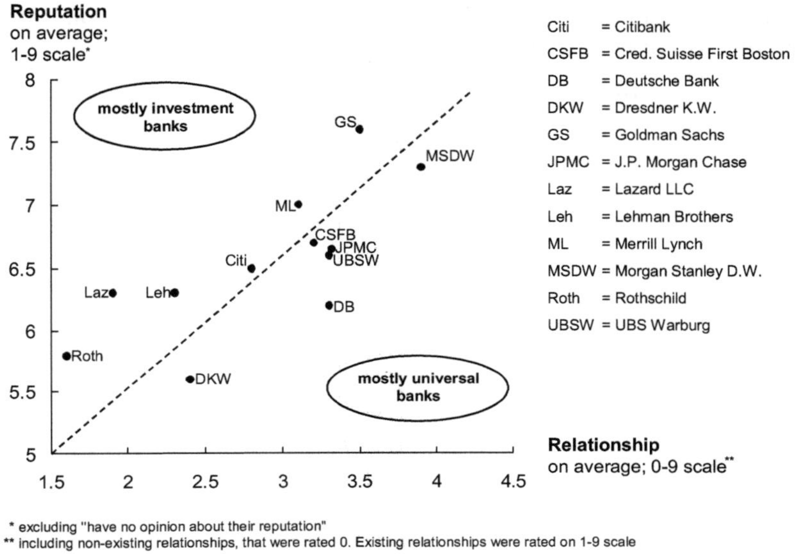

Figure 11.16: Market positioning by bank
(Extended sample)

tackle specific bank groups' most urgent development needs, better insights when using a more granular basis can be expected. Due to small sample size and according data constraints, such an assessment can only be given for reputation and relationship, see figure 11.16.

Deutsche Bank for instance being relatively strongly positioned on relationship, but relatively weakly on reputation, it is likely to be frequently included in the consideration set, but also likely to have a relatively low selection rate, in particular in competitive selection. Conversely, Lazard being relatively strongly positioned on reputation, but relatively weakly on relationship, opposite results may be expected. Indeed, comparing consideration and selection rate in the core sample for the two banks, Deutsche Bank is found to have a high consideration rate (34 percent), but low selection rate (33 percent; 20 percent in competitive solicitation), while the opposite holds for

Lazard (10 percent consideration, and 66 percent selection rate; 33 percent in competitive solicitation)[60].

60 Since bases along the purchase funnel get increasingly smaller on a bank by bank basis, these analyses shall not be extended any further.

12 Synthesis and outlook

Chapter 10 has assessed the empirical validity of hypothesised relationships between risk and information concepts. Thereby, the assessment of test results was complemented by the discussion of inferences on a very granular, namely hypothesis basis. Chapter 11 was meant to provide the reader with a background on what buyer perceptions and behaviour typically looked like in the market.

In the remainder of this thesis, empirical findings shall be reviewed from more of a high-level perspective, and their implications shall be discussed.

12.1 Theoretical perspective

To start, let us revisit results by taking a theoretical perspective. This shall comprise an assessment of the explanatory power of the theoretical frameworks applied, and an identification of limitations and corresponding research needs for the future.

12.1.1 Power of applied frameworks and further explanation needs

Empirical research has shown that perceived risk and risk relievers play highly important roles in a company's selection of its M&A advisor – this may be particulary emphasised from the perspective that industrial markets have often been considered "expert buyer" markets. Risk and risk reduction playing important roles in M&A advisor choice, one can contend a risk-information perspective on the marketing of M&A advisory proved highly appropriate.

Operationalising the risk associated with the choice of the M&A advisor by two components (uncertainty and consequence), the propositions of respectively different antecedents have been widely supported by empirical findings. On the other hand, it was found that the widely established proposition that an increase in *either* risk component increases the importance of *either* risk component reliever, was not generally supported. While operationalisation inexactitudes may have contributed to such findings – for instance might it be argued that beauty contests do not solely serve the purpose of additional information search –, there are also good reasons to believe that, while, *factually*, overall risk can be decreased by decreasing either component, the human mind *perceives* their utility in linkage with the risk component they relief. Apart from that, two other propositions which might help explain these observations, have been discussed. First, it was suggested that one of the risk components may categorically surmount the threshold above which "it pays" to further reduce risk. Alternatively, it was suggested a company may assign changing relative importance to risk relievers, dependent on the level of risk perceived[1]. The latter proposition seems highly plausible from the perspective of the illustrative example given[2], and may constitute an interesting field of research, as well as the deepening of the topic how risk relievers link to risk components. Both research areas may provide interesting complementary insights to the risk reliever research conducted so far, which has been highly concentrated on linking risk relievers to risk types, such as financial risk, ego loss, etc.[3]

Another topic that ought to be addressed is represented by the newly introduced concepts of primary risk, underlying risk, and transfer lever. While one can easily contend that the proposed relationships are most likely to hold for highly related product classes – in particular services that consist in the giving of advice on other transactions –, it ought to be explored, from a theoretical, as well as an empirical perspective, how well claimed relationships can be generalised and hold in less related contexts.

Further, many of the propositions on the utility increasers of information types, derived in section 5.2, may constitute interesting fields of research themselves. To give an example, one may want to conduct field research on buyers' perception of how and why the "reli-

1 Cf. also footnote 21 on page 230.

2 See discussion of hypotheses R13 and R14 on page 193.

3 Cf. for instance Cox[61], pp. 619–626, Roselius[198], Derbaix[72]. Cf. also Ross[200], page 8, for a review of selected studies on this topic.

ability" of experience type information varies, dependent on provider and product characteristics[4]. Similarly, the research of the preconditions under which a bank's capability assessment for one product class may be easily transferred to other product classes, dependent on product classes, benefit focus, and buyer knowledge, may constitute an interesting research topic[5]. This kind of research may put existing frameworks and fragments into a broader and more ready-to-apply perspective.

Eventually, concept operationalisation has been parsimonious, due to the multiplicity of assessments to be made by survey respondents. In order to increase the utility of findings on how these concepts interrelate, the research of factors within the explored concepts may provide practitioners with an even better understanding why their institution is being perceived well or badly positioned with respect to specific concepts. To give an example, factors making up the "activity/intensity of investment banking relationship" may provide practitioners with concrete levers which ought to be tackled, in case an overall better relationship quality is being envisioned.

Last but not least, research on the interrelation of explored concepts over time would be desirable.

12.1.2 Limitations and broadening research needs

Obvious limitations of the research presented in this thesis consist in the fact that propositions were empirically tested only in a specific industry and geography, namely the European M&A advisory market, and in the relatively small data basis used for that purpose.

The former limitation means that the question in how far this thesis' findings are generalisable to other industries, must be left open. As a starting point, corresponding research in the top management consulting industry, which shows a high degree of similarity with M&A advisory, would be desirable. Further broadening research should then extend to other industrial core services. Further, the question how propositions transfer to or change in markets dependent on their maturity and geography, respectively – examples

4 Cf. paragraph 5.2.1.
5 Cf. paragraph 5.2.3.

for the M&A advisory business may be provided by the US (more mature) and Asian (less mature) market –, may constitute an interesting research topic.

As to the data basis employed, it should be mentioned that, while non-parametric test methods allow a statistically accurate assessment also in the case of small data sets, a cross-validation of results by means of another data set would be highly desirable.

12.2 Practical perspective

What can investment banks learn from this thesis' findings? – Taking into account their current and potential customers' perceptions, the remaining sections want to discuss what banks could change in order to be in a better position to win customers and retain them. Some of the issues discussed may be considered particularly crucial for major bracket universal banks, while others may be considered to be of equal concern to all banks.

Practical recommendations shall be developed from the following three perspectives:

- The risk and risk relief perspective
- The signal vehicle perspective
- The individual-corporation antagonism perspective.

One paragraph shall be devoted to each of these perspectives – and, where appropriate, the discussion of direct implications shall be embedded into a broader perspective.

12.2.1 Risk and risk relief perspective

Field research indicates that risk and risk relief play a highly important role in the selection of M&A advisors. Thus, it should lie in an investment bank's interest to lower risk barriers that may endanger its selection as M&A advisor. Reputation playing an important role as risk reliever, this means that banks not extremely well positioned with respect to reputation, may find it useful to provide their potential customers with additional risk relievers, possibly other than the ones currently available in the market.

Making use of the mode of action risk reliever systematisation developed in paragraph 4.2.3, the following can be observed and suggested regarding the potential provision and utility of such risk relievers.

Intrinsic quality indicators

Intrinsic quality indicators are not available, and it is out of a bank's power to provide the buyer with intrinsic quality indicators, due to M&A advisory's sales occurring before production and its low task programmability.

Probabilistic quality indicators

Probabilistic quality indicators, in contrast, are available – in fact, quality indicators of probabilistic character can always be generated for any kind of product.

As show empirical results, reputation plays the most important role for first time buyers as selection criterion[6], while repeat buyers rely to an equal extent on reputation, relationship, and previous execution. Further, it was found that companies perceiving high uncertainty were more likely to employ competitive selection procedures than were others. Thereby, competitive selection decreased uncertainty only modestly, albeit significantly. Another finding was that buyers that widely based their M&A advisor choice on previous execution were most satisfied with their M&A advisors' subsequent execution. Last but not least, the importance of previous execution as selection criterion has been found to increase when the M&A advisor choice was based on the banker, rather than the bank.

These observations induce the proposition that banker-specific references might help out-suppliers to gain mandates. More specifically, it is proposed that banks that have not been engaged by a

6 Thereby, one should not forget that reputation can also be considered a vehicle through which self-selection becomes effective, and that reputation's overall role surmounts its role as uncertainty reliever.

company before, may want to provide the individuals that form the buying centre with the names and details of contact persons whose companies have used the bank in question – and who are willing to talk with peers about the experience they have made with the bank[7]. As shows this thesis' research, such *referrals* might be most useful if the *banker* to lead the project in question *is the same* as the one that had been engaged by the referral company in question.

Such referrals can be considered an important complement to information displayed in tombstone advertisements. While the latter may help a lot in reputation building, by displaying which transactions respective banks have advised on, the former may be considered an important tool for providing companies with more specific information on a bank's actual project management and performance, all the more, since these sources are not provider-controlled. In contrast to tombstone advertisements, references offer the buyer the opportunity to ask questions, to find out what the process behind a successful project outcome looked like, and, by "providing faces that have dealt with the investment bank's faces", may make the service offer in question more tangible.

This, of course, premises that a bank does have satisfied customers that might be used as referrals, and who are willing to spend some time to their service provider's benefit.

Self-selection mechanisms

Self-selection mechanisms are currently not available on the M&A advisory market, apart from reputation, which also serves as probabilistic quality indicator. While reputation constitutes a "naturally given" self-selection mechanism, there are others that can be created by market participants.

An example for such a mechanism is provided by *variable compensation, dependent on the buyer's satisfaction* with the service delivered.

7 That is, it is suggested that experience type information may be made more broadly accessible by means of providing companies that have not made own experience with the bank with third party experience type information.

Since "just" quantitative performance metrics do not exist in the case of M&A advisory – due to its intangibility, the buyer's influence on production, influence of exogenous factors on product quality –, investment banks may consider to offer their potential clients the possibility to adjust remuneration, based on their satisfaction. This requires the investment bank be ready to be paid the lower fees in case perspectives on the execution quality diverge, since power over the "hostage" must be given to the client. This may sound a risky undertaking for an investment bank, but, if having pleased customers is one important marketing goal, provider's acknowledgement of own failures is only the first step on the long way to reach that goal. Since fair client-provider interactions also imply, in return, that clients acknowledge provider performance[8], it seems sensible that clients should not only be provided with the opportunity to "punish", but also to "reward" their service provider[9]. That way, provided decent quality delivery, banks should – on an average basis – financially be no worse off than nowadays.

Variable remuneration components may reinforce the bank's service mentality, and clients may more consciously think about whether blaming a bank for a project's failures is always fair. Through such "review dialogue", which should be initiated at the beginning of the project by defining a compact set of qualitative evaluation criteria[10], banks and clients may learn a lot about each other, from which the longer-term relationship quality may only profit.

From a future business point of view, there is hardly anything worse than a customer who thinks he has paid by far too much for

8 The investment banks' IPO business during the 1998–2000 boom years constitutes an example for a business where such financial rewards were being given from companies to investment banks. If banks outreached their expectations, some of the companies were ready to give the banks a higher share of stock capital than originally agreed.

9 Thereby, rewards should be considered a "may", rather than a "must".

10 It is suggested that such a set should comprise a handful of criteria, in order to focus project activities, and make a meaningful evaluation as feasible a task as possible. Evaluation criteria may for instance comprise the client's project leaders' overall satisfaction with the project, their evaluation of how well the bank has managed to keep client decision makers informed and use their time in an adequate manner, their judgement about the bank's ability to develop an appropriate, innovative deal structure, and about the bank's ability to deliver against commonly agreed milestones.

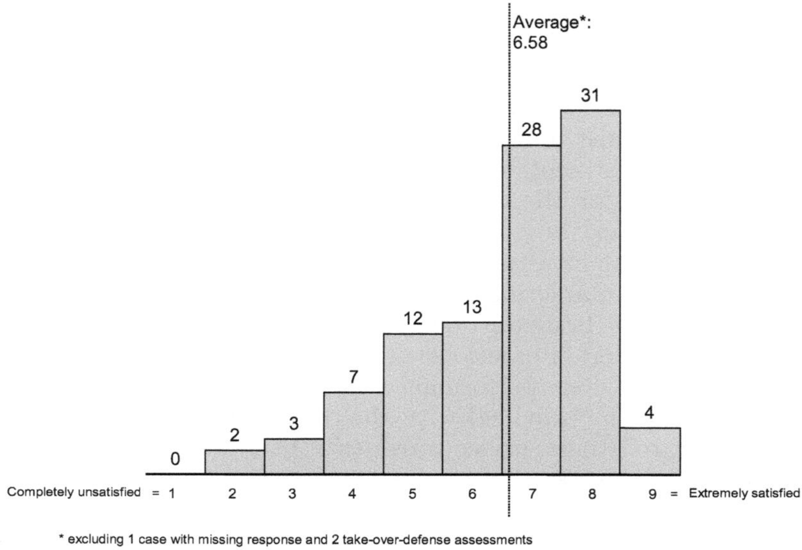

Figure 12.1: Satisfaction with the lead bank's execution
(On a 1–9 scale; percent of main sample)

by far too bad a performance. From that perspective, lower fees in the case of a company's dissatisfaction with the execution may provide a placebo for other, in the mid-term by far costlier activities through which the client may vent his anger, such as the damaging of the bank's reputation through bad word-of-mouth. Conversely, if a bank's execution offers repeatedly high satisfaction rates, nothing is being lost by offering such instruments. In contrast, they underline the bank's ongoing commitment to continuous quality management, and may thus help its reputation building.

The example of consumer goods, where many products can be returned within some time to merchants without the necessity of any explanation, or the accommodating handling of consumer complaints by producers, may serve as examples where similar mechanisms are being used to gain the customer's confidence, and help the merchant or producer to build goodwill.

As illustrated by figure 12.1, the respondent sample comprised a small, though significant share of companies that were not satisfied with the bank's execution[11], and for which – assuming client assessment not to be biassed – such instrument would have yielded a reduction in compensation. Conversely, for another significant share of projects[12], some "extra-reward" may have been paid.

Eventually, it seems sensible that variable remuneration components should be of moderate size, and that the "punishment" should surmount the "reward" component in size, in order to symbolise the bank's self-selection willingness, and to make such scheme attractive to clients[13]. While variable compensation should provide the buyer with a means to express his dissatisfaction and "punish" the bank accordingly, it should not put the bank's existence at stake, nor should huge variable compensation components lead to long-lasting, time-consuming debates about performance quality between bank and client – which indeed would damage the bank's reputation. Rather, the decision, which of the fees should be paid, should mostly be left to the client in the case of variable compensation schemes. Similarly, the decision of whether or not to incorporate variable compensation components at all into a remuneration system should be left to the buyer. – Already the offer of a variable compensation scheme may help to gain the buyer's confidence.

Reparations

Reparations in their purest form are out of question due to their association with enormous risk shifting from the company to the bank, and the strong influence that external factors have on an M&A's success. Further, it clearly lies outside the bank's financial power to provide adequate compensation for losses in case the propositions made by the bank during an M&A project turn out to be bad

11 At least 12 percent (assessments of 1–4), but the 12 percent of neutral assessments in this bucket should also be included, since a bank should clearly aspire a higher customer satisfaction rate.

12 The M&A advisory user survey hints at 4–35 percent.

13 To indicate a bandwidth, reduction by 40 percent in the case of dissatisfaction, and increase by 20 percent in the case of high satisfaction.

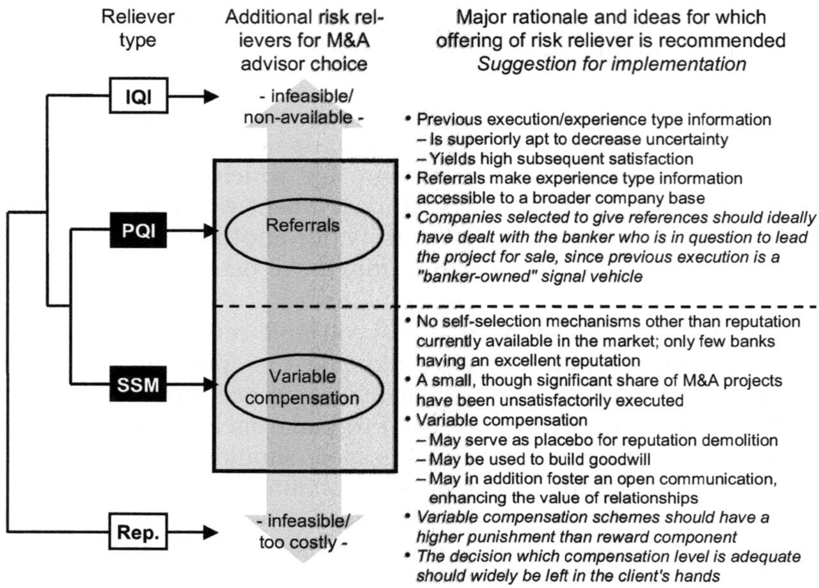

Figure 12.2: Recommendations from a risk/risk relief perspective

or "wrong" from ex post[14]. From such perspective, it should also be clear that the major purpose of offering variable compensation components, as discussed above, lies in potential punishment of the quality provider, rather than in compensation for the buyer's losses.

Figure 12.2 illustrates the main ideas of this paragraph's discussion.

12.2.2 A broader perspective on remuneration schemes

To finish the review of M&A advisory's marketing from a mode of action risk reliever perspective, remuneration schemes shall be discussed from a broader perspective.

14 The lever between fees and actual value creation or destruction is by far too big for such endeavours.

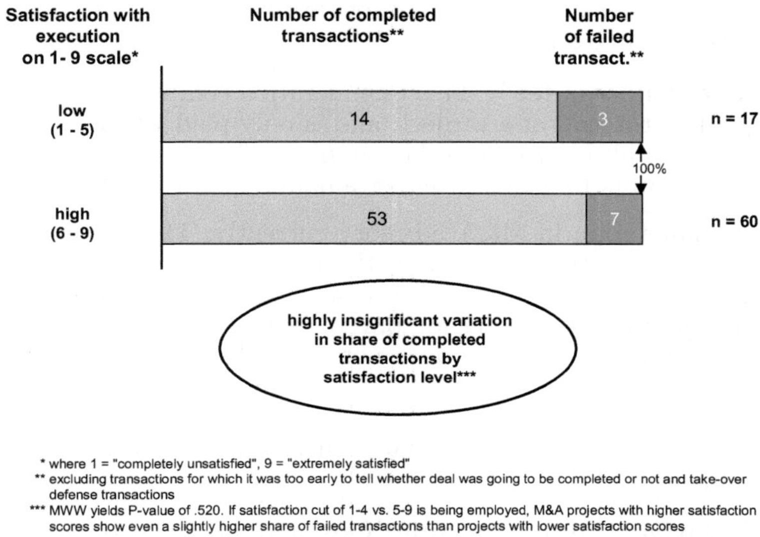

Figure 12.3: Share of completed transactions by satisfaction bucket *(Main sample)*

As shows figure 12.3, the survey data indicate that a company's satisfaction with the bank's execution is not correlated with the question whether a transaction has actually been completed, or whether such completion has failed. This indicates external factors may play a decisive role for a transaction's completion or not.

But, on the other hand, the level of compensation for an investment bank's M&A advice, as common in the market, strongly depends on the question whether transactions are being completed or not[15]. Currently, compensations systems are typically composed of two items

- **The "retainer".** This remuneration component is usually paid on an ongoing basis from the start of an M&A project to

15 For simplicity reasons, take-over-defense advice is being left out in this discussion, since the avoidance of a transaction may, in this case, and in contrast to other M&A mandates, be indicative of a bank's success.

its end, and it is meant to provide coverage for the costs the investment bank incurs

- **The "success fee".** This remuneration component is usually paid at the end of a project, and is only paid when the transaction is likely or sure to be completed[16]. Usually, the success fee amounts to a by far higher amount than the retainer.

Thus, remuneration in M&A advisory currently (1) involves lots of risk shifting from the company to the investment bank[17], (2) puts a bank into the pressure to close deals "no matter what", possibly undermining its striving for purely fact-driven approaches and recommendations[18], and (3) does not depend on the client's satisfaction[19].

Alternatively, banks could thus consider remuneration systems that comprise

- **Relatively higher retainer fees**, and relatively lower success fees[20]. This may help to put banks into a more objective posi-

16 Dependent on contract specifics, remuneration fees are already paid upon announcement of a transaction, or only upon its closing. While investment banks favour the former, companies usually favour the latter.

17 At least, when the closing of a transaction represents an important goal per se. From such perspective, the height of success fees can be considered to represent a risk premium.

18 Such incitements may be appropriate when banks are mostly used for the execution of pre-drafted deal propositions. When the strategic scope of the investment bank's tasks is broader though, including the assessment of whether suitable transaction counterparts exist at all, the bank's objectivity may be endangered by such remuneration system.

19 Fee margins usually do increase when a bank succeeds in selling a business at a superior price – the latter of which can be assumed to increase customer satisfaction –, but such effects are negligible from an overall customer satisfaction perspective.

20 Interestingly, companies are frequently ready to pay the high success fees, since they want to avoid the incurring of high costs in the case the transaction does not happen, while they can easily accommodate (high) success fees in the bunch of costs being incurred in case transactions are being settled. Companies should seriously review their investment banking remuneration schemes from the perspective whether such practices are in their self-interest in the mid- and longer-term.
It is clear that, with risk shifting back to the companies, average investment bank remuneration should decrease.

tion to agitate in the company's strategic interest[21]. Further, risk-shifting may be moderated that way

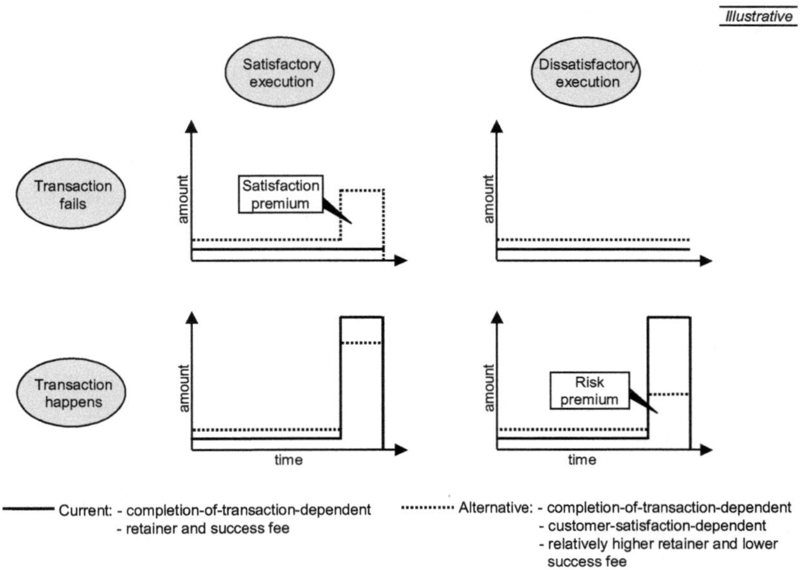

Figure 12.4: Alternative M&A advisory remuneration scheme

- **Variable success components that depend on customer satisfaction**. This may provide the buyer with an additional self-selection mechanism. The fact that, as illustrated by figure 12.3, a company's satisfaction with a bank's execution is usually only marginally affected by the question whether a transaction is happening or not, strongly substantiates such proposition

- **Variable success components that depend on the question whether a transaction has been closed**. Such re-

21 Note that this aspect addresses mostly uncertainty of compliance, rather than quality uncertainty.

muneration component would maintain (some of) the risk-of-closing shifting from the company to the investment bank.

The data[22] of the M&A advisory user survey suggest that a company's satisfaction with a bank's execution hardly depends on the question whether a transaction is being completed or not. This means that current completion-of-transaction-dependent remuneration systems *cannot* be considered self-selection mechanisms, but rather constitute exogenous risk shifting devices. This means that customer-satisfaction-dependent success fees may significantly enlarge the range of endogenous risk relief devices currently available in the market. On the other hand, completion-of-transaction-dependent compensation system's popularity in the market hints that endogenous risk-shifting may constitute an important benefit a company receives from engaging an investment bank. Thus, a combination of completion-of-transaction- and customer-satisfaction-dependent success fees may look most promising as alternative remuneration scheme.

Figure 12.4 illustrates such a customer-satisfaction- and completion-of-transaction-dependent remuneration scheme with a retainer over market level, thus success fee below market level, and compares remuneration under such alternative system with today's remuneration, dependent on customer satisfaction and completion or failure of transaction.

12.2.3 Signal vehicle perspective

Let us next revisit research results from a signal-vehicle perspective, that is, let us take a look at what has been learnt about the roles that reputation, investment banking relationship, previous execution, sales presentation or discussion, and commercial banking relationship play. This paragraph's recap of findings and potential implications shall be organised around these topics.

Reputation

Reputation has been found to play the most important role for advisor selection in the buyer's perception. This was no surprising from

22 Cf. figure 12.3.

both the perspective of the multiplicity of its roles (uncertainty decrease through probabilistic quality indication or self-selection, justification device, device by means of which the buyer may save signalling costs himself), as well as from an availability perspective. While it was proposed that reputation be among the most important selection criteria for these reasons, it was also suggested that reputation may represent a makeshift rather than an "actively chosen and preferred" signal vehicle for its abstract character[23]. This proposition was substantiated by the finding that companies relying widely on reputation in their M&A advisor choice, showed significantly higher uncertainty scores than others.

Further, it was found that, if a highly renowned bank[24] was chosen, the importance of previous execution as selection criterion did not depend on whether choice was based on the banker, or on the bank. This contrasted with the cases in which less renowned banks were selected, where perceived importance of previous execution increased when choice was based on the banker rather than the bank. Vice versa, if previous execution was among the top choice criteria and one of the most renowned banks was being chosen lead advisor, companies were found to relatively less "cherry-pick" the banker, than when less renowned banks were chosen. These findings were in the expected way from the perspectives that (1) reputation may serve as non-intrinsic utility increaser for experience type information, and that (2) reputation may provide reassurance on the quality of individuals employed by a bank.

As to the importance that reputation, as opposed to relationship, plays along the steps of the customer decision funnel, it was found to play a relatively more important role in the later (from invitation to selection) than the earlier (to consideration) steps of the funnel[25].

Reputation being perceived by buyers to constitute the most important selection criterion, and reputation being most universally available, it clearly constitutes an asset banks should be keen to

23 Reputation is mostly based on third party information, and has only a moderate degree of affinity.

24 Goldman Sachs, Morgan Stanley Dean Witter, or Merrill Lynch.

25 An exception to this finding provided first time purchases, where the bank chosen lead (and thus also considered) usually had not maintained that strong a relationship with the bank before selection.

build. The observations that reputation goodwill stretches across buyers, that it reassures clients about the capabilities of individuals to lead the project in question, and that it is "corporation-" rather than "individual-owned", can only underline this imperative. From a bank corporation perspective, an insufficient reputation quality and strength hold the threat that companies may "cherry-pick" bankers, and be loyal towards bankers rather than banks – which, from a bank perspective, is highly indesirable[26].

As already discussed in the previous paragraph, investment banks that are not highly renowned may consider the offering of alternative pledges to their buyers in order to increase selection chances. Against the background of the multiplicity of benefits that a strong and high quality reputation offers, it is clear that the offering of alternative pledges cannot fully compensate such deficit. But it was also proposed that such alternative devices may, conversely, help reputation-building themselves.

Vice versa, if banks *are* being chosen for their reputation, banks may want to cement and strengthen the favourable image for which they originally had been chosen, through an excellent execution – all the more, since reputation – while constituting the most universally available risk reliever –, does not represent a very reliable one[27].

Investment banking relationship

Investment banking relationship has been shown to play an important, though not as decisive a role as reputation, in a company's choice of its M&A advisor. As to repeat buyers, investment banking relationship has been found to figure among the most important selection criteria. The "evoked set of investment banks", that is, the set of investment banks that a company considers potential advisor candidates for an M&A transaction, has been found to widely be composed of relationship banks. Again, this proved at most partially true for M&A advisor choices in which an investment bank was selected for the first time. Investment banking relationship's goodwill character, as well as the observation that banks maintaining dia-

26 Paragraph 12.2.5 shall expand on this topic.

27 From the perspective of its ability to increase uncertainty. Reputation was discussed to represent a "makeshift", rather than an "actively chosen" uncertainty reliever.

logue with a company offer the latter a higher familiarity with its potential, in particular organisation[28], provided the major reasons for which these findings were no surprising.

But the role of relationships for mandate acquisition should be relativised by the finding that only a small share of M&A mandates had *actively* been acquired by banks[29], which may be found indicative for banks' at most moderate success to engage into a sound strategic dialogue with their (potential) clients on M&A. Thus, investment banking relationships may have mostly constituted an important vehicle for banks to "keep in touch" with companies and to react to their needs. At the worst, this may indicate companies consider investment banks "executing forces", rather than sparring partners.

While the reacting to customer needs and the taking-further of their problem approaches should clearly lie in an investment bank's endeavours, a more active shaping of customer relationships and business portfolio may be desirable from both the bank's and the (potential) client's perspective. These findings induce the proposition that banks should reinforce their *targeting* of efforts, by using dedicated corporate resources. More specifically, it is proposed that project proposals should not be left in a single banker's responsibility, but that teams should be assigned to systematically analyse market segments, and to draft market perspectives and project proposals, in order to provide the (potential) client with "outside-in" perspectives. In short, banks should not only provide answers to the questions the company asks them, but they should also define questions themselves, and use systematic processes to shape their (potential) client's M&A agenda.

28 Relationships provide the companies with own type information.

29 This can be derived from the low share of active mandate solicitation. The comparatively high share of non-competitive solicitation, on the other hand, may be interpreted to indicate banks have managed to establish "privileged relationships". A competing interpretation of the latter is that companies rotate mandates within their "evoked set", dependent on tactical and situational factors.

Previous execution

For companies that chose a bank for repeat time, previous execution was found to figure among the most important signal vehicles. This was no surprising from the perspective that previous execution offers a high degree of own specific experience type information[30], and that the joint production experience, i. e., the M&A project, gives the highly intangible M&A advisory product tangible aspects. These observations also provided a substantiation for the finding that, if previous execution was among the most important signal vehicles, perceived uncertainty associated with the M&A advisor choice was significantly lower than in other cases. It was also found that if M&A advisor choice had been widely based on previous execution, subsequent satisfaction proved significantly higher than in other cases[31]. This finding was in the expected way, since companies using a bank for repeat time as their M&A advisor can be assumed to "better know what to expect" than do others – in particular when one takes into account that the smoothness of an M&A project's process supposedly plays a decisive role for the satisfaction with an M&A advisor's execution[32].

Further, the importance of the banker as opposed to the bank was found to strongly increase when previous execution figured among the most important selection criteria. The latter was highly sensible from the perspective that availability (in general) and non-identity of individual (in the case of non-automated services) are likely to constitute experience type's major utility setbacks, the latter of which may be overcome by virtue of choosing the same individual for repeat time. Reputation had been proposed to provide an alternative device by means of which the utility of experience type informa-

30 And that all these information types can be considered superior over their alternatives, due to high congruence in points of reference and in buyer-specific external factors (M&A advisory is individualised by both transaction *and* buyer), high affinity to the product for sale in question, and non-existence of the product at sales.

31 While, in general, low perceived uncertainty did not necessarily yield significantly higher satisfaction with subsequent execution.

32 Due to M&A advisory's high share of credence qualities. Indeed, the main sample data yield the following *Spearman* correlations for satisfaction with the bank's execution: .632 for satisfaction with the smoothness and clarity of the M&A project's process, .555 for satisfaction with the M&A project overall, and (only) .489 for the satisfaction with the M&A project's outcome.

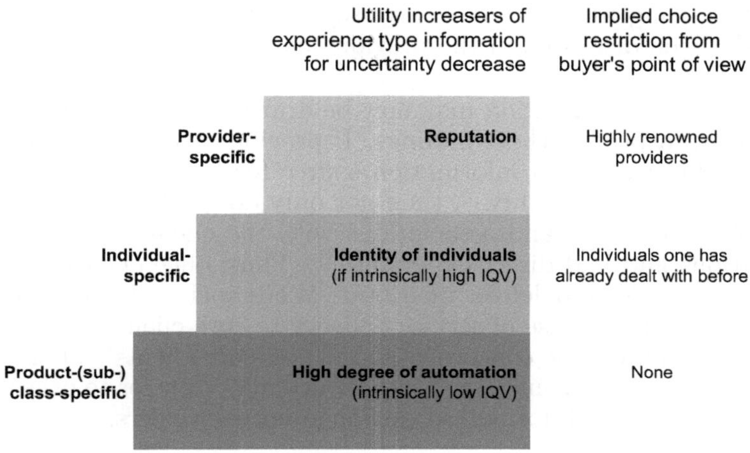

Figure 12.5: Escalation of experience type utility increasers

tion – more specifically, its reliability for uncertainty decrease –, may be increased. Therefore, it was proposed that the positive relationship between importance of previous execution and importance of the banker (as opposed to the bank) for advisor selection be of significantly weaker strength for highly renowned, than for other banks[33]. Indeed, the survey data did substantiate this proposition. Figure 12.5 depicts the three types of utility increasers for experience type information, and assesses their implied choice restriction, respectively.

Finally, previous execution was – contrarily to expectations – found to play an important role in both non-competitive *and* competitive selection, and a highly satisfactory execution was found to constitute the most important prerequisite for re-engagement intention.

One practical implication from these findings on the role that previous execution plays for future selection, namely the potential

33 Cf. also page 262 and following on the role of reputation.

benefit arising from an increased usage of reference-marketing, has already been discussed in the previous paragraph.

The reader's attention may now be drawn to another potentially important aspect of these findings. If previous execution represents such highly valued an information source for lead advisor selection – provided its availability –, then not only do *good* executions leave "deep" impressions and associations with the client, but so do *bad* executions and bad direct experience[34]. Thus, once engaged, banks should be anxious to deliver their best. While such endeavour may be self-evident in the case of service delivery to core-clients, investment banks should also be concerned about non-core clients' satisfactory product experience, since their experience may transfer to other (potential) buyers by information exchange between peers.

Sales presentation/discussion

Empirical data revealed that M&A advisory users did not consider solicitation events to represent any of the most important signal vehicles. As hypothesised, companies applied competitive solicitation primarily in cases where they perceived high uncertainty, where the employment of competitive selection procedures offered a significant, though relatively small uncertainty relief.

The observations that the demanding of some solicitation event[35] lies in the ad hoc power of the buyer – and differs in this respect from some of the more reliable uncertainty relievers, like previous execution –, but that it, conversely, has a high degree of plasticity (low task programmability), elucidated this behaviour. Discriminant analyses revealed solicitation events may play a decisive role in the last step of the customer decision funnel (from invitation to selection).

The combination of these findings suggests that sales presentation or discussion constitute a "hygiene factor", that is, a vehicle that mainly bears downside potential. Put differently, it is proposed

34 Due to the test set-up, previous execution's downside potential could not be assessed to the same extent as its upside potential, cf. footnote 23 on page 159. Propositions by prospect theory suggest that potential downsides can even be expected to outweigh potential upsides in the buyer's perception, cf. for instance Herrmann[112], pp. 6–8.

35 Which offers the buyer the opportunity for additional information search.

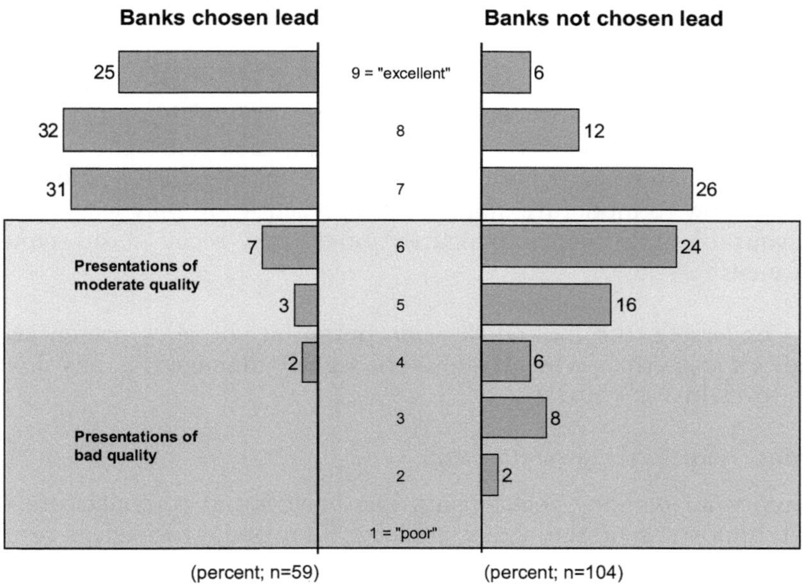

Figure 12.6: Perceived quality of sales presentation/discussion *(On a 1–9 scale; respondents of core sample that employed and assessed sales presentation/discussion)*

that banks are unlikely to win a business exclusively based on their sales presentation, but that they may loose it exclusively for its bad quality.

Indeed, and as illustrated by figure 12.6 on page 269, only a very low share[36] of lead mandates was awarded to banks whose sales presentation was considered of moderate or low quality in the respondent sample, while many a bank that delivered an excellent presentation was not awarded the mandate[37].

36 12 percent of lead mandates were given to banks whose sales presentation was assessed by 6 or less on a 1–9 scale.

37 The latter limits the indicated suspicion of dissonance reduction, cf. page 243 of paragraph 11.3.3.

Thus, if going for a pitch, a bank should be convinced it wants to win it; never should bankers go to pitches – for instance in times of capacity constraints –, only because their bank *was asked* by the buyer. The scenario of bankers "showing up" without being convinced they want to get the mandate in question holds the high risk that they, indeed, are not going to get that mandate. And, a lot worse, a low to moderate quality sales presentation may leave highly infavourable impressions, which the buyer may recall at subsequent instances[38].

Conversely, the limited "upside potential" of sales presentation quality means that, while it should be tightly managed, banks should not "over-invest" into it.

Commercial banking relationship

Commercial banking relationship has been found to constitute the least important of the signal vehicles discussed. Empirical results were thus in line with expectations, which had been developed from the observation of the low congruence between commercial and investment banking's production and success factors, as well as the low benefits that the one-stop-shopping of investment and commercial banking services could provide to the buyer.

Thus, there is no such thing like easy cross-selling between commercial banking and M&A advisory. Accordingly, universal banks should consider it imperative to convince buyers based on their investment banking capabilities, and not based on bartering expectations or even implicit threats. While commercial banking relationships may be used as natural starting points for investment banking dialogues, the substance of topics brought up in such dialogue should decide over whether a universal bank is going to be its commercial client's M&A advisor or not.

38 Already *Luffman* has mentioned, in the context of industrial goods, that "the fact that a certain supplier was not appointed on a certain occasion should be reviewed in the light of the on-going nature of the purchasing process and that the information obtained may be stored and used on future occasions; thus an unfavorable impression of a supplier at this stage may have a long term detrimental effect on his potential future business with the customer. Thus marketeers should beware of such activities as 'quoting a high price because we don't want the business at the moment'.", see Luffman[162], page 100.

	Most important insights	Recommendations
Reputation	• Most important for advisor selection • May increase experience type information utility, reassure on banker quality • Important for selection and first time consideration • Unable to strongly decrease uncertainty ex ante • Bank-owned	• **Foster and handle with care for its prominent role. Manage actively** • **Flank with other signal vehicles more apt to decrease uncertainty**
Investment banking relationship	• Plays particularly important role in repeat purchase decisions • Particularly important for consideration • Low share of active mandate acquisition questions quality of relationships	• **Let relationship management not lie in a single banker's responsibility** • **Enhance dialogue and target efforts by using corporate resources**
Previous execution	• Highly decisive, if available. Satisfaction with execution is crucial for re-engagement intention • If applied as major selection criterion, high subsequent satisfaction with execution • For non-bulge-bracket banks, incrementally stronger banker- than bank-owned	• **Accept mandates only when you have appropriate resources** • **Either carefully manage quality of projects at non-core-clients, or do not do them at all**
Sales presentation/ discussion	• Preferrably requested when uncertainty is high • Hygiene factor, rather than "mandate winner", for its low task programmability	• **If you give a presentation, give a good one** • **But do not overinvest into presentations**
Commercial banking relationship	• Plays only marginal role in M&A advisor choice • May provide the starting point to initiate an investment banking relationship	• **Earn investment banking mandates by virtue of your investment banking, rather than your commercial banking skills**

Figure 12.7: Recommendations from a signal vehicle perspective

Figure 12.7 summarises the major findings and implications on the marketing on M&A advisory from a signal vehicle perspective.

12.2.4 A broader perspective on goodwill creation

The previous paragraph has shown that all of reputation, investment banking relationship, previous execution, and sales presentation/discussion do play significant roles for a bank's acquisition of M&A business. While it has been the previous paragraph's endeavour to elaborate on signal vehicle specifics, it is evident they cannot be considered in isolation from each other. For instance should repeatedly high customer satisfaction with a bank's execution and high quality sales presentations have positive impact on the quality of reputation, and so should active investment banking relationships.

Reputation, on the other hand, may render the relationship acquisition task easier; dissatisfactory executions may provide a setback to relationship quality, and also damage reputation.

While the research of mutual influence has been out of this thesis' scope, the reputation-relationship interplay shall be briefly expanded on in the following.

Reputation and relationship may be considered the most fundamental, most universally available, and most complementary vehicles of the five considered in this thesis[39]. Taking up the reputation-relationship matrix from figure 11.16 on page 247, figure 12.8 represents a schematised version.

As discussed earlier[40], the goodwill built in relationships can be expected to transfer to reputation, while reputation goodwill offers a bank easier access to companies and company relationships, respectively, which means reputation goodwill also serves the building of relationship goodwill[41]. That way, company-specific goodwill feeds and is fed by goodwill that stretches over markets. This mutual reinforcement suggests that banks might most efficiently turn from what figure 12.8 calls "light weights" into "heavy weights"[42] by moving up the matrix diagonal.

Now, as illustrated by figure 11.16, many a bank's positioning deviates from this ideal path. More specifically, universal banks have

39 Most fundamental because previous execution(s) may be considered one component of the investment banking relationship, while sales presentation is only decisive in the latter steps of the purchase funnel; further, commercial banking has been shown to at most slightly influence the choice of an M&A advisor. Reputation and relationship can be considered most complementary, since a buyer's reputation assessment reflects what he thinks that other thinks about a bank – which means it is strongly driven by third party information, while his relationship assessment reflects own type information.

40 See page 111 of paragraph 5.3.3.

41 *Sweeney* notes that "[t]he importance of personal relationships in marketing to business is well established. The research supports the concept that establishing a relationship between the customer and the brand can deliver part of the same benefits", see Sweeney[227].

42 The "heavy weight" position is currently occupied by Goldman Sachs and Morgan Stanley Dean Witter (one may also want to include Merrill Lynch, whose positioning is somewhat weaker).

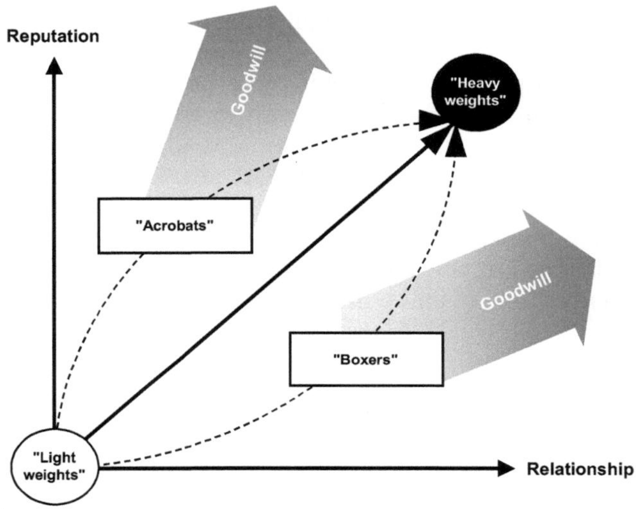

Figure 12.8: Moving up the reputation-relationship matrix

most frequently been found to be positioned relatively strong in relationship, but not that strong in reputation. Such positioning has been called a "boxer" positioning for the "aggressiveness" and mass necessary to build and maintain such relationships without a proportionate reputation support[43]. Correspondingly, boxers may reconsider improving their skills, by aspiring a higher consistency in delivered quality, and employing a more rigid quality management[44].

43 From a corporate perspective, it is good news that most of these banks have, due to their sizes, been able to attract buyers by means of "corporate power", rather than specific individuals' skills, cf. figure 10.9 on page 217.

44 One can argue here that reputation quality may be under-proportionate since execution quality is too variable and spills, respectively has spilled, back on reputation. Figures 10.8 on page 214 and figure 10.9 on page 217 substantiate this proposition. In particular, the finding that for major bracket, but not for bulge bracket banks, subsequent satisfaction with execution was significantly lower when companies chose major bracket banks for corporate reasons, than when they chose these banks for the specific banker in question to lead the project, hints at a comparatively high inhomogeneity of product quality, and thus a necessity for more rigid quality management.

Conversely, pure investment banks have mostly been found to be positioned comparatively strong in reputation quality, but rather weak in relationship. Such positioning has been called an "acrobat" positioning, to hint at these banks' supposedly over-proportionate skill development, in comparison to "demand adhesion". Correspondingly, acrobats should be concerned about how to better exploit and leverage their skills. In particular, the initiation of new customer relationships may be helpful to achieve higher demand adhesion. One might suspect that, in the longer run, acrobats may not be able to further move up the diagonal when maintaining their relatively small sizes.

12.2.5 Individual-corporation antagonism perspective

Empirical results have shown that bankers play highly important a role in M&A advisor selection – one third of respondents indicated their bank choice had been based on the banker, rather than the bank. This finding was in the expected way against the background that individuals play highly important a role in M&A advisory service delivery due to the product class' low degree of automation. Further, it has been seen that basing one's choice on the banker, rather than the bank, proved a successful risk reduction strategy for buyers. Not only was perceived uncertainty smaller when the M&A advisor choice was based on the banker, rather than the bank, but also was subsequent satisfaction with the execution significantly higher[45].

It was also proposed that, while individual goodwill may transfer on corporation goodwill, banks cannot wholly rely on this transfer process. Again, this proposition was supported by test results: in particular, data showed that when a company had chosen the banker rather than the bank, this yielded higher subsequent satisfaction and higher re-engagement intention of both the banker and the bank. But, on the other hand, companies that had based their choice on the banker, rather than the bank, were significantly more willing to follow their banker to another bank, provided he would leave his current employer.

---

45 Only the highly renowned banks provided an exception to this finding.

The most basic findings of the research conducted on the individual-corporation antagonism were thus that bankers "make the difference" in product delivery, and that therefore a bank's popularity strongly depends on the quality of its employees.

From a bank corporation perspective, these observations yield two potential imperatives for a successful go-to-market:

- To attract, develop, and retain gifted individuals, and
- To generate, respectively enhance corporation-owned customer benefits.

The latter means a bank should create offers that benefit a company (potentially) using its M&A advisory services, but which a banker or a group of bankers cannot take with him or them in case he or they leave.

In the following, a concretion of potential starting points, and discussion of their implications shall be given.

Attracting, developing, and retaining talent

If individuals are highly influential on product experience and quality, then it is imperative to banks to attract, develop, and retain highly gifted persons.

Theorists as well as practitioners have suggested a variety of ways through which this goal may be achieved. Important corner stones provide the building of a strong corporate culture and shared values, as well as the creation of a transparent, stimulating work environment in which employees' skills are being valued, fostered, and freed[46].

46 Cf. for instance Manville[167], where a model for motivation is drafted by learning from the system of self-governance that the ancient Athenians developed 2,500 years ago, based on the cornerstones of "participatory structures for making decisions", "communal values", and "practices of engagement [to ensure] broad participation of the entire citizenry", or the research by *Kim* and *Mauborgne*, which found that employees are most likely to commit to managerial decisions if they believe processes by means of which such decisions were derived were fair, where fairness is characterised by "engagement, explanation, and expectation clarity", see Kim[142].

An important managerial decision consists in whether to grow by acquisitions, or whether to grow organically, where organic growth may be implemented in a more or less rigid way, dependent on whether the rate of experienced hires is kept low or moderate to high. While an obvious advantage of external growth is provided by the flexibility to quickly adapt own resources to demand in times of booming markets, an obvious disadvantage and danger is provided by its dilution of a company's culture, which holds the danger of a boom and bust scenario.

As show extraordinarily high and variable compensation schemes, and many a bank's head-hunting activities for whole banker teams from competitors – at least during M&A booms –, the highly important role that individuals play in business acquisition and execution has long been recognised by practitioners. But the question is, whether most promising practices have been implemented to attract, develop, and retain gifted individuals.

So far, many a major bracket bank has mostly tried to increase its attractiveness by offering highly attractive compensation packages. But many of the top bankers attracted that way have left their new employers after some time, not infrequently taking the bait of even higher salary offers from other banks hunting in the market[47]. As a result, the market looks spoiled from an employee loyalty perspective, and the question of whether the salary path is the most and exclusively salutary one, is highly legitimate.

As *Berry* notes, "[b]uilding an organizational climate for marketing will fail to deliver intended results if employees constantly turn over and customers continually must deal with different or inexperienced service providers [...]. High employee turnover discourages management from investing much in hiring, training, and other commitment-building activities"[48]. So how can a bank build an attractive organisation that is able to retain individuals? – *Herzberg* found that the reasons for which employees leave are quite different from the reasons for which they stay with a firm. Accordingly, he differentiated between "extrinsic motivators" constituting "hygiene factors" in the sense that their non-delivery would grow an

47 To use *Herzberg*'s provocative words,"[h]ave spiraling wages motivated people? Yes, to seek the next wage increase", cf. Herzberg[116], page 88.

48 See Berry[27], page 241.

employee's dissatisfaction with his job, while their delivery would hardly affect his satisfaction with his job, and contrasted these with "intrinsic motivators". Intrinsic motivators constituting factors for which employees felt satisfied with their job, rather than that their absence induced them to high dissatisfaction, *Herzberg* indentified these factors to be highly related to "that unique human characteristic, the ability to achieve and, through achievement, to experience psychological growth", while he found that hygiene factors were mostly related to "humankind's animal nature"[49]. Not very surprisingly, salary figured among the hygiene factors, as well as status, work conditions, relationship with supervisor, supervision, and company policy/administration. Conversely, achievement, recognition, work itself, and responsibility figured among the most popular intrinsic motivators.

Thus, it is proposed that many a bank should reconsider its practice of "buying" experienced hires during boom times from the market. Such practice may be helpful to earn the euros in the short-term, but it does not help to build a value-based, purpose-driven corporate culture. In particular, broadly implementing such practices, a bank will never earn the buyers' credibility for being able to cultivate talent on its own. This implies a bank has to trade off short-term benefits with mid-term ones, and may have to give away some of its business in the short-term, in order to be more credibly and consistently positioned in the mid-term. In particular, many a major bracket bank should consider it imperative to

- Foster *long-term* personal growth
- Retain key skills[50]
- Put a stronger emphasis on building, rather than buying talent
- Balance incentives.

49 Cf. Herzberg[116], page 91.

50 As *Berry* and *Parasuraman* note, "[i]nternal marketing has been emphasized in the services marketing literature because the services product is a performance and the performers are employees. Thus service firms must focus attention and resources on attracting, developing, motivating, and retaining qualified employees through job-products that satisfy their needs", see Berry[26], page 151.

The latter means banks should seek to retain talent also by offering other than purely financial benefits. A stronger build as opposed to buy philosophy may already constitute an element of such culture, since it yields a higher share of "promotions from within", which may encourage junior talent to stay. In accordance with that, banks may also put a stronger emphasis on training other than "on the job", thus expressing their commitment to further develop their employees' capabilities. Last but not least, banks may consider offering their employees more room for developing in the way they like[51]. The "fellowship program" by consulting company McKinsey, which offers university graduates a three years paid contract, of which the first two years are being passed on the job, and the third can be used for MBA or doctoral studies, may be considered an example for such balancing of incentives.

To conclude this paragraph, let us have a look at two effects that an excellent reputation has on the individual-corporation interplay.

- In a business environment where reputation is one of the most important prerequisites for customer acquisition, highly renowned banks will find it easier to attract talent, since talent will naturally feel attracted by the banks offering the most interesting client portfolio[52]. This suggests that less renowned banks may have to hire some key individuals and engage them in the longer term, in order to offer the knowhow and client portfolio necessary to attract top talent. This may provide then the basis for the building of a high-performing organisation that is able to cultivate and free talent on its own[53]

- Second, reputation makes a bank less vulnerable to losses of employees. If a bank has an excellent reputation and a company's key banker leaves the bank, the company will trust the bank's reputation that an equally suited banker will take over

51 As *Levinson* notes, an employee may choose not to be expendable "in an organization that he feels regards him as an instrument for reaching a goal. Many young people are refusing to enter large organizations for just this reason", see Levinson[158], page 112.

52 Put differently, reputation on the customer market transfers to reputation on the talent market.

53 One may want to add that such efforts may be taken during "bearish" phases, in order to be in good shape once markets are up again.

the leaving banker's role. That way, reputation helps a bank to retain customers when individuals leave.

Thus, an excellent reputation renders the task of acquiring gifted individuals a lot easier, while making the company less dependent on specific individuals. On the other hand, if a bank manages to hire, develop, and retain gifted individuals, positive spill-backs on reputation can be expected. This means reputation and people management can be considered reinforcing devices.

Generating and enhancing corporation-owned customer benefits

In addition to hiring, developing, and retaining the right people, a bank may seek to increase corporation-owned customer benefits in order to increase its attractiveness to potential clients. This means a bank should generate offers whose benefits a banker cannot easily copy or take with him when he leaves the bank, and which thus would be, from a (potential) client's view, at stake if he followed the banker to another bank. To use *Berry*'s terms, banks may want to aim at a transition from "level two relationship marketing" whose primary bond is "social", to "level three relationship marketing" whose primary bond is "structural"[54].

M&A advice constituting a highly intangible, knowledge- and knowhow-driven product, such corporation-owned customer benefits may most likely be based on the transfer of M&A-related knowledge and skills to corporations. For instance may banks want to give perspectives on the client-specific industry development and according success factors of M&A, or they may want to share their insights as to in what the most important prerequisites for the successful execution of an M&A transaction consist. The generation of knowledge to be shared should e not left in the responsibility of few bankers, but systematic processes and dedicated teams, possibly in "rotation

54 *Berry* differentiates in total three levels of relationship marketing, where level three offers target customers "value-adding benefits that are difficult or expensive for customers to provide and that are not readily available elsewhere", which means "the solution to the customer's problem is designed into the service-delivery system rather than depending upon the relationship-building skills of individual service providers. The problem solution is 'structural' and thus binds the customer to the company instead of – or in addition to – an individual service provider who may leave the firm", cf. Berry[27], pp. 240, 241.

schemes", should be put into place to institutionalise the generation of knowledge on an ongoing basis[55]. Thereby, knowledge may be shared in the form of oral or written communication, be it, for instance, through publications in renowned magazines, reports shared only with a selection of companies, seminars to which companies are being invited, or presentations at respective companies' sites.

Beyond that, and probably even more important, banks may want to transfer knowhow. In contrast to knowledge sharing, this comprises the enabling of a company to perform tasks on its own which it formerly was unable to perform without the help of third parties. The offering of negotiation skill seminars to core clients, or the coaching of their M&A department members, for instance on the purpose and usage of a newly developed valuation tool, may represent examples for such knowhow transfer. Again, these efforts should be anchored in systematic institutional processes, and be offered on an ongoing basis.

Systematic knowledge sharing and transfer may provide the starting point of a "partnership" between companies and banks, rather than one-sided dependency, and may thus be considered yet another means of goodwill creation. Such knowhow transfer can be expected to strengthen client relationships in the mid-term, rather than cannibalising business away from investment banks to the companies that use their advice – provided banks do have the intellectual power to stay on the "cutting edge" of knowledge and skill development.

It is here where the circle to complementary measures to be taken, namely to create an environment that attracts, develops, and retains suited individuals, closes. While the establishment of systematic processes lies in a bank's corporate power, the success of its endeavours to generate and transfer knowledge and knowhow on a regular basis – with the purpose of tightening corporate bonding – strongly depends on its employees' motivation and capability to develop and advance according skills and "fill" these tools with contents. Again, if a bank succeeds in offering knowledge and knowhow transfer, a positive spill-back on reputation can be expected.

55 Some of this task is already being accomplished by a bank's research department, which is separated by Chinese walls from the bank's "executing arms", though.

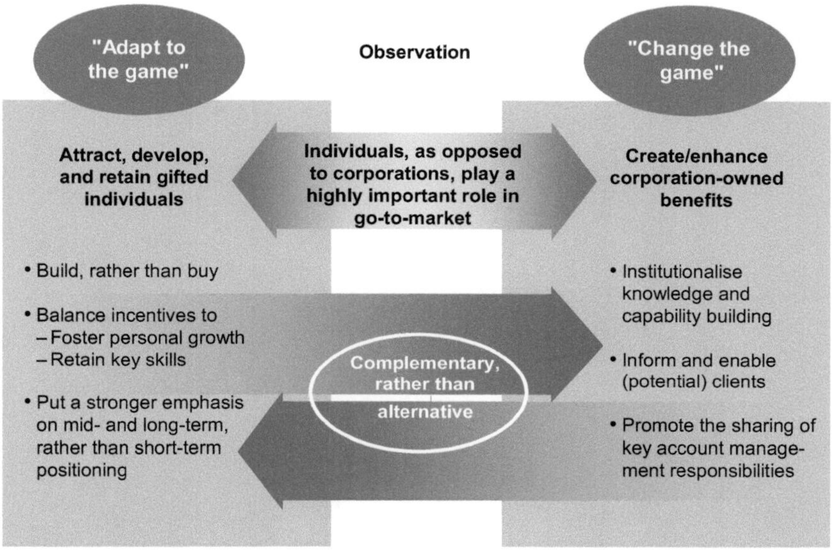

Figure 12.9: Recommendations from an individual-corporation perspective

In addition, banks may want to think about a more pronounced sharing of key account management responsibilities between several bankers, in order to be less vulnerable to the leaving of a banker.

Figure 12.9 summarises this paragraph's discussion. As illustrated, the importance of individuals in a bank's go-to-market yields two basic starting points for a bank's successful positioning. Where the first imperative, namely to attract, develop, and retain the right people, reflects a bank's deliberate *adaption* to the "rules of the game", the second, namely to enhance corporation-owned customer benefits, makes use of its potential to *change* the "rules of the game" in its own favour. These two paths should be considered complements, rather than alternatives.

Appendix

Questionnaire

Your company has made an M&A project between July 2000 and now. This questionnaire deals with your opinion about certain banks, as well as the process by means of which you selected one of the banks to act as M&A advisor to you on this project.

In the case where your company has made **several** M&A projects between July 2000 and now, please pick a **single** one of these projects*, and give your opinion on **this specific** one.
The technical terms that this questionnaire uses are underlined, and a clarification of the terms (in case you are not familiar with them) can be found on page 10. Please note in particular that, unless specified differently, the term investment bank is used to denote a pure investment bank or the investment banking division of a universal bank.

This questionnaire takes about 20 minutes to complete. All you have to do is to check the applying boxes. Please do also choose a username and password, in order to be able to later access the results (a dummy is provided on page 11).

Thank you for your participation!

*** but one for which you used a bank's advice**

YOU AND YOUR COMPANY

What geography is your company (its headquarter) in? Please check.

O UK
O France
O Germany
O Scandinavia
O Other. Please specify: ____________

What about were your company's annual revenues **before** the M&A project? Please check.

O less than 50m
O 50m - 99m
O 100m - 249m
O 250m - 499m
O 500m - 999m
O 1.0b - 2.4b
O 2.5b - 4.9b
O 5.0b - 15.0b
O More than 15.0b

Which of the following applied to your company before the transaction? Please check.

O Publicly owned
O Privately owned

What is your position in your company? Please check.

O CFO/Financial Director
O Treasurer
O Member of the strategic M&A department
O Other. Please specify: ____________

THE M&A PROJECT

What was your company's role in the M&A project? Please check.

O To acquire a company
O To acquire some business of a company
O To sell our company
O To sell one of our businesses
O To fend off take-over
O To merge with a company
O Other. Please specify: ____________

What about the geographic reach of the M&A project? Please check what applies.

O Domestic
O Cross-border within Europe
O Cross-border trans-atlantic

What about was the M&A transaction volume in question?

O less than 50m
O 50m - 99m
O 100m - 249m
O 250m - 499m
O 500m - 999m
O 1.0b - 2.4b
O 2.5b - 4.9b
O 5.0b - 15.0b
O More than 15.0b

Has the transaction been completed?

O Completed
O Failed/fended off
O Too early to tell. Project still alive

How big was the M&A project's **potential impact** on the corporate governance and organization of **your company**? Please check.

Very low = 1 O 2 O 3 O 4 O 5 O 6 O 7 O 8 O 9 O = Very high

How would you rate your company's risk that was associated with the M&A project/ transaction itself?

Very low = 1 O 2 O 3 O 4 O 5 O 6 O 7 O 8 O 9 O = Very high

How would you rate the importance of your investment bank choice decision for your company's future welfare?

Very low = 1 O 2 O 3 O 4 O 5 O 6 O 7 O 8 O 9 O = Very high

Who in your company was involved in selecting the advising investment bank(s)? Please check.

O CEO/Chairman
O CFO/Financial director
O Treasury department
O Members of the strategic M&A department
O Others. Please specify: ____________

How easy was it for you to make up your mind about the capabilities of different banks

	Very easy = 1	2	3	4	5	6	7	8	9 = Very difficult
... **before** the solicitation events	O	O	O	O	O	O	O	O	O
... **after** the soliciation events?	O	O	O	O	O	O	O	O	O

How difficult was it for you to decide yourself for one of the banks as opposed to others as your advisor?

Not difficult at all = 1 O 2 O 3 O 4 O 5 O 6 O 7 O 8 O 9 O = Very difficult

How big was the role the lead bank was supposed to play in the course of the M&A project?

Not that important a role = 1 O 2 O 3 O 4 O 5 O 6 O 7 O 8 O 9 O = Highly important a role

Which of the following tasks was the lead bank supposed to carry out/assist your company in? Please check **all that apply**.

- O Identify potential transaction counterpart(s)
- O Establish contact to potential counterpart(s)
- O Valuate potential counterpart(s)
- O Support negotiations with potential counterpart(s)
- O Advise on deal structure/contraction
- O Provide financing for deal

How big was your time pressure to choose the advising bank(s)?

Very low = 1 O 2 O 3 O 4 O 5 O 6 O 7 O 8 O 9 O = Very high

Please give us your opinion about the following investment banks' public reputation.

Please mark one check for each bank.

	Poor reputation = 1	2	3	4	5	6	7	8	Excellent reputation = 9	Have no opinion about their reputation
ABN Amro	O	O	O	O	O	O	O	O	O	O
Credit Suisse First Boston	O	O	O	O	O	O	O	O	O	O
Deutsche Bank	O	O	O	O	O	O	O	O	O	O
Dresdner Kleinwort Wasserst.	O	O	O	O	O	O	O	O	O	O
Goldman Sachs	O	O	O	O	O	O	O	O	O	O
J.P. Morgan Chase	O	O	O	O	O	O	O	O	O	O
Lazard LLC	O	O	O	O	O	O	O	O	O	O
Lehman Brothers	O	O	O	O	O	O	O	O	O	O
Merrill Lynch	O	O	O	O	O	O	O	O	O	O
Morgan Stanley DW	O	O	O	O	O	O	O	O	O	O
Rothschild	O	O	O	O	O	O	O	O	O	O
Schroder Salomon Smith Barney	O	O	O	O	O	O	O	O	O	O
UBS Warburg	O	O	O	O	O	O	O	O	O	O
Other:____________	O	O	O	O	O	O	O	O	O	O
Other: ____________	O	O	O	O	O	O	O	O	O	O

"The quality of M&A advice given by the big investment banks (as the ones mentioned above) is very much alike."

Fully disagree = 1 O 2 O 3 O 4 O 5 O 6 O 7 O 8 O 9 O = Fully agree

"Regarding the M&A lead bank, our company is always seriously interested in alternatives to the banks we have already used."

Fully disagree = 1 O 2 O 3 O 4 O 5 O 6 O 7 O 8 O 9 O = Fully agree

Which of these **investment banks** did your company have an investment banking relationship (i.e., an exchange of ideas on an ongoing basis) with, **ahead of the M&A project?**

Please indicate the type of relationship, if any, your company had with the following investment banks, and indicate the duration of this relationship.

	Had no relationship with this bank	Only for key banks you had a relationship with: Character of relationship (loose/inactive … intense/active)									Duration of relationship (in years ahead of transaction)			
		1	2	3	4	5	6	7	8	9	<1	1 to 2	3 to 5	more than 5
ABN Amro	O	O	O	O	O	O	O	O	O	O	O	O	O	O
Credit Suisse First Boston	O	O	O	O	O	O	O	O	O	O	O	O	O	O
Deutsche Bank	O	O	O	O	O	O	O	O	O	O	O	O	O	O
Dresdner Kleinwort Wasserstein	O	O	O	O	O	O	O	O	O	O	O	O	O	O
Goldman Sachs	O	O	O	O	O	O	O	O	O	O	O	O	O	O
J.P. Morgan Chase	O	O	O	O	O	O	O	O	O	O	O	O	O	O
Lazard LLC	O	O	O	O	O	O	O	O	O	O	O	O	O	O
Lehman Brothers	O	O	O	O	O	O	O	O	O	O	O	O	O	O
Merrill Lynch	O	O	O	O	O	O	O	O	O	O	O	O	O	O
Morgan Stanley DW	O	O	O	O	O	O	O	O	O	O	O	O	O	O
Rothschild	O	O	O	O	O	O	O	O	O	O	O	O	O	O
Schroder Salomon Smith Barney	O	O	O	O	O	O	O	O	O	O	O	O	O	O
UBS Warburg	O	O	O	O	O	O	O	O	O	O	O	O	O	O
Other: ____________	O	O	O	O	O	O	O	O	O	O	O	O	O	O

How about these banks' **key bankers?** You might have had a relationship with certain key bankers* **ahead of the M&A project.**

Please indicate the type of relationship, if any, your company had with the key bankers, and indicate the duration of this relationship.

	Had no relationship with him/her	Only for key bankers you had a relationship with: Character of relationship (loose/inactive … intense/active)									Duration of relationship (in years ahead of transaction)			
											<1	1 to 2	3 to 5	more than 5
ABN Amro's banker	O	O	O	O	O	O	O	O	O	O	O	O	O	O
Credit Suisse First Boston's banker	O	O	O	O	O	O	O	O	O	O	O	O	O	O
Deutsche Bank's banker	O	O	O	O	O	O	O	O	O	O	O	O	O	O
Dresdner Kleinwort Wasserstein's banker	O	O	O	O	O	O	O	O	O	O	O	O	O	O
Goldman Sachs' banker	O	O	O	O	O	O	O	O	O	O	O	O	O	O
J.P. Morgan Chase's banker	O	O	O	O	O	O	O	O	O	O	O	O	O	O
Lazard LLC's banker	O	O	O	O	O	O	O	O	O	O	O	O	O	O
Lehman Brothers' banker	O	O	O	O	O	O	O	O	O	O	O	O	O	O
Merrill Lynch's banker	O	O	O	O	O	O	O	O	O	O	O	O	O	O
Morgan Stanley DW's banker	O	O	O	O	O	O	O	O	O	O	O	O	O	O
Rothschild's banker	O	O	O	O	O	O	O	O	O	O	O	O	O	O
Schroder Salomon Smith Barney's banker	O	O	O	O	O	O	O	O	O	O	O	O	O	O
UBS Warburg's banker	O	O	O	O	O	O	O	O	O	O	O	O	O	O
Other: ____________'s banker	O	O	O	O	O	O	O	O	O	O	O	O	O	O

* such relationship may have been built at times when this banker was with another bank

What applies to the **lead bank** to which you finally awarded the mandate? Please check **all that apply.**

- O Bank did previous M&A project with us
- O Was the first time we used this bank for M&A
- O We had used another bank for previous M&A
- O Bank had already done IPO for us
- O Bank had already led equity offerings or debt offerings for us
- O Bank we always use for investment banking
- O Had an investment banking relationship with bank prior to selection
- O Had a commercial banking relationship with them
- O Bank we had never used for anything before
- O Bank has members on our board

If the lead bank had already worked on one of your M&A projects before: How good was the execution of the most recent M&A project it had done for you?

Poor = 1 O 2 O 3 O 4 O 5 O 6 O 7 O 8 O 9 O = Excellent

What applies to the bank's **key banker** of the team, to which you finally awarded the mandate? Please check all that apply.

- O He/she did the previous M&A project with us
- O We had never worked with her/him before
- O We always use this banker for M&A
- O We had a relationship with her/him prior to selection
- O The banker had changed the bank, and we had followed the banker to her/his new bank
- O The banker is very well known in industry

If the key banker had already worked on one of your M&A projects before: How good was his/her execution of the most recent project he/she avised you on?

Poor = 1 O 2 O 3 O 4 O 5 O 6 O 7 O 8 O 9 O = Excellent

Who initiated the M&A project/transaction?

- O The investment bank that advised us
- O Our company
- O Our (potential) transaction counterpart, resp. the investment bank they worked with
- O Other. Please specify: ____________________

What applied to the investment banking experience of your company, **prior** to the M&A project?

- O First time we dealt with investment banking
- O Had some, but not much experience with investment banking
- O Had considerable experience with investment banking
- O Were already very experienced with investment banking

Which was the selection procedure your company applied to select the advising investment bank? Please check what applies.

- O We invited several banks to make presentations, and selected thereafter
- O We discussed the transaction with several banks, and selected thereafter
- O We contacted only one bank for the transaction, and this was
  - O our existing investment banking relationship
  - O our existing commercial banking relationship
  - O some bank we did not have a relationship with
  - O the bank who brought us the idea
  - O the bank that has members on our board
- O We have a rotation scheme among a special set of investment banks, and assigned the mandate to the bank whose turn it was
- O We gave the mandate to the bank that was on <u>retainer</u>
- O Other. Please specify: ____________________

How important was it that no information about you planning an M&A project would leak out in the market?

Not important = 1 O 2 O 3 O 4 O 5 O 6 O 7 O 8 O 9 O = Extremely important

Which banks did you consider as advisor candidates for the transaction? Who did you invite to pitch, and who did you award the mandate to?

Please check all that apply for each of the banks listed.

(**EXAMPLE**: If you awarded UBS Warburg the lead mandate following a presentation, check all of the following for UBS Warburg:

- We considered at some point in time this bank
- We invited this bank for pitch/discussion
- This bank presented its ideas to us
- We chose this bank to be part of the syndicate
- We awarded this bank our lead mandate)

	We considered at some point in time this bank as advisor for the transaction*	We would have liked to invite/ use this bank, but it was not available**	We invited this bank for pitch/ discussion	This bank presented its ideas to us (through pitch or discussion)	We chose this bank to be part of the syndicate	We awarded this bank our lead mandate	This bank provided financing only
ABN Amro	O	O	O	O	O	O	O
CS First Boston	O	O	O	O	O	O	O
Deutsche Bank	O	O	O	O	O	O	O
Dresdner KW	O	O	O	O	O	O	O
Goldman Sachs	O	O	O	O	O	O	O
J.P. Morgan Chase	O	O	O	O	O	O	O
Lazard LLC	O	O	O	O	O	O	O
Lehman Brothers	O	O	O	O	O	O	O
Merrill Lynch	O	O	O	O	O	O	O
Morgan Stanley DW	O	O	O	O	O	O	O
Rothschild	O	O	O	O	O	O	O
Schroder Salomon SB	O	O	O	O	O	O	O
UBS Warburg	O	O	O	O	O	O	O
Other: ____________	O	O	O	O	O	O	O
Other: ____________	O	O	O	O	O	O	O

* for example: we considered the bank at the very beginning, but then decided not to contact it for this transaction

** for example: the bank was already engaged by a competitor or our potential counterpart, did not have the capacity for another mandate, or was not interested in the mandate

Looking at the **banks and their key bankers that you considered***. Please indicate which of the following applies to them.

Please check for all that you considered.

	We considered at some point in time this bank for the transaction*	For the **banks that you did not select**: If their key banker had been more convincing, we might have taken that bank	For the **banks that you did not select**: The key banker was great, but we did not want to use the bank	For the **bank(s) that you selected****: Their key banker was so great we would have liked her/him to do the deal, also if he had been with another bank
ABN Amro	O	O	O	O
Credit Suisse First Boston	O	O	O	O
Deutsche Bank	O	O	O	O
Dresdner Kleinwort Wass.	O	O	O	O
Goldman Sachs	O	O	O	O
J.P. Morgan Chase	O	O	O	O
Lazard LLC	O	O	O	O
Lehman Brothers	O	O	O	O
Merrill Lynch	O	O	O	O
Morgan Stanley DW	O	O	O	O
Rothschild	O	O	O	O
Schroder Sal. Smith Barney	O	O	O	O
UBS Warburg	O	O	O	O
Other: ______	O	O	O	O
Other: ______	O	O	O	O

Please assess for each of the **banks that solicited the M&A project***** the quality of their sales presentation(s) resp. discussion you had with them about the transaction in question.

Please check for each bank that gave a presentation to you, resp. had a discussion with you.

	This bank presented its ideas to us (through presentation or discussion)***	Poor presentation / discussion 1	2	3	4	5	6	7	8	Excellent presentation/ discussion 9
ABN Amro	O	O	O	O	O	O	O	O	O	O
Credit Suisse First Boston	O	O	O	O	O	O	O	O	O	O
Deutsche Bank	O	O	O	O	O	O	O	O	O	O
Dresdner Kleinwort Wass.	O	O	O	O	O	O	O	O	O	O
Goldman Sachs	O	O	O	O	O	O	O	O	O	O
J.P. Morgan Chase	O	O	O	O	O	O	O	O	O	O
Lazard LLC	O	O	O	O	O	O	O	O	O	O
Lehman Brothers	O	O	O	O	O	O	O	O	O	O
Merrill Lynch	O	O	O	O	O	O	O	O	O	O
Morgan Stanley DW	O	O	O	O	O	O	O	O	O	O
Rothschild	O	O	O	O	O	O	O	O	O	O
Schroder Sal. Smith Barney	O	O	O	O	O	O	O	O	O	O
UBS Warburg	O	O	O	O	O	O	O	O	O	O
Other: ______	O	O	O	O	O	O	O	O	O	O
Other: ______	O	O	O	O	O	O	O	O	O	O

* cf. previous page, first column from left (please copy into this column)

** as syndicate member or lead bank, cf. previous page, second and third column from right

*** cf. previous page, fourth column from right (pls. copy into this column)

Please rate the **importance** of the following factors for your final **selection of the lead bank.**

Please mark one check for each factor.

	Not at all important = 1	2	3	4	5	6	7	8	Extremely important = 9
Knowledge/Research on our company	O	O	O	O	O	O	O	O	O
Knowledge/Research on our industry	O	O	O	O	O	O	O	O	O
Knowledge/Research on our domestic market	O	O	O	O	O	O	O	O	O
Understanding of our company's needs	O	O	O	O	O	O	O	O	O
Fee	O	O	O	O	O	O	O	O	O
Bank's ability to challenge and contradict us	O	O	O	O	O	O	O	O	O
Bank's network in the industry	O	O	O	O	O	O	O	O	O
Geographical proximity of bank/banker	O	O	O	O	O	O	O	O	O
Bank's ability to network globally	O	O	O	O	O	O	O	O	O
Bank's ideas on the transaction in question	O	O	O	O	O	O	O	O	O
Bank's experience with similar deals	O	O	O	O	O	O	O	O	O
Bank's reputation	O	O	O	O	O	O	O	O	O
Bank's investment banking relationship with us	O	O	O	O	O	O	O	O	O
Bank's commercial banking relationship with us	O	O	O	O	O	O	O	O	O
Key banker's relationship with our company	O	O	O	O	O	O	O	O	O
Bank had well executed one of our previous deals	O	O	O	O	O	O	O	O	O
Quality of sales presentation	O	O	O	O	O	O	O	O	O
Bank is pure investment bank	O	O	O	O	O	O	O	O	O
Bank is on our company's board	O	O	O	O	O	O	O	O	O
Other. Please specify: ______________________	O	O	O	O	O	O	O	O	O

Considering the **lead bank** that won your mandate. Was it more the **bank corporation** which made you choose this bank, or was it more due to the **key banker** that you awarded them the mandate?

The **key banker** was by far most important = 1	2	3	4	Key banker and bank were **equally** important 5	6	7	8	The **bank** was by far most important = 9
O	O	O	O	O	O	O	O	O

How many <u>solicitation events</u> did your company have with the lead bank, before awarding them the mandate?

O None
O 1 event
O 2 events
O 3 events
O 4 events
O 5 events
O 6 or 7 events
O 8 or 9 events
O 10 or more

		Completely unsatisfied = 1	2	3	4	5	6	7	8	Extremely satisfied = 9	Not applicable
How satisfied were you with...	... the M&A project **overall**?	O	O	O	O	O	O	O	O	O	
	... the **outcome** of the project?	O	O	O	O	O	O	O	O	O	
	... the smoothness and clarity of its **process**?	O	O	O	O	O	O	O	O	O	
	... the **lead bank's overall** contribution/execution?	O	O	O	O	O	O	O	O	O	
Thinking about the performance of the **lead bank** more in detail, how satisfied were you with its ability to...	... meet deadlines?	O	O	O	O	O	O	O	O	O	
	... keep you informed about the state of the project/ communicate interim results internally?	O	O	O	O	O	O	O	O	O	
	... derive clear-defined milestones/responsibilities and deliver against them?	O	O	O	O	O	O	O	O	O	
	... document interim results in a meaningful way?	O	O	O	O	O	O	O	O	O	
	... react to your concerns/input and adapt the project accordingly?	O	O	O	O	O	O	O	O	O	
	... motivate the whole M&A team?	O	O	O	O	O	O	O	O	O	
	... perform the promised tasks dependably and accurately?	O	O	O	O	O	O	O	O	O	
How satisfied were you with its...	... use of your management's time?	O	O	O	O	O	O	O	O	O	
	... style of interaction with your management?	O	O	O	O	O	O	O	O	O	
	... willingness to provide prompt answers to your questions and follow-through?	O	O	O	O	O	O	O	O	O	
	... knowhow of employees?	O	O	O	O	O	O	O	O	O	
	... willingness to understand your company's needs?	O	O	O	O	O	O	O	O	O	
	... courtesy of the bankers?	O	O	O	O	O	O	O	O	O	
	... ability to identify potential transaction counterparts?	O	O	O	O	O	O	O	O	O	O
	... ability to establish contact to the counterpart(s)?	O	O	O	O	O	O	O	O	O	O
	... valuation skills?	O	O	O	O	O	O	O	O	O	O
	... negotiation skills?	O	O	O	O	O	O	O	O	O	O
	... deal structuring/contraction skills?	O	O	O	O	O	O	O	O	O	O

Thinking about some future transaction to come, what applies to the **bank to which you awarded the lead mandate**? Please check **all that apply**.

- O Would avoid using them again
- O May possibly invite them to pitch
- O Would definitely invite them to pitch
- O Have <u>shortlisted</u> them for the next transaction
- O Would probably award them the mandate
- O Would most likely award them the mandate, without seriously considering other banks
- O Would recommend them to others

How likely would you re-engage this bank?

Definitely **not** re-engage = 1 O 2 O 3 O 4 O 5 O 6 O 7 O 8 O 9 O = Definitely re-engage

Thinking about a future transaction, what applies to the **key banker** to which you awarded the mandate? Please check **all that apply**.

- O Would avoid using this key banker
- O Would like to engage her/him also in future
- O Would like to engage only her/him in future
- O Would like to engage only her/him, independent of the bank she/he may be with then
- O Would recommend her/him to others

How likely would you re-engage this banker?

Definitely **not** re-engage = 1 O 2 O 3 O 4 O 5 O 6 O 7 O 8 O 9 O = Definitely re-engage

What, if any, would you want the lead bank do better if you were to use them again? Please state the most important single amendment.

____

____

YOUR COMPANY'S PREVIOUS M&A PROJECT

Was the project that you have assessed throughout the questionnaire your company's first M&A project?

- O Yes
- O No

If no: Please let us know which bank, if any, you had chosen as the lead bank for your previous M&A project.

- O ABN Amro
- O Credit Suisse First Boston
- O Deutsche Bank
- O Dresdner Kleinwort Wass.
- O Goldman Sachs
- O J.P. Morgan Chase
- O Lazard LLC
- O Lehman Brothers
- O Merrill Lynch
- O Morgan Stanley DW
- O Rothschild
- O Schroder Sal. Smith Barney
- O UBS Warburg
- O Other. Please specifiy: ________________

O We had not used a bank for our previous M&A project

As to this previous M&A project you did with the bank you just indicated: How satisfied were you with ...

	Completely unsatisfied = 1	2	3	4	5	6	7	8	Extremely satisfied = 9
... the M&A project **overall**?	O	O	O	O	O	O	O	O	O
... the **outcome** of the project?	O	O	O	O	O	O	O	O	O
... the smoothness and clarity of its **process**?	O	O	O	O	O	O	O	O	O
... the **lead bank's** contribution/execution?	O	O	O	O	O	O	O	O	O

TECHNICAL TERMS USED (IN ALPHABETICAL ORDER)

Investment bank	By the term ***investment bank,*** we denote a pure investment bank or the investment banking division of a universal bank.
Key banker	The ***key banker*** is the banker who leads the bank's team during solicitation resp. execution. The ***key banker*** is the main contact between the bank and the advised company's senior management.
Lead mandate/ lead bank	The ***lead mandate*** is the principal M&A mandate that a company awards to one of the investment banks. In the case where only one bank is chosen to advise the company on a transaction, this bank is the company's ***lead bank*** in the transaction, and it holds the ***lead mandate***. When there are several banks (thus, a so-called *syndicate* of banks) advising a company on a certain transaction, the main advisor is called the ***lead bank***. The lead bank earns more fees than any other of the advising banks, and it holds the ***lead mandate*** for the transaction.
M&A project	By the term ***M&A project***, we denote the activities that you and the advising investment bank(s) undertook in order to prepare the M&A transaction, respectively - in the case of take-over-defense - to avoid the M&A transaction in question.
Relationship	A ***relationship*** provides the means for a regular exchange of thoughts between your company and the bank. Such thoughts may for instance comprise concerns and ideas as to how to further develop your business, or industry perspectives in general. Since a ***relationship*** is not transaction-focused, it is characteristic for ***relationships*** that they also do exist <u>between</u> transactions, resp. when no specific transaction is in sight. ***Relationships*** foster an ongoing dialogue between your company's senior management and the banks' *key bankers*.
Retainer	If a bank is on ***retainer***, your company had promised them already before the concrete M&A project was alive, that they would get the lead mandate for this project. (Such promises may have been made during solicitation of some previous M&A project, where you seriously considered choosing the bank, but eventually awarded the mandate to someone else.)
Shortlisted	If your company has ***shortlisted*** an investment bank for the next *M&A project*, then this bank is on the list of banks which your company wants to contact when the next M&A project comes up (in order to possibly award it the advisory mandate).
Solicitation event	A ***solicitation event*** is a meeting (presentation, discussion) between you and the bank, by means of which the bank wants to convince you of its capabilities to advise you on a specific deal. Solicitation events happen before you make your choice as to which investment bank(s) to choose, and banks consequently want to influence you in their favour.
Syndicate/ syndicate member	If a company selects more than one bank as advisor for a certain transaction, the total of selected banks is called the ***syndicate.*** The banks that constitute the syndicate are called ***syndicate members.***
Transaction volume	If a company acquires some business, the ***transaction volume*** denotes the amount that the acquiring company pays for it (in cash, shares, etc.). If companies A and B merge, such merger can technically be considered a take-over, say A takes over B, and A's shareholders hold 55% of the newly created company, while B's hold 45%. The ***transaction volume*** then denotes the value of the company whose shareholders are going to hold the minority in the newly created company (in our example: B) - thus, the transaction volume amounts to half or less (in our case: 45%) of the newly created company's market cap.

My username and password

PLEASE PRINT and use no more than 10 and no less than 5 letters for each word

My **username** to later access the results of this study is: □□□□□□□□□□

My **password** to later access the results of this study is: □□□□□□□□□□

(Results will be accessible on http://www.uni-mainz.de/~keilbach starting April 2002)

Bibliography

[1] Aaker, David A./Jacobson, Robert, *The Strategic Role of Product Quality*, Journal of Marketing (October 1987), pp. 31–44.

[2] Aaker, David A., *Managing Brand Equity – Capitalizing on the Value of a Brand Name*, The Free Press (1991).

[3] Aaker, David A., *Building Strong Brands*, The Free Press (1996).

[4] Aaker, David A./Joachimsthaler, Erich, *Brand Leadership*, The Free Press (2000).

[5] Achleitner, Ann-Kristin, *Handbuch Investment-Banking*, Gabler, Wiesbaden (1999).

[6] Akerlof, George A., *The Market for 'Lemons'. Qualitative Uncertainty and the Market Mechanism*, Quarterly Journal of Economics, Vol. 84 (1970), pp. 488–500.

[7] Alchian, Armen A./Woodward, Susan E., *The Firm is Dead; Long Live the Firm – A Review for Oliver E. Williamsons's 'The Economic Institutions of Capitalism'*, Journal of Economic Literature, Vol. 26 (1988), pp. 65–79.

[8] Anderson, Erin/Chu, Wujin/Weitz, Barton, *Industrial Purchasing: An Empirical Exploration of the Buyclass Framework*, Journal of Marketing, Vol. 51 (1987), pp. 71–86.

[9] Anderson, Eugene W./Sullivan, Mary W., *The Antecedents and Consequences of Customer Satisfaction*, Marketing Science, Vol. 12 (1993), pp. 125–143.

[10] Anderson, Eugene W./Fornell, Claes/Lehmann, Donald R., *Customer Satisfaction, Market Share, and Profitability: Findings from Sweden*, Journal of Marketing, Vol. 58 (July 1994), pp. 53–66.

[11] Arndt, Johan *Perceived Risk, Sociometric Intetration, and Word-of-Mouth in the Adoption of a New Food Product*, in:

Cox, D. F. (Ed.), *Risk Taking and Information Handling in Consumer Behavior*, Harvard University Press, Boston (1967), pp. 289–316.

[12] Arnthorsson, Arni/Berry, Wendall E./Urbany, Joel E., *Difficulty of Prepurchase Quality Inspection – Conceptualization and Measurement*, in: Holman, R. H./Solomon, M. R. (Eds.), *Advances in Consumer Research*, Vol. 18 (1991), pp. 217–224.

[13] Arora, Neeraj/Allenby, Greg M., *Measuring the Infuence of Individual Preference Structures in Group Decision Making*, Journal of Marketing Research, Vol. 36 (November 1999), pp. 476–487.

[14] Arrow, Kenneth J., *Agency and the Market*, in: Arrow, K. J./Intriligator, M. D. (Eds.) *Handbook of Mathematical Economics*, North-Holland Amsterdam, Vol. 3 (1986), pp. 1183–1195.

[15] Atkins, Ralph, *Germany casts some light on takeover law*, Financial Times, Companies & Finance International (March 23, 2001), page 23.

[16] Backhaus, Klaus, *Investitionsgütermarketing – Theorieloses Konzept mit Allgemeinheitsanspruch?*, Zeitschrift für betriebswirtschaftliche Forschung, Vol. 44 (1992), pp. 771–791.

[17] Backhaus, Klaus, *Industriegütermarketing*, 6th edition, Vahlen, München (1999).

[18] Backhaus, Klaus/Erichson, Bernd/Plinke, Wulff/Weiber, Rolf, *Multivariate Analysemethoden – eine anwendungsorientierte Einführung*, 9th edition (1st edition 1980), Springer (2000).

[19] Bauer, Hans H./Huber, Frank, *Der Wert der Marke*, Institut für Marktorientierte Unternehmensführung der Universität Mannheim, Reihe Management-Knowhow Nr. 31, Mannheim (1997).

[20] Bauer, Raymond A., *Consumer Behavior as Risk Taking*, in Hancock, R. S., *Dynamic Marketing for a Changing World*, Chicago – American Marketing Association (1960), pp. 389–398 [Cited from Cox, Donald F. (Ed.), *Risk Taking and Information-Handling in Consumer Behavior*, Harward University Press, Boston (1967), pp. 23–24].

[21] Bearden, William O./Netemeyer, Richard G./Mobley, Mary F., *Handbook of Marketing Scales – Multi-Item Measures for Marketing and Consumer Behavior Research*, Sage Publications (1993).

[22] Becker, Gernot, *Mergers & Acquisitions als Instrument zur Umsetzung von Konzernstrategien*, WISU (1994), pp. 198–200.

[23] Benkenstein, Martin/Güthoff, Judith, *Typologisierung von Dienstleistungen – ein Ansatz auf der Grundlage system- und käuferverhaltenstheoretischer Überlegungen*, Zeitschrift für Betriebswirtschaft, 12, Vol. 66 (1996), pp. 1493–1510.

[24] Benston, George J./Smith, Clifford W., *A Transactions Cost Approach to the Theory of Financial Intermediation*, Journal of Finance, Vol. 31 (May 1976), pp. 215–231.

[25] Berry, Leonard L., *Services Marketing is Different*, Business, Vol. 30(3) (May/June 1980), pp. 24–29.

[26] Berry, Leonard L./Parasuraman, A., *Marketing Services – Competing through Quality*, New York, Free Press (1991).

[27] Berry, Leonard L., *Relationship Marketing of Services – Growing Interest, Emerging Perspective*, Journal of the Academy of Marketing Science, Vol. 23 (1995), pp. 236–245.

[28] Bettman, James R., *Perceived Risk and Its Components: A Model and Empirical Test*, Journal of Marketing Research, Vol. 10 (May 1973), pp. 184–190.

[29] Bettman, James R., *Decision Net Models of Buyer Information Processing and Choice – Findings, Problems, and Prospects*, in: Hughes, G. D./Ray M. R. (Eds.), *Buyer/Consumer Information Processing*, University of North Carolina Press, Chapel Hill, North Carolina (1974), pp. 59–74.

[30] Bettman, James R., *Information Integration in Consumer Risk Perception: A Comparison of Two Models of Component Conceptualization*, Journal of Applied Psychology, Vol. 60 (June 1975), pp. 381–385.

[31] Bettman, James R./Park, C. Whan, *Effects of Prior Knowledge and Experience and Phase of the Choice Process in Consumer Decision Processes – a Protocol Analysis*, Journal of Consumer Research, Vol. 7 (December 1980), pp. 234–48.

[32] Bitner, Mary J., *Building Service Relationships: It's All About Promises*, Journal of the Academy of Marketing Science, Vol. 23 (1995), pp. 246–251.

[33] Bitz, Michael, *Erscheinungsformen und Funktionen von Finanzintermediären*, Wirtschaftswissenschaftliches Studium, Heft 10 (Oktober 1989), pp. 430–436.

[34] Bloch, Peter H./Richins, Marsha L., *A Theoretical Model for the Study of Product Importance Perceptions*, Journal of Marketing, Vol. 47 (1983), pp. 69–81.

[35] Bloemer, José M./Lemmink, Jos G. A. M., *The Importance of Customer Satisfaction in Explaining Brand and Dealer Loyalty*, Journal of Marketing Management, Vol. 8 (1992), pp. 351–364.

[36] Bössmann, Eva, *Unternehmungen, Märkte, Transaktionskosten: Die Koordination ökonomischer Aktivitäten*, Wirtschaftswissenschaftliches Studium, Vol. 12 (1983), pp. 105–111.

[37] Bolton, Ruth N./Drew, James H., *A Multistage Model of Customers' Assessments of Service Quality and Value*, Journal of Consumer Research, Vol. 17 (March 1991), pp. 375–384.

[38] Booth, James R./Smith, Richard L., *Capital Raising, Underwriting, and the Certification Hypothesis*, Journal of Financial Economics, Vol. 15 (1986), pp. 261–281.

[39] Bower, Joseph L., *Not All M&As Are Alike – and That Matters*, Harvard Business Review (March 2001), pp. 93–101.

[40] Bradley, James V., *Distribution-Free Statistical Tests*, Prentice-Hall, Englewood Cliffs, New Jersey (1968).

[41] Breuer, Wolfgang, *Finanzintermediation und Reputationseffekte*, Kredit und Kapital, Vol. 28(4) (1995), pp. 516–534.

[42] Brosius, Gerhard/Brosius, Felix, *SPSS Base System und Professional Statistics*, International Thomson Publishing (1995).

[43] Brossard, Hubert L., *Information Sources Used by an Organization During a Complex Decision Process – An Exploratory Study*, Industrial Marketing Management, Vol. 27 (1998), pp. 41–50.

[44] Brown, Jonathan, *Team Players and Star Performers*, Euromoney (December 2000), pp. 108–111.

[45] Bruhn, Manfred, *Qualitätssicherung im Dienstleistungsmarketing – eine Einführung in die theoretischen und praktischen Probleme*, in: Bruhn, M./Stauss, B. (Eds.), *Dienstleistungsqualität – Konzepte, Methoden, Erfahrungen*, Wiesbaden (1991), pp. 19–47.

[46] Buchanan, Robin W. T./Gillies, Crawford S., *Value Managed Relationships: The Key to Customer Retention and Profitability*, European Management Journal, Vol. 8 (1990), pp. 523–526.

[47] Bühl, Achim/Zöfel, Peter, *SPSS Version 10 – Einführung in die moderne Datenanalyse unter Windows*, 7th edition, Addison-Wesley (2000).

[48] Burnkrant, Robert E./Unnava, H. Rao, *Effects of Self-Referencing on Persuasion*, Journal of Consumer Research, Vol. 22 (1995), pp. 17–26.

[49] Caminiti, Susan, *The Payoff from a Good Reputation*, Fortune (February 10, 1992), pp. 74–77.

[50] Campbell, Tim S./Kracaw, William A., *Information Production, Market Signalling, and the Theory of Financial Intermediation*, Journal of Finance, Vol. 35 (1980), pp. 863–882.

[51] Cannon, Joseph P./Perreault, William D., *Buyer-Seller Relationships in Business Markets*, Journal of Marketing Research, Vol. 36 (1999), pp. 439–516.

[52] Cardozo, Richard N./Cagley, James W., *Experimental Study of Industrial Buyer Behavior*, Journal of Marketing Research, Vol. 8 (August 1971), pp. 329–334.

[53] Carter, Richard B./Dark, Frederick H., *An Empirical Examination of Investment Banking Reputation Measures*, The Financial Review, Vol. 27(3) (1992), pp. 355–374.

[54] Chemmanur, Thomas J./Fulghieri, Paolo, *Investment Bank Reputation, Information Production, and Financial Intermediation*, Journal of Finance, Vol. 49(1) (1994), pp. 57–79.

[55] Choffray, Jean-Marie/Lilien, Gary L., *Assessing Response to Industrial Marketing Strategy*, Journal of Marketing (April 1978), pp. 20–31.

[56] Choffray, Jean-Marie/Johnston, Paul E., *Measuring Perceived Pre-Purchase Risk for a New Industrial Product*, Industrial Marketing Management, Vol. 8 (1979), pp. 333–340.

[57] Coombs, Clyde H./Huang, Lily, *Tests of a Portfolio Theory of Risk Preference*, Journal of Experimental Psychology, Vol. 85 (1970), pp. 23–29.

[58] Copeland, Melvin T., *Principles of Merchandising*, 3rd edition, Chicago – New York (1925).

[59] Corsten, Hans, *Zur Diskussion der Dienstleistungsbesonderheiten und ihrer ökonomischen Auswirkungen*, Jahrbuch der Absatz- und Verbrauchsforschung, Vol. 32(1) (1986), pp. 16–41.

[60] Cox, Donald F., *Risk Handling in Consumer Behavior – an Intensive Study of Two Cases*, in: Cox, D. F. (Ed.), *Risk Taking and Information Handling in Consumer Behavior*, Harvard University Press, Boston (1967), pp. 34–81.

[61] Cox, Donald F., *Synthesis: Risk Taking and Information Handling in Consumer Behavior*, in: Cox, D. F. (Ed.), *Risk Taking and Information Handling in Consumer Behavior*, Harvard University Press, Boston (1967), pp. 604–639.

[62] Craven, John A., *Mergers & Acquisitions*, in: Gerke W./Steiner, M. (Eds.), *Handwörterbuch des Bank- und Finanzwesens*, 2nd edition, Stuttgart (1995), pp. 1443–1453.

[63] Cunningham, Scott M., *The Major Dimensions of Perceived Risk*, in: Cox, D. F. (Ed.), *Risk Taking and Information Handling in Consumer Behavior*, Harvard University Press, Boston (1967), pp. 82–108.

[64] Currie, Antony, *Ganging Up Against the Big Boys*, Euromoney (October 2000), pp. 50–68.

[65] Currie, Antony, *Brawn Takes on Brains in the Battle for the Corporates*, Euromoney (October 2001), pp. 92–100.

[66] Darby, Michael R./Karni, Edi, *Free Competition and the Optimal Amount of Fraud*, Journal of Law and Economics, Vol. 16 (April 1974), pp. 67–88.

[67] Dawes, Philip L./Dowling, Grahame R./Patterson, Paul G., *Information Sources Used to Select Different Types of Management Consultancy Services*, Asia Pacific Journal of Management, Vol. 8 (1991), pp. 185–199.

[68] Decker, Reinhold/Temme, Thorsten, *Diskriminanzanalyse*, in: Herrmann, A./Homburg, C.(Eds.), *Marktforschung – Methoden, Anwendungen, Praxisbeispiele*, 2nd edition (first edition 1999), Gabler, Wiesbaden (2000), pp. 295–335.

[69] Deering, Barbara J./Jacoby, Jacob, *Risk Enhancement and Risk Reduction as Strategies for Handling Perceived Risk*, in: Venkatesan, M. (Ed.), Proceedings, 3rd Annual Convention of the Association for Consumer Research (1972), pp. 404–416.

[70] Deiß, Christian, *M&A-Beratung in Deutschland – Funktionen und Akteure*, M&A Review (November 1997), pp. 488–498.

[71] Dempsey, William A., *Vendor Selection and the Buying Process*, Industrial Marketing Management, Vol. 7 (1978), pp. 257–267.

[72] Derbaix, Christian, *Perceived Risk and Risk Relievers: An Empirical Investigation*, Journal of Economic Psychology, Vol. 3 (1983), pp. 19–38.

[73] Dibelius, Alexander, *Mergers & Acquisitions aus Sicht der Kapitalmärkte*, in: Picot, Gerhard (Ed.), *Handbuch Mergers & Acquisitions – Planung, Durchführung, Integration*, Schäfer-Poeschel, Stuttgart (2000), pp. 33–51.

[74] Dietzsch-Doertenbach, Maximilian, *Fusionen – Bildung von Gemeinschaftsunternehmen*, in: Achleitner, Ann-Kristin/ Thoma, Georg F. (Eds.), *Handbuch Corporate Finance*, Dt. Wirtschaftsdienst, Köln (1997), paragraph 10.1.5.

[75] Diller, Hermann/Kusterer, Marion, *Beziehungsmanagement – Theoretische Grundlagen und explorative Befunde*, Marketing ZFP, Vol. 10 (1988), pp. 211–220.

[76] Douglas, Torin, *The Power of Branding*, in: Lovelock, Christopher H. (Ed.), *Services Marketing*, 3rd edition, Prentice Hall, New Jersey (1996), pp. 398–401.

[77] Dowling, Grahame R., *Perceived Risk: The Concept and Its Measurement*, Psychology and Marketing (Fall 1986), pp. 193–210.

[78] Dowling, Grahame R./Staelin, Richard, *A Model of Perceived Risk and Intended Risk-handling Activity*, Journal of Consumer Research, Vol. 21 (June 1994), pp. 119–134.

[79] Eisenhardt, Kathleen M., *Agency Theory: An Assessment and Review*, Academy of Management Review, Vol. 14(1) (1989), pp. 57–74.

[80] Elschen, Rainer, *Gegenstand und Anwendungsmöglichkeiten der Agency-Theorie*, Zeitschrift für betriebswirtschaftliche Forschung, Vol. 43 (1991), pp. 1002–1012.

[81] Emons, Winand, *Warranties, Moral Hazard, and the Lemons Problem*, Journal of Economic Theory, Vol. 46 (1988), pp. 16–33.

[82] Engelhardt, Werner H./Backhaus, Klaus/Günter, Bernd, *Investitionsgüter-Marketing – Eine kritische Bestandsaufnahme und Ansatzpunkte zur Weiterentwicklung*, Zeitschrift für Betriebswirtschaft, Vol. 47 (1977), pp. 153–166.

[83] Engelhardt, Werner H./Dichtl, Erwin, *Investitionsgütermarketing*, Wirtschaftswissenschaftliches Studium, Vol. 9 (1980), pp. 145–153.

[84] Engelhardt, Werner H./Witte, Petra, *Konzeptionen des Investitionsgüter-Marketing – eine kritische Bestandsaufnahme ausgewählter Ansätze*, in: Kliche, M. (Ed.), *Investitionsgütermarketing – Positionsbestimmung und Perspektiven*, Festschrift zum 60. Geburtstag von Karl-Heinz Strothmann (1990), pp. 3–17.

[85] Engelhardt, Werner H./Kleinaltenkamp, Michael/Reckenfelderbäumer, Martin, *Leistungsbündel als Absatzobjekte – ein Ansatz zur Überwindung der Dichotomie von Sach- und Dienstleistungen*, Zeitschrift für betriebswirtschaftliche Forschung, Vol. 45 (1993), pp. 395–426.

[86] Esch, Franz-Rudolf/Wicke, Andreas, *Herausforderungen und Aufgaben des Markenmanagements*, in: Esch, Franz-Rudolf (Ed.), *Moderne Markenführung*, Gabler 1999, 2nd edition, Wiesbaden (2000), pp. 3–55.

[87] Esch, Franz-Rudolf, *Ansätze zur Messung des Markenwerts*, in: Esch, Franz-Rudolf (Ed.), *Moderne Markenführung*, Gabler 1999, 2nd edition, Wiesbaden (2000), pp. 937–965.

[88] Farquhar, Peter H., *Managing Brand Equity*, Marketing Research (September 1989), pp. 24–33.

[89] Festinger, Leon, *A Theory of Cognitive Dissonance*, Stanford (1957).

[90] Fischer, Marc et al., *Marketing und neuere ökonomische Theorie: Ansätze zu einer Systematisierung*, Betriebswirtschaftliche Forschung und Praxis, Vol. 45(4) (1993), pp. 444–470.

[91] Ford, Gary T./Smith, Darlene B./Swasy, John L., *An Empirical Test of the Search, Experience and Credence Attributes Framework*, in: Houston, M. J. (Ed.), *Advances in Consumer Research*, Vol. 15 (1988), pp. 239–243.

[92] Fornell, Claes, *A National Customer Satisfaction Barometer: The Swedish Experience*, Journal of Marketing, Vol. 56 (January 1992), pp. 6–21.

[93] Ganesan, Shankar, *Determinants of Long-Term Orientation in Buyer-Seller Relationships*, Journal of Marketing, Vol. 58 (1994), pp. 1–19.

[94] Garbe, Bernd, *Marktforschung im Industriegütersektor – vom Kundenwunsch zum Produktkonzept*, in: Herrmann, A./Homburg, C. (Eds.), *Marktforschung – Methoden, Anwendungen, Praxisbeispiele*, 2nd edition (first edition 1999), Gabler, Wiesbaden (2000), pp. 1107–1126.

[95] Gemünden, Hans G., *Perceived Risk and Information Search: A Systematic Meta-Analysis of the Empirical Evidence*, International Journal of Research in Marketing, Vol. 2(2) (1985), pp. 79–100.

[96] Gerpott, Torsten R., *Feindliche Übernahme*, Marktforschung und Management, Vol. 41(6) (1997), pp. 246–247.

[97] Gibbons, Jean D., *Nonparametric Methods for Quantitative Analysis*, Holt, Rinehart and Winston (1976).

[98] Gibbons, Jean D., *Nonparametric Statistics – An Introduction*, Sage Publications (1993).

[99] Gierl, Heribert/Stich, Armin/Strohmayr, Marcus, *Einfluss der Glaubwürdigkeit einer Informationsquelle auf die Glaubwürdigkeit der Information*, Marketing ZFP, Vol. 19 (1997), pp. 27–31.

[100] Grönhaug, Kjell, *Autonomous vs. Joint Decisions in Buying Organizations*, Industrial Marketing Management, Vol. 4 (1975), pp. 265–271.

[101] Grönroos, Christian, *Value-Driven Relational Marketing: From Products to Resources and Competencies*, Journal of Marketing Management (1997), pp. 407–419.

[102] Grünbichler, Andreas, *Reputation oder implizite Ansprüche? – Anmerkungen*, Zeitschrift für Betriebswirtschaft, Vol. 59(4) (1989), pp. 440–442.

[103] Günter, Bernd, *Die Referenzanlage als Marketing-Instrument*, Zeitschrift für betriebswirtschaftliche Forschung – Kontaktstudium, Vol. 31 (1979), pp. 145–151.

[104] Günter, Bernd *Systemdenken und Systemgeschäft im Marketing*, Marktforschung und Management, Vol. 32 (1988), pp. 106–110.

[105] Hakansson, Hakan/Wootz, Björn, *Risk Reduction and the Industrial Purchaser*, European Journal of Marketing, Vol. 9 (1975), pp. 35–53.

[106] Hardie, Bruce G. S./Johnson, Eric J./Fader, Peter S., *Modeling Loss Aversion and Reference Dependence Effects on Brand Choice*, Marketing Science, Vol. 12 (Fall 1993), pp. 378–394.

[107] Harris, Milton/Raviv, Arthut, *Optimal Incentive Contracts with Imperfect Information*, Journal of Economic Theory, Vol. 20 (1979), pp. 231–259.

[108] Hartmann-Wendels, Thomas, *Principal-Agent-Theorie und asymmetrische Informationsverteilung*, Zeitschrift für Betriebs-wirtschaft, Vol. 59 (1989), pp. 714–734.

[109] Haugtvedt, Curtis P./Leavitt, Clark/Schneier, Wendy L., *Cognitive Strength of Established Brands: Memory, Attitudinal, and Structural Approaches*, in: Aaker, D./Biel, A. (Eds.), *Brand Equity and Advertising: Advertising's Role in Building Strong Brands*, Lawrence Erlbaum Associates, Hillsdale NJ (1993), pp. 247–261.

[110] Heide, Jan B., *Interorganizational Governance in Marketing Channels*, Journal of Marketing, Vol. 58 (1994), pp. 71–85.

[111] Herbig, Paul/Milewicz, John/Golden, Jim, *A Model of Reputation Building and Destruction*, Journal of Business Research, Vol. 31(1) (1994), pp. 23–31.

[112] Herrmann, Andreas/Bauer, Hans H./Huber, Frank, *Wenn Käufer auch verkaufen – Preispolitische Implikationen der 'prospect'-Theorie*, Marketing ZFP, Vol. 19(1) (1997), pp. 5–14.

[113] Herrmann, Andreas/Johnson, Michael D., *Die Kundenzufriedenheit als Bestimmungsfaktor der Kundenbindung*, Zeitschrift für betriebswirtschaftliche Forschung, Vol. 51(6) (1999), pp. 579–598.

[114] Herrmann, Andreas/Homburg, Christian, *Marktforschung: Ziele, Vorgehensweise und Methoden*, in: Herrmann, A./ Homburg, C. (Eds.), *Marktforschung – Methoden, Anwendungen, Praxisbeispiele*, 2nd edition (first edition 1999), Gabler, Wiesbaden (2000), pp. 13–32.

[115] Herrmann, Andreas/Huber, Frank/Fischer, Marc, *Kundenzufriedenheit, Kundenbindung und Unternehmenserfolg – Wie*

prägnant ist dieser Zusammenhang tatsächlich?, Kostenrechnungspraxis, special issue 3 (2000), pp. 15–21.

[116] Herzberg, Fred, *One More Time: How Do You Motivate Employees?*, Reprint of an article published in 1968, Harvard Business Review, Special Issue (January 2003), pp. 87–96.

[117] Hildebrandt, Lutz, *Hypothesenbildung und empirische Überprüfung*, in: Herrmann, A./Homburg, C. (Eds.), *Marktforschung – Methoden, Anwendungen, Praxisbeispiele*, 2nd edition (first edition 1999), Gabler, Wiesbaden (2000), pp. 33–57.

[118] Holström, Bengt, *Moral Hazard and Observability*, Bell Journal of Economics, Vol. 10 (1979), pp. 74–91.

[119] Homburg, Christian/Herrmann, Andreas/Pflesser, Christian, *Methoden der Datenanalyse im Überblick*, in: Herrmann, A./Homburg, C. (Eds.), *Marktforschung – Methoden, Anwendungen, Praxisbeispiele*, 2nd edition (first edition 1999), Gabler, Wiesbaden (2000), pp. 101–125.

[120] Hopf, Michael, *Ausgewählte Probleme der Informationsökonomie*, Wirtschaftswissenschaftliches Studium, Vol. 12 (1983), pp. 313–318.

[121] Hunt, David, *What Future for Europe's Investment Banks?*, McKinsey Quarterly, No. 1 (1995), pp. 104–117.

[122] Jackson, Barbara B., *Build Customer Relationships that Last*, Harvard Business Review, Vol. 63 (1985), pp. 120–128.

[123] Jackson, Ralph W./Cooper, Philip D., *Unique Aspects of Marketing Industrial Services*, Industrial Marketing Management, Vol. 17 (1988), pp. 111–118.

[124] Jacob, Adolf-Friedrich/Klein, Sebastian, *Investment Banking – Bankpolitik, Methoden und Konzepte*, Gabler, Wiesbaden (1996).

[125] Jacob, Frank, *Produktindividualisierung als spezielle Form des Dienst-leistungsmarketing*, in: Kleinaltenkamp, M. (Ed.), *Dienstleistungsmarketing – Konzeptionen und Anwendungen*, Wiesbaden (1995), pp. 193–223.

[126] Jacoby, Jacob/Kaplan, Leon B., *The Components of Perceived Risk*, in: Venkatesan, M. (Ed.), *Proceedings, Third Annual Convention of the Association for Consumer Research*, Association for Consumer Research, Chicago (1972), pp. 382– 393.

[127] Jansen, Stephan A., *Mergers & Acquisitions – Unternehmensakquisitionen und -kooperationen*, 2nd edition (1st edition 1998), Gabler, Wiesbaden (1999).

[128] Jensen, Michael C./Meckling, William H., *Theory of the Firm: Managerial Behavior, Agency Costs, and Ownership Structure*, Journal of Financial Economics, Vol. 3 (1976), pp. 305–360.

[129] Johnson, Michael D./Herrmann, Andreas/Gustafsson, Anders, *Comparing Customer Satisfaction across Industries and Countries*, Journal of Economic Psychology, Vol. 23(6) (2002), pp. 749–769.

[130] Kaas, Klaus P., *Marketing als Bewältigung von Informations- und Unsicherheitsproblemen im Markt*, Betriebswirtschaft, Vol. 61 (1990), pp. 539–548.

[131] Kaas, Klaus P., *Kontraktgütermarketing als Kooperation zwischen Prinzipalen und Agenten*, Zeitschrift für betriebswirtschaftliche Forschung, Vol. 44 (1992), pp. 884–901.

[132] Kaas, Klaus P./Schade, Christian, *Bindungsstärke in Kooperations- und Geschäftsbeziehungen am Beispiel der Dienstleistung Unternehmensberatung*, in: Thelen, E. M./Mairamhof, G. B. (Eds.), *Dienstleistungsmarketing – eine Bestandsaufnahme* (1993), pp. 73–99.

[133] Kahneman, Daniel/Tversky, Amos, *Prospect Theory: An Analysis of Decision Under Risk*, Econometrica, Vol. 47 (March 1979), pp. 263–291.

[134] Kahneman, Daniel/Tversky, Amos, *The Framing of Decisions and the Psychology of Choice*, Science, No. 211 (1981), pp. 453–458.

[135] Kahneman, Daniel/Tversky, Amos, *Loss Aversion and Riskless Choice: A Reference-Dependent Model*, Quarterly Journal of Economics, Vol. 106 (November 1991), pp. 1039–1061.

[136] Kapferer, Jean-Noël, *Strategic Brand Management – Creating and Sustaining Brand Equity Long Term*, 2nd edition (1st edition 1992), Les Editions d'organisation, Kogan Page (1997).

[137] Kaplan, Leon B./Szybillo, George J./Jacoby, Jacob, *Components of Perceived Risk in Product Purchase: A cross-validation*, Journal of Applied Psychology, Vol. 59 (1974), pp. 287–291.

[138] Kaplanski, Guy/Kroll, Yoram, *VaR Risk Measures versus Traditional Risk Measures: an Analysis and Survey*, Journal of Risk, Vol. 4(3) (spring 2002), pp. 1–27.

[139] Keep, William W./Hollander, Stanley C./Dickinson, Roger, *Forces Impinging on Long-Term Business-to-Business Relationships in the United States: An Historical Perspective*, Journal of Marketing, Vol. 62 (1998), pp. 31–45.

[140] Keller, Kevin L., *Conceptualizing, Measuring, and Managing Customer-Based Brand Equity*, Journal of Marketing, Vol. 57 (1993), pp. 1–22.

[141] Keller, Kevin L., *Strategic Brand Management – Building, Measuring, and Managing Brand Equity*, Prentice-Hall (1998).

[142] Kim, W. Chan/Mauborgne, Renée, *Fair Process: Managing in the Knowledge Economy*, Reprint of an article published in 1997, Harvard Business Review, Special Issue (January 2003), pp. 127–136.

[143] Klein, Benjamin/Crawford, Robert G./ Alchian, Armen A., *Vertical Integration, Appropriable Rents, and the Competitive Contracting Process*, Journal of Law and Economics, Vol. 22 (1978), pp. 297–326.

[144] Kleinaltenkamp, Michael, *Investitionsgütermarketing aus informationsökonomischer Sicht*, Zeitschrift für betriebswirtschaftliche Forschung, Vol. 44 (1992), pp. 809–829.

[145] Kleinaltenkamp, Michael, *Typologien von Business-to-Business-Transaktionen – Kritische Würdigung und Weiterentwicklung*, Marketing ZFP, Vol. 16(2) (1994), pp. 77–88.

[146] Klemm, Hanns-Alexander/Gehrt, Alexander, *Unerwünschte Übernahmen aus Sicht des übernehmenden Unternehmens*, in: Achleitner, A.-K./Thoma, G. F. (Eds.), *Handbuch Corporate Finance*, Dt. Wirtschaftsdienst, Köln (1997), paragraph 10.2.5.1.

[147] Kotler, Philip/Armstrong, Gary, *Marketing – an Introduction*, 3rd edition (1st edition 1987), Prentice-Hall, New Jersey (1993).

[148] Kotler, Philip/Connor, Richard A., *Marketing Professional Services*, Journal of Marketing, Vol. 41 (1977), pp. 71–76.

[149] Kreps, David M./Wilson, Robert, *Reputation and Imperfect Information*, Journal of Economic Theory, Vol. 27 (1982), pp. 253–279.

[150] Krishnan, H. Shanker, *Characteristics of Memory Associations: A Consumer-Based Brand Equity Perspective*, International Journal of Research in Marketing (October 1996), pp. 389–405.

[151] Kutschker, Michael, *Verhandlungen als Elemente eines verhaltenswissenschaftlichen Bezugsrahmens des Investitionsgütermarketing*, disseration, Mannheim (1972).

[152] Lavidge, Robert J./Steiner, Gary A., *A Model for Predictive Measurements of Advertising Effectiveness*, Journal of Marketing, Vol. 25 (October 1962), pp. 59–62.

[153] Lechler, Thomas, *Die Bedeutung der Personen für den Projekterfolg – Erkenntnisse aus 448 Projekten*, Marktforschung und Management, Vol. 41(6) (1997), pp. 228–233.

[154] Leigh, Thomas W./Rethans, Arno J., *A Script-Theoretic Analysis of Industrial Purchasing Behavior*, Journal of Marketing, Vol. 48 (1984), pp. 22–32.

[155] Lehmann, Donald R./O'Shaughnessy, John, *Differences in Attribute Importance for Different Industrial Products*, Journal of Marketing, Vol. 38 (1974), pp. 3–42.

[156] Lehmann, E. L./d'Abrera, H. J. M., *Nonparametrics – Statistical Methods Based on Ranks*, Holden-Day, McGraw-Hill (1975).

[157] Leland, Hayne E./Pyle, David H., *Informational Asymmetries, Financial Structure, and Financial Intermediation*, Journal of Finance, Vol. 32(2) (May 1977), pp. 371–281.

[158] Levinson, Harry, *Management By Whose Objectives?*, Reprint of an article pulished in 1970, Harvard Business Review, Special Issue (January 2003), pp. 107–116.

[159] Lovelock, Christopher H., *Services Marketing*, 3rd edition, Prentice Hall, New Jersey (1996).

[160] Lovelock, Christopher H./Wright, Lauren, *Principles of Service Marketing and Management*, Prentice Hall, New Jersey (1999).

[161] Low, George S./Fullerton, Ronald A., *Brands, Brand Management, and the Brand Manager System: a Critical-Historical Evaluation*, Journal of Marketing Research, Vol. 31 (May 1994), pp. 173–190.

[162] Luffman, George A., *Industrial Buyer Behavior: Some Aspects of the Search Process*, European Journal of Marketing, Vol. 8 (1974), pp. 93–107.

[163] Lutz, Richard J./Reilly, Patrick, *An Exploration of the Effects of Perceived Social and Performance Risk on Consumer Information Acquisition*, in: Ward, S./Wright, P. (Eds.), *Advances in Consumer Research*, Proceedings of the Fourth Annual Convention of the Association for Consumer Research, Vol. 1 (1973), pp. 393–405.

[164] Lutz, Richard J., *Affective and Cognitive Antecedents of Attitude Toward the Ad: A Conceptual Framework*, in: Alwitt, L. F./Mitchell, A. A., *Psychological Processes and Advertising Effects: Theory, Research and Application*, Hillsdale (1985), pp. 45–63.

[165] Lynn, Susan A., *Identifying Buying Influences for a Professional Service: Implications for Marketing Efforts*, Industrial Marketing Management, Vol. 16 (1987), pp. 119–130.

[166] Maister, David H., *Marketing to Existing Clients*, Journal of Management Consulting, Vol. 5(2) (1989), pp. 25–32.

[167] Manville, Brook/Ober, Josiah, *Beyond Empowerment: Building a Company of Citizens*, Harvard Business Review, Special Issue (January 2003), pp. 48–53.

[168] Marshall, Alfred, *Principles of Economics*, 8th edition (1st edition 1890), Macmillan, London (1936).

[169] Meffert, Heribert, *Marktorientierte Führung von Dienstleistungsunternehmen – neuere Entwicklungen in Theorie und Praxis*, Die Betriebswirtschaft, Vol. 54 (1994), pp. 519–541.

[170] Meffert, Heribert/Bruhn, Manfred, *Dienstleistungmarketing – Grundlagen, Konzepte, Methoden*, 2nd edition (1st edition 1995), Gabler, Wiesbaden (1997).

[171] Menon, Ajit, *Finding the Right Mix*, Gulf Marketing Review (October 2000), pp. 27–30.

[172] Merbold, Claus, *Marken-Wirkungen bei Investitionsgütern – Psychologische Effizienz bei Kaufentscheidungen*, Marktforschung & Management, Vol. 35 (3) (1991), pp. 109–112.

[173] Meyer, Anton, *Dienstleistungs-Marketing*, Die Betriebswirtschaft, Vol. 51 (1991), pp. 195–209.

[174] Millon, Marcia H./Thakor, Anjan V., *Moral Hazard and Information Sharing: A Model for Financial Information Gathering Agencies*, Journal of Finance, Vol. 40 (1985), pp. 1403–1422.

[175] Moriarty, Rowland T./Kimball, Ralph C./Gay, John H., *The Management of Corporate Banking Relationships*, Sloan Management Review, Vol. 24 (1983), pp. 3–18.

[176] Moriarty, Rowland T./Spekman, Robert E., *An Empirical Investigation of the Informationn Sources Used During the Industrial Buying Process*, Journal of Marketing Research, Vol. 21 (1984), pp. 137–147.

[177] Morris, Jennifer, *Customers Stick with Pick and Mix*, Euromoney (October 2001), pp. 97–100.

[178] Müller-Stewens, Günter/Spickers, Jürgen/Deiß, Christian, *Mergers & Acquisitions – Markttendenzen und Beraterprofile*, Schäfer-Poeschel, Stuttgart (1999).

[179] Nelson, Phillip, *Information and Consumer Behavior*, Journal of Political Economy, Vol. 78 (1970), pp. 311–329.

[180] Newall, John, *Industrial Buyer Behavior – A Model of the Implications of Risk Handling Behavior for Communication Policies in Industrial Marketing*, European Journal of Marketing, Vol. 11 (1977), pp. 165–211.

[181] Oliver, Richard L., *A Cognitive Model of the Antecedents and Consequences of Satisfaction Decisions*, Journal of Marketing Research, Vol. 17 (November 1980), pp. 460–469.

[182] Oliver, Richard L., *A Conceptual Model of Service Quality and Service Satisfaction: Compatible Goals, Different Concepts*, in: Swartz, T. A./Bowen, D. E./Brown, S. W. (Eds.), *Advances in Services Marketing and Management*, JAI Press, Greenwich, CT, Vol. 2 (1993), pp. 65–85.

[183] Peter, Sibylle Isabell, *Kundenbindung als Marketingziel – Identifikation und Analyse zentraler Determinanten*, 2nd edition (1st edition 1997), Gabler (1999).

[184] Picot, Arnold/Dietl, Helmut, *Transaktionskostentheorie*, Wirtschaftswissenschaftliches Studium, Vol. 19(4) (1990), pp. 178–184.

[185] Picot, Arnold, *Zur Bedeutung allgemeiner Theorieansätze für die betriebswirtschaftliche Information und Kommunikation: Der Beitrag der Transaktionskosten- und Principal-Agent-Theorie*, in: Kirsch, W./Picot, A. (Eds.) *Die Betriebswitschaftslehre im Spannungsfeld zwischen Generalisierung und Spezialisierung* (1989), pp. 361–379.

[186] Picot, Gerhard, *Wirtschaftliche und wirtschaftsrechtliche Parameter bei der Planung von Mergers & Acquisitions*, in: Picot, G. (Ed.), *Handbuch Mergers & Acquisitions – Planung, Durchführung, Integration*, Schäfer-Poeschel, Stuttgart (2000), pp. 3–32.

[187] Plinke, Wulff, *Investitionsgütermarketing*, Marketing ZFP, Vol. 13(3) (1991), pp. 172–177.

[188] Plinke, Wulff, *Ausprägungen der Marktorientierung im Investitionsgüter-Marketing*, Zeitschrift für betriebswirtschaftliche Forschung, Vol. 44 (1992), pp. 830–846.

[189] Popper, Karl R., *Logik der Forschung*, 10th edition (1st edition 1934), Mohr, Tübingen (1994).

[190] Pretzlitz, Charles, *The Bankers Who Are Living On Borrowed Time*, Financial Times, Companies & Markets (March 8, 2001), page 15.

[191] Puto, Christopher P./Patton, Wesley E./King, Ronald H., *Risk Handling Strategies in Industrial Vendor Selection Decisions*, Journal of Marketing, Vol. 49 (1985), pp. 89–98.

[192] Reed, Gary/Story, Vicky/Saker, Jim, *Marketing Theory in Business-to-Business Organisations*, Report by the Chartered Institute of Marketing (2002).

[193] Reichheld, Frederick F./Sasser, W. Earl, *Zero Defections: Quality Comes to Services*, Harvard Business Review, Vol. 68 (1993), pp. 105–111.

[194] Richter, Frank, *Unternehmensbewertung*, in: Picot, G. (Ed.), *Handbuch Mergers & Acquisitions – Planung, Durchführung, Integration*, Schäfer-Poeschel, Stuttgart (2000), pp. 255–287.

[195] Richter, Hans-Peter, *Investitionsgütermarketing – Business-to-business-Marketing von Industrieunternehmen*, Hanser (2001).

[196] Richter, Rudolf, *Sichtweise und Fragestellung der neuen Institutionenökonomik*, Zeitschrift für Wirtschafts- und Sozialwissenschaften, Vol. 110(4) (1990), pp. 571–591.

[197] Robinson, Patrick J./Faris, Charles W./Wind, Yoram, *Industrial Buying and Creative Marketing*, Allyn & Bacon, Boston (1967).

[198] Roselius, Ted, *Consumer Rankings of Risk Reduction Methods*, Journal of Marketing, Vol. 35 (January 1971), pp. 56–61.

[199] Ross, Ivan, *Structure of Information Seeking and Personality in Consumer Decision Making*, Journal of Business Administration, Vol. 3 (1972), pp. 55–67.

[200] Ross, Ivan, *Perceived Risk and Consumer Behavior: A Critical Review* in: Schlinger, M. J. (Ed.), *Advances in Consumer Research*, Association for Consumer Research, Urbana IL, Vol. 2 (1975), pp. 1–19.

[201] Sattler, Henrik, *Markenbewertung*, Zeitschrift für Betriebswirtschaft, Vol. 65(6) (1995), pp. 663–682.

[202] Sattler, Henrik, *Markentransfers bei Dienstleistungen*, Markenmanagement für Dienstleistungen, St.Gallen (1998), pp. 134–146.

[203] Sattler, Henrik, *Markenbewertung als Instrument der Wertorientierten Unternehmensführung*, Wertorientierte Unternehmensführung – Perspektiven und Handlungsfelder für die Wertsteigerung von Unternehmen, Festzeitschrift zum 10-jährigen Bestehen des WWZ, Gabler (1998), pp. 191–212.

[204] Sattler, Henrik, *Ein Indikatorenmodell zur langfristig monetären Markenwertbestimmung [1]*, DBW 59 (1999), pp. 633–653.

[205] Schade, Christion/Schott, Eberhard, *Kontraktgüter als Objekte eines informationsökonomisch orientierten Marketing*, Arbeitspapier Nr. 1 des DFG-Forschungsprojektes *Grundlagen einer informationsökonomischen Theorie des Marketing* (1991).

[206] Schade, Christian/Schott, Eberhard, *Kontraktgüter im Marketing*, Marketing ZFP, Vol. 15 (1993), pp. 15–25.

[207] Schade, Christian, *Marketing für Unternehmensberatung – ein institutionenökonomischer Ansatz*, 2nd edition (1st edition 1995), Deutscher Universitätsverlag, Gabler, Wiesbaden (1997).

[208] Scheffler, Hartmut, *Stichprobenbildung und Datenerhebung*, in: Herrmann, A./Homburg, C. (Eds.), *Marktforschung – Methoden, Anwendungen, Praxisbeispiele*, 2nd edition (first edition 1999), Gabler, Wiesbaden (2000), pp. 59–77.

[209] Schelling, Thomas C., *The Strategy of Conflict*, 2nd edition (1st edition 1960), Oxford University Press, New York (1963).

[210] Schiffman, Leon G., *Perceived Risk in New Product Trial by Elderly Consumers*, Journal of Marketing Research, Vol. 9 (1972), pp. 106–108.

[211] Schmidt, Reinhard H./Wagner, Gerd R., *Risk Distribution and Bonding Mechanisms in Industrial Marketing*, Journal of Business Research, Vol. 13 (1985), pp. 421–433.

[212] Schröder, Benedikt Freiherr von/Tschöke, Kai, *Unternehmenbewertung bei Mergers & Acquisitions*, in: Achleitner, A.-K./Thoma, G. F. (Eds.), *Handbuch Corporate Finance*, Dt.Wirtschaftsdienst, Köln (1997), paragraph 10.6.

[213] Shapiro, Carl, *Premiums for High Quality Products as Returns to Reputation*, Quarterly Journal of Economics, Vol. 98 (1983), pp. 659–679.

[214] Sheth, Jagdish N., *A Model of Industrial Buyer Behavior*, Journal of Marketing, Vol. 37 (October 1973), pp. 50–56.

[215] Shocker, Allan D./Srivastava, Rajendra K./Ruekert, Robert W., *Challenges and Opportunities Facing Brand Management: an Introduction to the Special Issue*, Journal of Marketing Research, Vol. 31 (May 1994), pp. 149–158.

[216] Skiera, Bernd/Albers, Sönke, *Regressionsanalyse*, in: Herrmann, A./Homburg, C. (Eds.), *Marktforschung – Methoden, Anwendungen, Praxisbeispiele*, 2nd edition (first edition 1999), Gabler, Wiesbaden (2000), pp. 203–236.

[217] Smith, Robert E./Swinyard, William R., *Attitude-Behavior Consistency: The Impact of Product Trial versus Advertising*, Journal of Marketing Research, Vol. 20 (1983), pp. 257–267.

[218] Spence, Michael A., *Job Market Signaling*, Quarterly Journal of Economics, Vol. 87 (1973), pp. 355–374.

[219] Spence, Michael A., *Informational Aspects of Market Structure: An Introduction*, Quarterly Journal of Economics, Vol. 90 (1976), pp. 591–597.

[220] Spremann, Klaus, *Reputation, Garantie, Information*, Zeitschrift für Betriebswirtschaft, Vol. 58 (1988), pp. 613–629.

[221] Spremann, Klaus, *Asymmetrische Information*, Zeitschrift für Betriebswirtschaft, Vol. 60 (1990), pp. 561–586.

[222] Staffelbach, Bruno, *Strategisches Marketing von Dienstleistungen*, Marketing ZFP, Vol. 10(4) (1988), pp. 277–284.

[223] Stauss, Bernd, *Dienstleistungsmarken*, in: Bruhn, M. (Ed.), *Handbuch Markenartikel*, Stuttgart (1994), pp. 79–103.

[224] Stem, Donald E./Lamb, Charles W./MacLachlan, Douglas L., *Perceived Risk: A Synthesis*, European Journal of Marketing, Vol. 11(4) (1977), pp. 312–319.

[225] Stigler, George J., *The Economics of Information*, Journal of Political Economy, Vol. 69 (1961), pp. 213–225.

[226] Stock, James R./Zinszer, Paul H., *The Industrial Purchase Decision for Professional Services*, Journal of Business Research, Vol. 15 (1987), pp. 1–16.

[227] Sweeney, Brian, *B2B Brand Management*, Brand Strategy, Centaur Communications (September 16, 2002), page 32.

[228] Taylor, James W., *The Role of Risk in Consumer Behavior*, Journal of Marketing, Vol. 38 (1974), pp. 54–60.

[229] Tolle, Elisabeth, *Informationsökonomische Erkenntnisse für das Marketing bei Qualitätsunsicherheit der Konsumenten*, Zeitschrift für betriebswirtschaftliche Forschung, Vol. 46 (1994), pp. 926–938.

[230] Tomkins, Richard, *The Last Temptation of Capitalism*, Financial Times (March 3/4, 2001), page 8.

[231] Ungern-Sternberg, Thomas von/Weizsäcker, Carl C. von, *Marktstruktur und Marktverhalten bei Qualitätsunsicherheit*, Zeitschrift für Wirtschafts- und Sozialwissenschaften, Vol. 101 (1981), pp. 609–626.

[232] Vasek, Thomas, *Marke, streck dich!*, McK Wissen, Vol. 1(3) (2002), pp. 72–75.

[233] Wilding, J./Bauer, R. A., *Consumer Goals and Reactions to a Communication Source*, Journal of Marketing Research, Vol. 5 (1968), pp. 73–77.

[234] Williamson, Oliver E., *Credible Commitments: Using Hostages to Support Exchange*, The American Economic Review, Vol. 73 (1983), pp. 519–540.

[235] Williamson, Oliver E., *Reflections on the New Institutional Economics*, Zeitschrift für die gesamte Staatswissenschaft, Vol. 141 (1985), pp. 187–195.

[236] Williamson, Oliver E., *The Economic Institutions of Capitalism*, The Free Press, New York (1985).

[237] Wind, Yoram, *Organizational Buying Behavior*, in: Zaltman, G./Bonoma, T. (Eds.), *Review of Marketing*, American Marketing Association, Chicago (1978).

[238] Wind, Yoram/ Thomas, Robert J., *Conceptual and Methodological Issues in Organizational Buying Behavior*, European Journal of Marketing, Vol. 14 (1980), pp. 239–263.

[239] Woratschek, Herbert, *Ein neues Positionierungsmodell für den Dienstleistungsbetrieb* in: Kleinaltenkamp, M. (Ed.), *Dienstleistungsmarketing – Konzeptionen und Anwendungen*, Wiesbaden (1995), pp. 34–62.

[240] Yankelovich Partners, *The Hill and Knowlton/Chief Executive Magazine/Yankelovich Partners Second Annual Corporate Reputation Report: CEOs On the Value of Corporate Reputation and Managing Corporate Reputation on the Internet*, Chief Executive Magazine (1998).

[241] Yoon, Eunsang/Guffey, Hugh J./Kijewski, Valerie, *The Effects of Information and Company Reputation on Intentions to Buy a Business Service*, Journal of Business Research, Vol. 27 (1993), pp. 215–228.

[242] Zeithaml, Valerie A./Parasuraman, A./Berry, L., *Problems and Strategies in Services Marketing*, Journal of Marketing, Vol. 49 (Spring 1985), pp. 33–46.

[243] Zeithaml, Valerie A., *How Consumer Evaluation Processes Differ between Goods and Services*, in: Lovelock, C. H. (Ed.), *Services Marketing*, Englewood Cliffs (1991), pp. 39–47.

[244] Zenz-Spitzweg, Stephan R., *Strategische Rahmenbedingungen von Unternehmenskäufen und -verkäufen*, in: Achleitner, A.-K./Thoma, G. F. (Eds.), *Handbuch Corporate Finance*, Dt. Wirtschaftsdienst, Köln (1997), paragraph 10.1.

[245] Zikmund, W. G./Scott, Jerome E., *A Multivariate Analysis of Perceived Risk, Self-confidence and Information Sources*, in: Ward, S./Wright, P. (Eds.), *Advances in Consumer Research*, Proceedings of the Fourth Annual Convention of the Association for Consumer Research, Vol. 1 (1973), pp. 406–416.

MIX
Papier aus verantwortungsvollen Quellen
Paper from responsible sources
FSC® C105338

If you have any concerns about our products,
you can contact us on
ProductSafety@springernature.com

In case Publisher is established outside the EU,
the EU authorized representative is:
Springer Nature Customer Service Center GmbH
Europaplatz 3, 69115 Heidelberg, Germany

Printed by Libri Plureos GmbH
in Hamburg, Germany